ASIAN STUDIES ASSOCIATION OF AUSTRALIA

Southeast Asia Publications Series

Colonial Law Making

ASIAN STUDIES ASSOCIATION OF AUSTRALIA
Southeast Asia Publications Series

Since 1979 the Southeast Asia Publications Series (SEAPS) has brought some of the best of Australian scholarship on Southeast Asia to an international readership. It seeks to publish leading-edge research by both young and established scholars on the countries and peoples of Southeast Asia across all disciplines of the humanities and social sciences with particular encouragement to interdisciplinary and comparative research.

SEAPS is published for the Asian Studies Association of Australia by NUS Press, a unit of the National University of Singapore.

Editorial Board

Professor Edward Aspinall (Australian National University) (Editor)
Professor Barbara Andaya (University of Hawai'i and University of Hawai'i Press)
Associate Professor Nick Cheesman (Australian National University) (Editor)
Professor Emeritus Robert Cribb (Australian National University)
Professor Melissa Crouch (University of New South Wales)
Professor Emeritus Howard Dick (University of Melbourne/Newcastle)
Professor Emeritus Robert Elson (University of Queensland)
Professor Michele Ford (University of Sydney)
Professor Emeritus Ariel Heryanto (Monash University)
Associate Professor Holly High (Deakin University)
Gerald Jackson (NIAS – Nordic Institute of Asian Studies)
Associate Professor Patrick Jory (University of Queensland)
Dr Paul Kratoska (NUS Press, National University of Singapore)
Professor Julian Millie (Monash University)
Professor Emerita Lyn Parker (University of Western Australia)
Professor Emeritus Anthony Reid (Australian National University)
Dr. Jayde Roberts (University of New South Wales)
Professor Emerita Kathryn Robinson (Australian National University)
Professor Mina Roces (University of New South Wales)
Peter Schoppert (NUS Press, National University of Singapore)
Associate Professor Maila Stivens (University of Melbourne)
Professor Adrian Vickers (University of Sydney)

Website: http://asaa.asn.au/book-series/southeast-asia/

Colonial Law Making
Cambodia under the French

Sally Frances Low

NUS PRESS
SINGAPORE

ASIAN STUDIES ASSOCIATION OF AUSTRALIA

in association with

NUS PRESS

© 2024 Sally Frances Low

Published by:

NUS Press
National University of Singapore
AS3-01-02, 3 Arts Link
Singapore 117569
Fax: (65) 6774-0652
E-mail: nusbooks@nus.edu.sg
Website: http://nuspress.nus.edu.sg

ISBN: 978-981-325-244-8 (paper)
ePDF ISBN: 978-981-325-245-5

All rights reserved. This book, or parts thereof, may not be reproduced in any form or by any means, electronic or mechanical, including photocopying, recording or any information storage and retrieval system now known or to be invented, without written permission from the Publisher.

National Library Board, Singapore Cataloguing in Publication Data
Name(s): Low, Sally Frances. | Asian Studies Association of Australia.
Title: Colonial law making: Cambodia under the French / Sally Frances Low.
Other Title(s): Southeast Asia publications series.
Description: Singapore: NUS Press [2024] | Asian Studies Association
    of Australia in association with NUS Press.
Identifier(s): ISBN 978-981-325-244-8 (paperback) |
    ISBN 978-981-325-245-5 (PDF)
Subject(s): LCSH: Law—Cambodia—History—19th century. |
    Law—Cambodia—History—20th century. | Cambodia—Colonization. |
    Cambodia—History—1863–1953. | France—Colonies—Asia.
Classification: DDC 349.596—dc23

Cover: The Cambodian Ministry of Justice building (formerly *Palais de Justice*) (Photo by Mick2770 / Shutterstock.com / Photo ID 1154514793).

Typeset by: Westchester Publishing Services UK
Printed by: Markono Print Media Pte Ltd

For

Peter

Contents

List of Figures		ix
List of Tables		xi
List of Maps		xi
Note on References		xv
Glossary of Khmer Transliterations		xvii
Foreword		xxi
Acknowledgements		xxv
1.	Colonial Narratives of Protection and Civilisation	1
2.	*Fonctionnaires*, Mandarins and Cosmologies of Law	27
3.	The Jurisdictional Dispossession of King Norodom	50
4.	Codification Begins	77
5.	Rural Jurisdictions and the 1916 Affair	101
6.	The Cambodian Courts after 1922	125
7.	Lawyers and Other Critics	150
8.	Constitutions and Independence	166
9.	Making Law in Colonial Protectorates	194
Bibliography		213
Index		235

List of Figures

2.1	Cambodian Court Hierarchy pre-colonisation	33
2.2	Provincial officials, Pursat 1896	34
3.1	King Norodom	65
4.1	François Baudoin	80
4.2	King Sisowath	81
6.1	Cambodian *Palais de Justice*	127
6.2	Plaque commemorating the inauguration of the *Palais de Justice* in 1925	128
7.1	Prince Monivong and Governor General Alexandre Varenne, Phnom Penh 1926	152
8.1	Prince Norodom Sihanouk and President Charles de Gaulle, Paris 1964.	184
8.2	Norodom Sihanouk meets Cambodian judges	188

List of Tables

6.1 Cases processed in the Cambodian jurisdiction,
1924–26 and 1936–39   138

6.2 Cases registered in Courts of First Instance,
1932 and 1939   139

List of Maps

Map 1 French Indochina (excluding Guangzhouwan)   xiii

Map 2 Cambodia 2013   xiv

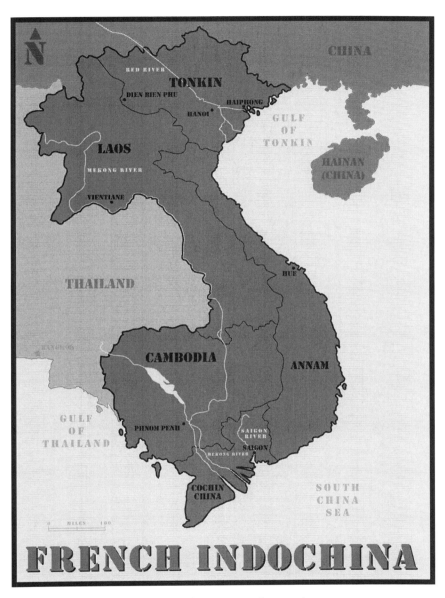

Map 1: French Indochina (excluding Guangzhouwan)
Source: CPA Media Pte Ltd/Alamy Stock

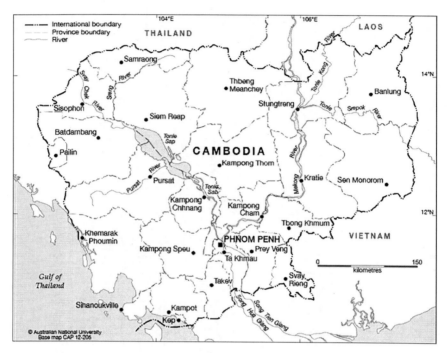

Map 2: Cambodia 2013

Source: Cartog GIS Australian National University https://cartogis.anu.edu.au/ (accessed 2 October 2022).

Note on References

Unless otherwise indicated, quotations from archival documents and French-language publications in the body of the text and in footnotes have been translated by the author.

Most of the archival documents, codes and ordinances cited are originally in French. Unless otherwise indicated, I have translated their titles into English. The abbreviation (trans) after the title of an archival document indicates that it was originally written in Khmer but translated by the French colonial authorities. Documents translated from Khmer are indicated.

Abbreviations used for archival references in footnotes are:

NAC RSC	National Archives of Cambodia Collection of the *Résident Supérieur* of Cambodia
NAC Doc	National Archives of Cambodia Documentation Collection
CAOM RSC	Centre des Archives d'Outre-Mer (France), Collection of the *Résident Supérieur* of Cambodia
CAOM GGI	Centre des Archives d'Outre-Mer (France), Collection of the Governor General of Indochina
CAOM FM NF	Centre des Archives d'Outre-Mer (France), Collection of the French Minister for Colonies (new)
CAOM FM AF	Centre des Archives d'Outre-Mer (France), Collection of the French Minister for Colonies (old)

Glossary of Khmer Transliterations

Transliteration Used in Text	Khmer Term	English Explanation
Balat	បាឡ្ញត់	Provincial official, second in seniority to governor
Chau Krom Sala	ចៅក្រមសាលា	Literally, "court of the judges". See explanation of *sala lukhun*
Chaufai Khet	ចៅហ្វាយខេត្ត	Provincial governor
Comchan	យុំច័ន្ទ	Provincial-level official
Cpap	ច្បាប់	Law / legal code
Derichan	តិរច្ឆាន	"Bestial". The name given to the village of Kraang Laev in Kompong Chhnang Province, after the 1925 murder of *Résident* Bardez
Khet	ខេត្ត	Province. Before 1922 there were between 50 and 54 provinces. After 1922 the provincial borders were redrawn to coincide with the 12–14 regions or *circonscriptions* of each French *résident*
Kram	ក្រម	During the protectorate, the French used this term to refer to the pre-colonial Cambodian legal codes After 1940, the term was used to designate a Royal Ordinance or decree
Krom Rathabal	ក្រមរដ្ឋបាល	Administrative services, established in 1919
Krom Tralakar	ក្រមត្រឡាការ	Judicial services, established in 1919 (came into effect in 1923)

xviii *Glossary of Khmer Transliterations*

Transliteration Used in Text	Khmer Term	English Explanation
Krom Viveat	ក្រមវិវាទ	Administrative chamber, established in 1933 to hear administrative law matters
Kromakar	ក្រមការ	Cambodian official or civil servant
Metheavy	មេធាវី	Lawyer
Namoeun	អ្នកម៉ឺន	General name for the class of Cambodian officials or mandarins
Oknha	ឧកញ៉ា	Title designating senior Cambodian official
Prea Thamma Sath	ព្រះ ធម្មសាធ	Ancient text from which Cambodian laws were said to derive
Sala Dambaung	សាលាតំបូង	Court/s of First Instance, established in 1923 in each province
Sala Domruot	សាលាតំរួត	Ancient court to which the king could refer matters if he chose. Traditionally presided over by a prince. Abolished in 1891
Sala Kromchot	សាលាក្រមឈ្នុត	Indictment chamber (*chambre des mises en accusation*) attached to the Court of Appeal. Established in 1923
Sala Lohuk	សាលាលហុ	Single judge tribunal established in some remote areas under the 1922 reforms of the judicial structures. Often presided over by a local administrative official, dealt with petty offences and civil matters of small value
Sala Lukhun	សាលា ល្ឈុន	Leclère claimed this was the oldest royal court. It had previously been known as the *Chau Krom Sala*, but Norodom used the Thai word, *sala lukhun*. Under the protectorate, the *sala lukhun* became the Court of First Instance of Phnom Penh
Sala Okret	សាលា ឧក្រិ ដ្ឋ	Criminal Court
Sala Outor	សាលា ឧទ្ទរណ៍	Court of Appeal
Sala Vinichhay	សាលាវិនិ ច្ឆ័យ	Court of Cassation or Annulment, first established in 1912
Sampot	សំពត់	Cambodian sarong

Glossary of Khmer Transliterations xix

Transliteration Used in Text	Khmer Term	English Explanation
Sophea	សោភា	Judge. Also provincial official (up to 1923)
Srok	ស្រុក	Became the name for a specific administrative division, commonly translated as "district", in 1923. The term is used flexibly and can also mean "country" or "region"
Yokebat or Yoskebat	យសគេប៉ ត្រ	Provincial-level official charged with the duties of clerk of the provincial courts under the 1911 *Code of Criminal Procedure and Judicial Organisation*

Foreword

Dr Sally Low has written an original sociopolitical study of the making of colonial law in the French protectorate of Cambodia (1863–1953/54). The work provides fresh insights into an important period of Cambodian legal and constitutional history, tests the Cambodian experience against the hypotheses of a number of eminent scholars of colonial law and draws comparisons with neighbouring countries, particularly Thailand/Siam, Malaysia and Vietnam.

This book began as a doctoral thesis, reflecting the questions arising for the author from significant time spent in Cambodia as well as Vietnam and Indonesia. Dr Low's work in Southeast Asia was always accompanied by curiosity, particularly about the history of the legal systems in which she worked. And our understanding of Cambodia's complex legal past is all the richer for her decision, ultimately, to undertake a thesis which focused on the French colonial system of "justice" in Cambodia and its early legacies.

Dr Low first visited me to propose a doctoral study of the Cambodian system of "justice" in 2012. I suggested we see if Emeritus Professor David P. Chandler was interested in the project, as one of the few scholars globally with an august reputation for the study of Cambodian history. David was smitten by the scope and focus of the study from its inception. Each of us involved in this project (two as supervisors) felt it was a privilege to meet and discuss the issues. Sally's diligence about the research and its sources was evident from the beginning, as was her excellent writing. David's enthusiasm for the project only increased, as did mine.

Dr Low's tenacity in seeking, accessing and reading the vast sources held in the Cambodian National Archives and the French Archives Nationales d'Outre-Mer is a testament to her patience and her zeal. These documentary sources were digested alongside existing French-language doctoral theses of the French administration in Cambodia, particularly Adrien Blazy's 2012 history of the administration of justice in French Indochina, Ernest Hoeffel's 1932 thesis on the legal status of foreigners in the protectorate and the work of several Cambodian scholars, including Dr Khin Sok and Dr Sorn Samnang. In transforming the thesis into a manuscript, Sally returned to the archives, including those held in La Contemporaine, in the University of Paris, Nanterre. She has also drawn on further French resources, including the works of several eminent legal scholars who advised the newly independent Royal Government of Cambodia during the 1960s, particularly Claude-Gilles Gour and Jean Imbert.

As this publication amply demonstrates, very little scholarly attention had been given to the way law was imagined and practised in Cambodia by the French, and how that interacted with local conceptions of justice, across the relevant colonial period, 1863–1953/54 and in the decade after independence. This publication is a major contribution to our understanding of colonial impacts on Southeast Asian legal systems.

Drawing on post-colonial critiques of European colonial law, Dr Low asks to what extent French rule delivered the "noble achievements" of French law, a term adapted from Ranajit Guha when writing on India. She concludes that the French and the Cambodian elites each had distinct conceptions of "justice". The French incursions into the administration of justice in the protectorate, and the Cambodian reactions across the period 1863 to 1940, produced less than altruistic concessions on both sides. While the bargaining power of the Cambodian elite was severely constrained by their colonial masters, they concurrently sought to secure their own interests.

Colonial narratives claimed that, despite France's best efforts, Cambodians were not yet ready to adapt to a fully modern (French-derived) system of laws and courts. Dr Low meticulously explains that the French proudly proclaimed that they had reformed and reimagined law and its practice in colonial Cambodia: for example, by separating judicial and administrative powers, rationalising laws and courts, and introducing a range of guarantees for Cambodian litigants. Dr Low argues these claims need to be assessed in light of colonial French domination, which challenged idealised French justice. To take one example explored in the book, from 1901 the French colonial authorities thwarted any attempt to foster a robust Cambodian legal profession.

Continuing the account into the period immediately following independence, Dr Low interrogates the post-1954 Cambodian legal complex, arguing that the protectorate's heritage was a highly dependent, only partially secular, legal system. Dr Low argues that, despite increasingly direct French control, Cambodia's status as a colonial protectorate

Foreword xxiii

affected the structure and pace of colonial reforms, creating legacies that included a dependent legal system and that placed the Cambodian monarchy in an arguably ambiguous constitutional position. This played out in the early years of independence when King Norodom Sihanouk built on this legacy to argue that the constitution was his to change, and later abdicated the throne to become a nominally secular politician while continuing to build on his royal cachet.

Dr Low's work during the thesis and in the finalisation of this publication is exemplary: she looks to the stories to assemble the whole, with an acute judgement about how to evaluate what she discovers. I heartily recommend *Colonial Law Making: Cambodia under the French*.

Professor Pip Nicholson
Deputy Vice-Chancellor (People and Community),
University of Melbourne

Acknowledgements

This book diverges considerably from the original thesis on which it is based, but I owe a great debt to my two thesis supervisors, Professor Pip Nicholson, now Deputy Vice-Chancellor (People and Community) at the University of Melbourne, and Professor Emeritus David Chandler of Monash University. I profited immeasurably from Pip's expertise in Asian law, her ability to see the nub of things, her understanding of legal theory and her generosity as I made my own conceptual and analytical journey. David Chandler, for whom the study of Cambodian history has been the basis of a distinguished career, was unfailingly generous with his time and feedback, comprehensive knowledge of Cambodian and Asian history, and humorous asides. Pip and David have both supported my subsequent work on the project.

I am indebted to the staff of the National Archives of Cambodia (NAC) for their work in preserving and making available the material in their charge. I particularly want to pay tribute to the late Madame Y Dari, former director of the NAC. I am one among many researchers whom she helped and encouraged. The Archives d'Outre Mer (CAOM) in France is a great resource for researchers, and its staff were always helpful and professional.

Countless friends and colleagues have shared material, provided support, feedback and stimulating exchanges over the years, including Peter Arfanis, the late Daryl Collins, Mathieu Guérin, Mick Houlbrook, Helen Jarvis, Allen Myers, Menh Nimmith, Nay Dina, Ros Sokunthy, Sim Socheata, and John Tully. Greg Muller and Karine Benyahia generously provided accommodation in Aix-en-Provence. A number of scholarly reviewers have provided invaluable comment including: Sarah Biddulph, Penny Edwards, Craig Reynolds, and Amanda Whiting and my initial thesis examiners.

My love and gratitude goes to Peter Annear for his belief in the project and in me, and for the intellectual and emotional support without which I would not have completed this book. He also made invariably useful comments and suggestions on numerous drafts of each chapter, helped me to find a way through tangled structures and put in an almost superhuman final proofing effort.

Thanks to Nick Cheesman and Ed Aspinall of the Asian Studies Association of Australia for valuable ideas and encouragement, and to the editorial staff at NUS Press. I am responsible for the content of the book and for any errors or omissions.

1

Colonial Narratives of Protection and Civilisation

When French and Cambodian dignitaries gathered in Phnom Penh on 25 April 1925 to inaugurate the new *Palais de Justice*, Cambodia had been a French protectorate for 62 years and was a component of the broader colony of Indochina. Cambodia's King Sisowath and the acting governor general of French Indochina, François Baudoin, presided. Sisowath had been placed on the throne by the French, who treated him as their puppet. Yet without him, the event would have lacked legitimacy. The French relied on the Cambodian monarch to authorise their presence and to endorse their proclaimed dual mission to civilise and to protect his realm.

François Baudoin had dominated the colonial administration in Cambodia since 1914, when he took up the post of *résident supérieur*. Baudoin was despotic and allegedly corrupt. His pet project had been an expensive colonial retreat on Mount Bogor, south-west of Phnom Penh, built during the height of the First World War, when the French government was desperately trying to raise funds and troops to support the war effort in Europe. Up to 2000 Cambodian labourers, some of them prisoners, died constructing this colonial holiday resort.[1]

The ceremony to inaugurate the *Palais de Justice* celebrated more than a new building. It marked the end of a phase during which Cambodia's courts and laws had been transformed. Baudoin's bitter struggle against the then prosecutor general of Indochina, Gabriel

---

[1] John Tully, *Cambodia under the Tricolour: King Sisowath and the "Mission Civilisatrice" 1904–1927* (Clayton: Monash Asia Institute, 1996), pp. 276–7.

Michel, had directly affected some of those reforms. He had defeated the prosecutor general's attempts to establish a network of French judges and courts across rural Cambodia. Instead, beyond the capital, colonial administrators, known as *résidents*, who answered to Baudoin, acted as magistrates in local French courts and supervised the Cambodian judges in a separate indigenous jurisdiction.

Reflecting Baudoin's hostility to the French colonial judiciary, the courts housed in the new building were not French, but Cambodian, presided over by Cambodian judges. The two keynote speakers at the ceremony each stressed that this was an unusual situation, presenting it as a benefit granted to Cambodians by a wise and benevolent French administration. His Excellency (*Oknha*) Penn, the president of the Cambodian Court of Annulment (*sala vinichhay*), thanked Baudoin for having ensured that "it is Khmer who judge Khmer".[2] The other main speaker that day, Maurice Habert, told the assembled crowd that Cambodians were the only colonial subjects to whom the French had devolved their own independent jurisdictional power.[3] Habert was a French judge but had been seconded from the judicial corps to work for the *résident supérieur* of Cambodia, overseeing indigenous justice. King Sisowath, François Baudoin, Judge Penn and Maurice Habert each contributed to the legal system that Cambodia inherited at independence. They also represented the social and professional layers—Cambodian monarchy, Cambodian elites, and the administrative and judicial arms of the colonial apparatus—whose variously competing and coinciding interests had, on a quotidian basis, shaped justice institutions in the protectorate.

Using largely colonial archives, this book studies the role of law and justice administration in French-ruled Cambodia. It is a case study of the making and the workings of law in colonial rule, and of legal legacies. Each instance of colonisation was unique, but what took place was also determined by structural economic and political factors common to many European colonies in the late 19th and early 20th centuries. The nature of indirect colonial rule and the role of the monarchy are central to what transpired in Cambodia. The kingdom's formal status as a protectorate, and contests between the colonial administration and the local elite, which were carried out in the language of protection, encouraged

---

[2] "Inauguration du Palais de Justice cambodgien" [Inauguration of the Cambodian Palace of Justice], *Echo du Cambodge* [Echo of Cambodia], 25 April 1925, NAC RSC 11850.
[3] Ibid.

Colonial Narratives of Protection and Civilisation

hybridised concepts of law and of the state. These contests, and interpretations of protection, laid the basis for future disputes over the king's place within or above the constitution of 1947. Related to the role of the king, the separation of state law and religion remained ambiguous.

The impact of French rule (from 1863 to 1953/54) on Cambodian law and justice has been, until now, one of the lesser-told stories of that time. Law was one of the foundations of modern European colonial states and was arguably one of their most important legacies.[4] Colonial law justified, established, authorised, ordered and influenced colonial rule. International law created rules for relations between competing colonial powers and sanctioned European expansion.[5] Globally, the way law and justice evolved in each colonial situation varied according to many influences. Local resistance and the legal traditions of each colonial power played out within the context of international events and the evolving needs of each colonial power.

The process of imposing a Western-style legal system in Cambodia was part of a sometimes subterranean struggle between colonial power and the colonised elites for control of the state apparatus that emerged as a result of foreign occupation. Archives in Cambodia and France reveal some of the exchanges and transactions that were part of that struggle. Their contests shaped colonial law in Cambodia, which in turn influenced post-colonial law and the constitution of the post-colonial state. At first, under the reign of King Norodom (r. 1864–1904), contests were quite open. As French control expanded, Cambodian resistance became less overt, but continued in various forms. These exchanges demonstrate some of the ways by which both the dominating French and the seemingly submissive Cambodians influenced colonial law. They also raise

---

[4] Nick Cheesman, "Rule-of-Law Lineages in Colonial and Early Post-Colonial Burma", *Modern Asian Studies* 50, 2 (2016): 564–601, see 574. For a critical view of the colonial legal heritage, see Upendra Baxi, "The Colonialist Heritage", in *Comparative Legal Studies: Traditions and Transitions*, ed. Pierre Legrand and Roderick Munday (Cambridge: Cambridge University Press, 2003), pp. 46–75.

[5] Antony Anghi, *Imperialism, Sovereignty, and the Making of International Law* (particularly chapter 2—"Finding the Peripheries: Colonialism in Nineteenth-Century International Law") (Cambridge: Cambridge University Press, 2005), pp. 32–114; Charles Henry Alexandrowicz, "The Afro-Asian World and the Law of Nations: Historical Aspects", *Collected Courses of the Hague Academy of International Law*, vol. 123 (Leiden: Martinus Nijhoff, 1968); Jennifer Beard, *The Political Economy of Desire: International Law, Development and the Nation State* (New York: Routledge, 2006).

broader questions about the impact of economics and politics on the constitution of the colonial state, its law and its legacies.

Legal sociologists Yves Dezalay and Bryant Garth link colonial investment in law with trade, giving rise to indigenous legal professions whose elite members went on to dominate and to shape post-colonial law. These colonial foundations influenced the degree to which law and the legal field were embedded and influential in post-independence society.[6] Terence Halliday and Lucien Karpik also consider that lawyers were a key ingredient for resilient post-colonial legal systems, but argue that lawyers had to be supported by a broader "legal complex" in which judges, too, played an important role.[7] Post-colonial scholar Upendra Baxi disputes the idea of a colonial legal legacy, arguing that in India, colonial law left behind a "bricolage of alien ideologies and institutions".[8] On the other hand, Matthew Lange finds a correlation between direct colonial rule in British colonies and post-independence economic prosperity and liberal democracy. He maintains that some directly ruled British colonies established legal-administrative institutions that became the pillars of robust post-colonial democratic and relatively prosperous states. Lange argues that indirect rule left local elites in power and led to weak post-independence states undermined by systems of personalised patronage.[9] Dezalay and Garth's broad study of the origins, evolution and influence of legal professionals (lawyers) in a range of Asian countries provides highly persuasive insights into the connections between elite members of the legal profession and political and economic power. They take a sociological approach, using Pierre Bourdieu's theoretical concept of the field and social capital. Of particular interest for colonial law in Cambodia is their analysis linking colonial investments in law, particularly legal education for local elites, with the development

---

[6] Yves Dezalay and Bryant Garth, *Asian Legal Revivals: Lawyers in the Shadow of Empire* (Chicago: University of Chicago Press, 2010), pp. 1–15.

[7] Terence C. Halliday and Lucien Karpik, "Political Liberalism in the British Post-Colony", in *Fates of Political Liberalism in the British Post-Colony: The Politics of the Legal Complex*, ed. Terence C. Halliday, Lucien Karpik and Malcolm M. Feeley (Cambridge: Cambridge University Press, 2012), pp. 3–55.

[8] Upendra Baxi, "The Colonialist Heritage", pp. 46–7. See also Upendra Baxi, "Postcolonial Legality", in *A Companion to Postcolonial Studies*, ed. Henry Schwartz and Sangeeta Ray (Oxford: Blackwell, 2000), pp. 540–55, see p. 541.

[9] Matthew Lange, *Lineages of Despotism and Development: British Colonialism and State Power* (Chicago Scholarship Online, 2009), DOI:10.7208/chicago/9780226 470702.001.0001.

of a legal field capable of wielding a degree of social and political capital.[10] Cambodia confirms their view that the economic basis of the colony had an important influence on colonial approaches to and investments in law.[11] The French sought to create a favourable legal environment for French investors in Cambodia. They imposed strict fiscal and economic controls, which arguably created distortions and dependencies in the Cambodian economy.[12] However, even though rice and later rubber became important exports, the protectorate did not become a major centre for French trade. Instead, taxes and imposts proved to be the most consistently rewarding method of colonial extraction.[13]

In these conditions, colonial law focused largely on controlling and administering the local population. Although French rule relied on coopted local elites, this did not lead them to invest in a local legal profession. On the contrary, their modus vivendi with the Cambodian elite facilitated a highly administrative and controlled indigenous legal system, a dependent judiciary and a weak legal profession. The lack of a legal field with any autonomy or influence became apparent during the short period of relative peace from independence in 1953 to the end of the 1960s.

For Lange, one of the key factors that differentiated direct from indirect rule in British colonies was the degree to which British civil servants replaced local elites in establishing and administering a legal bureaucratic state apparatus. Taking into account other variables such as the nature of the transition to independence, he finds a correlation between directly ruled colonies and future political stability, democracy and economic development.[14] The main point of Lange's analysis that is relevant to this study of Cambodia—an indirectly ruled French protectorate—is his proposition that indirect rule left pre-colonial

---

[10] Dezalay and Garth, *Asian Legal Revivals*, pp. 1–15.

[11] Ibid., p. 5.

[12] See translated extracts of Khieu Samphan's 1959 doctoral thesis in Khieu Samphan, "Underdevelopment in Cambodia", trans. Laura Summer, *Indochina Chronicle* (Sept.–Nov. 1976): 2–25.

[13] See Margaret Slocomb, *Colons and Coolies: The Development of Cambodia's Rubber Plantations* (Bangkok: White Lotus, 2007). For analyses of the economy of the protectorate, see John Tully, *France on the Mekong: A History of the Protectorate in Cambodia, 1863–1953* (New York: University Press of America, 2002), pp. 121–6; Pierre Brocheux and Daniel Hémery, *Indochina: An Ambiguous Colonisation, 1858–1954*, 2nd ed., trans. Ly Lan Dill-Klein (Berkeley: University of California Press, 2009), pp. 118–20.

[14] Lange, *Lineages of Despotism and Development*, pp. 1–20.

elites and pre-colonial patrimonial power structures in place, precluding the development of modern, stable legal bureaucratic state structures. On one level Cambodia fits this model, as the protectorate was built on collaboration in which a small French apparatus worked in parallel with members of the Cambodian elite. However, there was not a clear division between "old" Cambodian methods of rule and "new" French approaches, and the legal system developed under the protectorate melded the two.

Lange's definition of direct and indirect rule is ultimately restrictive. Cambodia remained a protectorate, but French control expanded well beyond the terms of the 1863 Treaty of Amity, Commerce and Protection (Treaty of Protection) signed by Cambodia's Prince (soon to be King) Norodom and representatives of Emperor Napoleon III.[15] The French claimed to rule in the name of the Cambodian king and to respect Cambodian tradition. They allowed Cambodian elites to retain much of their power, but the "French period" transformed the country's machinery of law and government.

The fact that the French constituted Cambodia as a protectorate was indeed key to colonial law making, but not only for the reasons that Lange suggests. One of the most important legacies of (semi-)indirect rule in Cambodia arose from the narrative of protection, or what Lauren Benton and Adam Clulow call "protection talk", particularly talk of protecting Cambodian tradition.[16] Even though the French disregarded many of its provisions, the 1863 Treaty of Protection provided the terminology for entwined contests to control law. The French claimed to protect non-elite Cambodians from exploitative rulers, but also to respect and protect Cambodian tradition. In turn Cambodian elites resorted to tradition to protect their privileges and to call for limits on French power. In the process, colonial and local elites each contributed to reinterpretations of tradition and in doing so influenced colonial law and laid the foundations for contests over the constitution of the post-colonial state.

---

[15] Clive Parry, ed., *Consolidated Treaty Series: 1648–1919*, vol. 128 (Oxford: Oxford University Press, 1969), p. 143. Norodom signed the treaty in 1863 and Napoleon III ratified it in 1864.

[16] Lauren Benton and Adam Clulow, "Introduction: The Long Strange History of Protection", in *Protection and Empire: A Global History*, ed. Lauren Benton, Adam Clulow and Bain Attwood (Cambridge: Cambridge University Press, 2018), pp. 1–9; Christina Twomey and Katherine Ellinghaus, "Protection: Global Genealogies, Local Practices", *Pacific Historical Review* 87, 1 (2018): 2–9.

The Cambodian monarchy lay at the centre of colonial encounters over protection and tradition. The French claimed to rule in the name of, and in order to protect, the king, but also the Cambodian people. The French usurped the king's temporal powers, but then went to great lengths to enhance his symbolic importance. They legitimised their rule by claiming to act in the name of the king and promoted the monarchy as the symbolic source of all laws, but also of Khmer tradition and identity. From 1897 onwards, the king and the French *résident supérieur* jointly promulgated all new laws, but the monarch formally remained the semi-divine source of law. As a result, the separation of state and religion, enacted into French law in 1905, did not travel to Cambodia. The cleavage between state law and custom, which historian Lauren Benton points out was a common legacy of European colonisation, remained at best contested as, for example, the French and the king insisted that new legal codes modernised rather than repealed pre-colonial, semi-religious texts.[17]

Following independence in 1954, King Norodom Sihanouk expanded on the notion that he was the semi-divine source of law, and that Cambodian tradition and identity were immutably linked to absolute monarchy. He claimed the right to rewrite the country's constitution, to take control of government and even to interfere in litigation. Cold War politics and the US-led war in Vietnam, as well as Sihanouk's personal bent, affected the fate of law and constitutionality in the early post-colonial years, but the colonial legacy provided the base on which Sihanouk built.

In neighbouring countries, those monarchs who survived the colonial encounter also retained, or since independence have been able to reassert, varying degrees of power. In her subtle and insightful work on the evolution of the royal rulers of the Malay Peninsula during and since British colonisation, Kobkua Suwannathat-Pian points out that, although the rulers came close to losing all their powers, they survived the struggle for independence and have at times exercised significant influence over Malaysia's constitution and politics, and, perhaps less directly, some aspects of law.[18] In Thailand, the Chakri dynasty, which used law and

---

[17] Lauren Benton, *Law and Colonial Cultures: Legal Regimes in World History, 1400–1900* (Cambridge: Cambridge University Press, 2002), pp. 127–8.

[18] Kobkua Suwannathat-Pian, *Palace, Political Party and Power: A Story of the Socio-Political Development of Malay Kingship* (Singapore: NUS Press, 2010), pp. 330–70; also, Piya Sukhani, "The Evolving Role of Malaysia's Royalty", *RSIS Commentary*

legal reforms to help to avoid direct colonisation, also consolidated its place in Thai politics by imposing uniform laws and a centralised state apparatus. Their claim to semi-divine authority was embedded constitutionally, and this arguably also occurred in Cambodia.

In 1978, the distinguished scholar of Southeast Asian studies, Benedict Anderson, provocatively questioned whether Siam/Thailand would have fared better if it had been directly rather than indirectly colonised, or semi-colonised.[19] Writing in the shadow of a military coup and the brutal suppression of student demonstrations in 1976, Anderson posited that Thailand had not become a modern constitutional monarchy, as had occurred in Japan. Instead, he claimed that the Thai monarchy was typical of other Southeast Asian kingdoms that had been indirectly, rather than directly, colonised. He argued that indirect colonial rule left a space for royals to remain as political actors, unlike more "modern" constitutional monarchies. Anderson's point regarding the residual, and varying, levels of political power enjoyed by monarchs in former indirect colonies of Southeast Asia is relevant to the colonial legal legacy in Cambodia, and to the role played by Norodom Sihanouk from independence in 1953, to the end of the 1960s and beyond. However, even in modern constitutional monarchies, a degree of royal power remains and operates in diverse ways. Moreover, monarchical institutions are the result of unique political and cultural histories, and the roles of monarchs and the levels of public support they enjoy are constantly changing.

Norodom Sihanouk's varied career, as king, prime minister, head of state, regent, head of a government in exile, and then again as king reflect his response to his country's turbulent post-independence history, characterised by civil war and great power rivalry. French rule over Cambodia, as part of the larger colony of Indochina, also exacerbated and gave nationalistic form to pre-existing ethnic antipathies, which would be important in post-independence politics.

107–21 (12 July 2021) https://www.rsis.edu.sg/wp-content/uploads/2021/07/CO21107.pdf (accessed 10 Sept. 2023); Hean Leng Ang and Amanda Whiting, "Federalism and Legal Unification in Malaysia", in *Federalism and Legal Unification: A Comparative Empirical Investigation of Twenty Systems*, ed. Daniel Halberstam and Mathias Reimann (Dordrecht: Springer, 2014), pp. 295–336.

[19] Benedict Anderson, *Exploration and Irony in Studies of Siam over Forty Years* (Ithaca, NY: Southeast Asia Program, Cornell University, 2014), pp. 15–45.

Cambodia in "Indochina"

From the late 1850s onwards, France incrementally laid claim to the culturally and politically disparate region it called *Indochine française*. The French first annexed a region in southern Vietnam, which they called *Cochinchine* (Cochin China). Next, they signed the Treaty of Protection with Cambodian Prince Norodom in 1863. By 1897, they had largely wrested control of the territory that approximates today's Cambodia, Laos and Vietnam.

The French established across this region a complicated and varied system of justice administration. A hierarchy of French courts, headed by two Courts of Appeal (or at times two chambers of the one court), one in Saigon and one in Hanoi, covered all Europeans living in Indochina.[20] The majority of local inhabitants were subject to separate indigenous jurisdictions, which varied across each of the five regions of Indochina. In Cochin China French courts and judges took over the indigenous jurisdiction in 1881. In Cambodia, the French placed ethnic Vietnamese and Chinese inhabitants within a "sub-jurisdiction" under the French courts but separate from Europeans, deeming ethnic Khmer people and Cambodian legal institutions unfit to deal with seemingly more sophisticated ethnic Vietnamese and Chinese inhabitants.

In return for Prince Norodom signing the 1863 Treaty of Protection, the French supported his claim to the throne, defeated rival claims by his brothers Sisowath and Sivotha, and suppressed local rebellions. Norodom likely also hoped that the French would afford him more space to manoeuvre between the royal courts of Siam and Hue, which had previously competed for hegemony in Cambodia. However, French rule would bring a very different kind of domination, not least by taking away the king's right to negotiate with other foreign powers.

As the French started to transgress the terms of the 1863 treaty, taking control of state revenues and state administration, King Norodom did what he could to resist. Although by 1897 he had largely lost that

---

[20] H. Morché, "Organisation Judiciaire de l'Indochine" [The Legal Organisation in French Indochina], *La justice en Indochine* [Justice in French Indochina], Indochine Français, Direction de L'Administration de la Justice (Hanoi: Imprimerie d'Extrême-Orient, 1931), pp. 9–39, see p. 13; Adrien Blazy, "L'Organisation judiciaire en Indochine française (1858–1945)" [The Legal Organisation in French Indochina (1858–1945)] (PhD dissertation, Université de Toulouse, 2012).

struggle, Norodom's efforts led the French to understand that their rule depended on the authority of the king and on local elites to implement their administrative and legal reforms. Having incrementally usurped Norodom's formal temporal powers, they assiduously enhanced the religious and symbolic authority of his more cooperative, hand-picked successors.[21]

France invested more in the Vietnamese territories, particularly Cochin China in the south and Tonkin in the north, than they did in Cambodia.[22] Nevertheless, they transformed its governance structures, going to considerable lengths to take charge of and to reshape Cambodia's legal institutions. They imposed a French-inspired state-based centralised hierarchy of courts and legal codes. Economic, political and cultural factors motivated the colonial drive to take control of Cambodia's courts and laws and underlay Cambodian resistance to and adaptations of colonial law. Cambodia largely remained a colony of taxation and monopolies rather than trade and investment.[23] The French attempted to facilitate more extensive colonial investment, for example by transforming land into a credit-worthy commodity and creating a system of land concessions for French commercial agriculture. Yet, even after French concessionaires began to profit from the rubber boom of the late 1920s, the main role of law was to enforce a complex array of charges and imposts, protect private property and punish all forms of dissent.

Whereas the French had often in the past used protectorates as a stepping stone to direct annexation, in the late 19th century, policy makers began to promote the protectorate as a more efficient means of colonisation.[24] Indirectly ruled protectorates were often more acceptable

---

[21] Milton E. Osborne, *The French Presence in Cochinchina and Cambodia: Rule and Response (1859–1905)* (Bangkok: White Lotus, 1997. First published Cornell University Press, 1969), p. 227.

[22] Regarding French neglect of Cambodia relative to other parts of Indochina, see Tully, *France on the Mekong*, pp. 215–28; Huy Kanthoul, *Mémoires* [Memoirs] (Chandler Papers, Monash University, 1988), p. 74.

[23] Dezalay and Garth, *Asian Legal Revivals*, pp. 1–34, make the distinction between trade and governance as motivations for colonial investment in law. Regarding Cambodia as a colony of taxation, see Brocheux and Hémery, *Indochina*, p. 81; Alain Forest, *Le Cambodge et la colonisation française: histoire d'une colonisation sans heurts (1897–1920)* [Cambodia and French Colonisation: History of a Smooth Colonisation (1897–1920)] (Paris: Harmattan, 1980), p. 252.

[24] Farid Lekéal and Annie Deperchin, "Le protectorat, alternative à la colonisation? Pistes de recherche pour l'histoire du droit" [The Protectorate, an Alternative to

Colonial Narratives of Protection and Civilisation   11

in international relations and among French public opinion. Some French protectorates, such as Tonkin in north Vietnam, became direct colonies in all but name, whereas others, such as Tunisia (1881–1956) and Morocco (1912–56) in north Africa, retained more elements of indigenous sovereignty.

In Cambodia, the French increasingly disregarded aspects of the 1863 Treaty of Protection, but the treaty continued to affect the way in which they ruled because it legitimised their presence in the kingdom to Cambodian people, to the French public and to other colonial powers. The treaty and the concept of protection therefore also framed the discourse by which King Norodom and the Cambodian elites resisted French encroachments on their power. King Norodom called for laws and customs to be protected as per the terms of the treaty. In turn, French officials took control of Cambodian laws and courts in order, they said, to protect Cambodian people from despotism and barbarism. Moreover, protection talk, which started with the treaty, absorbed non-legal notions of patronage that characterised both the colonial apparatus and the Cambodian social structures.[25]

The French validated their rule through two somewhat contradictory ideological narratives. They often justified legal reforms in terms of a mission to civilise, to guide Cambodians out of an era of feudal backwardness towards more advanced social and economic relations. At the same time, they reverted to the Treaty of Protection and to what they

---

Colonisation? Paths of Research for the History of Law], *Clio@Thiemis* [Online], 4, 2011, paras 1–5. Arthur Girault, *Principes de Colonisation et de Législation Coloniale* [Principles of Colonisation and of Colonial Legislation], vol. 2 (Paris: Librarie de la société du recueil général des lois et des arrêts, 1894, 2nd ed. 1904), p. 543.

[25] Regarding patronage and protection in the French colonial apparatus, see Paul Sager, "A Nation of Functionaries, a Colony of Functionaries: The Antibureaucratic Consensus in France and Indochina, 1848–1912", *French Historical Studies*, 39, 1 (2016): 145–82, see 145–6; Grégory Mikaelian, *Un* Partageux *au Cambodge: Biographie d'Adhémard Leclère. Suivie de l'inventaire du fonds Adhémard Leclère* [A *Partageux* in Cambodia: Biography of Adhémard Leclère. Followed by an Inventory of the Adhémard Leclère Collection] (Paris: Les Cahiers de Péninsule, vol. 12, Association Péninsule, 2011), pp. 1, 51, 66–7. Regarding patronage in Cambodia at the time of colonisation and French reactions to it, see, Gregor Muller, *Colonial Cambodia's "Bad Frenchmen": The Rise of French Rule and the Life of Thomas Caraman, 1840–87* (London: Routledge, 2006), p. 108; Khin Sok, *Le Cambodge entre le Siam et le Viêtnam* [Cambodia between Siam and Vietnam] (Paris: École Française d'Extrême-Orient, 1991), pp. 207–22.

called Cambodian tradition to justify their own authoritarianism and political compromises with local elites.

At the opening of the *Palais de Justice*, judicial adviser Habert's comments reflected these two themes of civilising and protecting. Under French guidance Cambodian people had, he said, been liberated from legal barbarism and despotism. Laws had been codified, courts restructured and, most importantly, judicial and administrative functions separated, in accordance with French legal practice. Yet, he said, Cambodia's traditions and culture had been respected and protected, its laws modernised rather than replaced.[26]

The French applied some common colonial tropes and approaches to legal reform in Cambodia, but contingent factors gave the indigenous jurisdiction a more important role than in other protectorates of Indochina and in many other European protectorates, for example, the British protectorates on the Malay Peninsular.

Colonial Comparisons

It is easy to find common trends in European colonial law. In particular, law helped to establish and justify racial hierarchies.[27] Colonial law commonly classified and divided people according to their race, culture or religion. Colonised peoples generally enjoyed a lesser legal status than Europeans and were subjected to discriminatory laws. However, each colonial power had its own distinct legal culture and constitutional history. Britain's pragmatic and precedent-based common law system, its status as a monarchy and its unwritten constitution led it to employ some different legal mechanisms than did France, the home of the Napoleonic Codes and of highly politicised, written constitutions. In Cambodia, France's approach was characterised by jurisdictions and codification of laws. The French colonial apparatus also emphasised the

---

[26] "Inauguration du Palais de Justice cambodgien", *Echo du Cambodge*, 25 April 1925, NAC RSC 11850.

[27] See, for example: Mahmood Mamdani, *Citizen and Subject: Contemporary Africa and the Legacy of Late Colonialism* (Princeton, NJ: Princeton University Press, 1996); Elizabeth Kolsky, *Colonial Justice in British India: White Violence and the Rule of Law* (Cambridge: Cambridge Studies in Indian History and Society, 2011); Elizabeth Kolsky, "Codification and the Rule of Colonial Difference: Criminal Procedure in British India", *Law and History Review* 23, 3 (2005): 631–85, see 631. DOI:10.1017/S0738248000000596.

separation of powers but applied that principle in a highly selective and restricted manner.

Law served to differentiate coloniser from colonised peoples, giving authority to the discrimination inherent in foreign domination. In Indochina, the French imposed different legal status partly by establishing jurisdictions based on ethnicity. In the protectorates of Cambodia, Tonkin and Annam and the semi-protectorate of Laos, they established separate court hierarchies and laws for Europeans and for colonised peoples. In directly annexed Cochin China and the three Vietnamese urban concessions of Hanoi, Haiphong and Tourane/Danang, all inhabitants came under the purview of French colonial courts, but French judges presided over two jurisdictions according to whether litigants were European or locals. In the protectorates of Tunisia and Morocco, the main divide was between French law, applicable to foreigners and locals in cases that also involved foreigners, and Islamic law and courts.[28] However, in Morocco, the French also used jurisdiction to enforce divisions between the ethnic Arab majority and the various Imazighen (Berber) minorities.[29]

The British also imposed separate jurisdictions, particularly in their indirectly ruled protectorates. In Britain's Asian colonies, however, the remit of indigenous courts was often limited to aspects of personal and religious law, whereas British courts applied modified forms of British common law in criminal, commercial and civil law matters. In India in the early days of British East India Company rule, separate jurisdictions existed for Indians and British people, largely as a result of a policy of non-interference in indigenous legal matters. However, as more British settlers moved into the interior of the country, colonial courts began to

---

[28] Layachi Messaoudi, "Grandeur et limites du droit musulman au Maroc" [The Scale and the Limits of Muslim Law in Morocco], *Revue internationale de droit comparé* [International Review of Comparative Law] 47, 1 (1995): 146–54; Farid Lekéal, "La Place de la justice française dans la distribution des pouvoirs au sein du protectrat tunisien: deux décennies d'adjustement (1883–1903)" [The Place of French Justice in the Distribution of Powers in the Tunisian Protectorate: Two Decades of Adjustment (1883–1903)] in *La Justice française et le droit pendant le protectorate en Tunisie* [French Justice and the Law during the Tunisian Protectorate], ed. Nada Auzary-Schmaltz (Rabat: Institute de recherche sur le Maghreb contemporain, 2007): pp. 43–63, see pp. 44–6.

[29] Adam Guerin, "Racial Myth, Colonial Reform and the Invention of Customary Law in Morocco, 1912–13", *The Journal of North African Studies* 16, 3 (2011): 361–80.

14   *Colonial Law Making*

administer indigenous jurisdictions.[30] In the nine British protectorates of the Malay Peninsula, indigenous courts, formally overseen by the Malay rulers, retained responsibility for matters of Malay custom, Islamic religion and some related aspects of family law. Similarly, in the Dutch East Indies colonial courts took control of all legal matters except personal and religious customary law or *adat*.[31] By contrast, in the French protectorates of Indochina, indigenous courts retained control of civil, commercial and many aspects of criminal law, at least at first instance.

This is not to say that indigenous courts in any colony remained independent of colonial control; the presence of colonial powers inevitably affected local justice, regardless of official policy. At appellate level France introduced French courts or judges to several indigenous jurisdictions in Indochina. This happened first in Cochin China and Tonkin but also in Laos, where, by 1927, a judge of the French Court of Appeal in Hanoi sat as president of the indigenous Court of Appeal and Annulment.[32] By contrast in Annam, an incrementally modified version of the pre-colonial court system continued to operate under the supervision of French administrators and Vietnamese ministers.[33]

The Cambodian indigenous jurisdiction stood out in Indochina because it was more radically transformed than in any of the other protectorates, but paradoxically, the indigenous courts remained in the hands of Cambodian judges, even at the highest level of appeal. Another distinctive but related feature of the colonial jurisdictions in Cambodia

---

[30] Kolsky, "Codification", p. 641; see also Cheesman, "Rule-of-Law Lineages", p. 588; Benton, *Law and Colonial Cultures*, pp. 127–66; M.B. Hooker, "English Law in Sumatra, Java, the Straits Settlements, Malay States, Sarawak, North Borneo and Brunei", in *Laws of South-East Asia*, vol. 2, ed. M.B. Hooker (Singapore: Butterworth, 1986–88), pp. 299–466, see pp. 305–8.

[31] Peter Burns, "The Netherlands East Indies: Colonial Legal Policy and the Definitions of Law", in *Laws of South-East Asia*, vol. 2, ed. M.B. Hooker, pp. 147–298, see pp. 147, 233–42; Daniel Lev, "Colonial Law and the Genesis of the Indonesian State", in Daniel Lev, *Legal Evolution and Political Authority in Indonesia: Selected Essays* (Leiden: Kluwer, 2000), pp. 13–32, see pp. 15–19.

[32] M.P.E. Cressent, "Administration mixte: le Laos" [Mixed Administration: Laos], in *La Justice en Indochine* (Hanoi: Imprimerie d'Extrême-Orient, 1931), pp. 82–112, see p. 94; L.A. Habert, "Le Tonkin" [Tonkin] in *La Justice en Indochine* (Hanoi: Imprimerie d'Extrême-Orient, 1931), pp. 175–210, see pp. 194–6; E.A.F. Garrigues, "Administration Unique: la Cochinchine" [A Unique Administration: Cochin China], in *La Justice en Indochine* (Hanoi: Imprimerie d'Extrême-Orient, 1931), pp. 41–81, see pp. 50–1.

[33] Blazy, "L'Organisation judiciaire", pp. 819–23.

was the importance of the French sub-jurisdiction that dealt with size-able ethnic Vietnamese and Chinese populations. Both of these aspects of Cambodian justice arose largely due to contests within the colonial apparatus, and between the French and Cambodian elite. The protectorate's jurisdictions would have a significant impact on the functioning of justice and contributed to debates over ethnicity and nationality after independence.

French and English legal traditions differed sharply on the question of codification. France saw the Napoleonic Codes as its gift to legal civilisation. The codes did away with feudal privileges, united all citizens under one set of laws and made male citizens equal before the law. By contrast, the legal codes the British imposed on India and exported to its other Asian colonies ran contrary to prevailing English common law, which was based on case law and judicial precedent. The British colonial law codes were an innovation, sometimes supported by those who, in the tradition of Jeremy Bentham, advocated for codification in England.[34]

For the French the question across Indochina was not whether or not codes were needed, but the extent to which to replace local laws with French law. In Cambodia the French claimed that they were modernising local codes rather than replacing them with new ones based on French law. This necessary fiction was a tip of the colonial hat towards the Treaty of Protection, indirect rule and respect for Cambodian tradition. It also placated local elites, reflecting the modus vivendi between Cambodian king and colonial power that had taken shape under the reign of King Norodom (1863–1904). It is therefore not surprising that in their speeches at the opening of the *Palais de Justice* in 1925, judicial adviser Habert and Judge Penn each enunciated the notion that the revised Criminal Code of 1924 and the Civil Code of 1922 modernised rather than replaced Cambodian law. Habert spoke of a perfect synthesis between French legal forms and procedure and Cambodia's pre-existing laws. Judge Penn asserted that only those aspects of French law that were compatible with Cambodian tradition had been introduced.[35]

---

[34] Nick Cheesman, *Opposing the Rule of Law: How Myanmar's Courts Make Law and Order*, Cambridge Studies in Law and Society (Cambridge: Cambridge University Press, 2015), pp. 38–41; Kolsky, "Codification", pp. 632–6; Cheesman, "Rule-of-Law Lineages", pp. 574–5.

[35] "Inauguration du Palais de Justice cambodgien", *Echo du Cambodge*, 25 Apr. 1925. Drafts of two speeches and a copy of the newspaper article are filed in NAC RSC 11850. The *Echo du Cambodge* was a semi-official French-language newspaper.

The new codes ostensibly represented indigenous law, but they bore no resemblance to the sacred Buddhist legal texts that they replaced, except in one respect: the authority under which they were issued. They cannot be equated with the colonial interpretations of Hindu, Buddhist and Islamic laws made by the British in India and Burma, or with attempts to codify *adat* laws in the Dutch East Indies.[36] Instead, the new Cambodian codes drew overwhelmingly on French law and so were analogous with the codified forms of English law introduced in British-ruled India, Burma, the Straits Settlements and the Federated Malay States.[37] But the myth that the new codes modernised rather than replaced the old legal texts perpetuated the notion that, like the old texts, they emanated from a semi-divine king.

The French sometimes likened their role in rewriting Cambodian law to that of the Belgian, British, American and French legal experts whom Siamese King Chulalongkorn (Rama V) and his successors engaged to draft new codes for Siam in the late 1800s and early 1900s.[38] The obvious difference is that the codes drafted by the French for Cambodia strengthened colonial rule, whereas the Siamese codes helped to lessen some aspects of European domination and to consolidate the Thai state. Yet in both countries, legal reforms enforced the connection between monarch, religion, law and the state.

---

[36] Hilary McGeachy, "The Invention of Burmese Buddhist Law: A Study in Orientalism", *Asian Law* 4 (2002): 30–52; Andrew Huxley, "Is Burmese Law Burmese? John Jardine, Em Forchhammer and Legal Orientalism", *Australian Journal of Asian Law* 10 (2008): 184–201, see 184; Muhammad Shafique Bhatti, "Empire, Law and History: The British Origin of Modern Historiography of South Asia", *Pakistan Journal of Social Sciences* 30, 2 (Dec. 2010): 389–400, see 389; Zezen Zaenal Mutaqin, "Indonesian Customary Law and European Colonialism: A Comparative Analysis on Adat Law", *Journal of East Asian and International Law* 4, 2 (2011): 351–78, see 351; Barry Hooker, *Legal Pluralism: An Introduction to Colonial and Neo-Colonial Laws* (Oxford: Clarendon Press, 1975), pp. 256–7; Lev, "Colonial Law and the Genesis of the Indonesian State", pp. 19–21.
[37] Kolsky, "Codification", p. 631; Cheesman, "Rule-of-Law Lineages", pp. 574–5; Wu Min Aun, *The Malaysian Legal System* (Malaysia: Longman, 1990), pp. 16–23, see p. 22; Andrew Harding, *The Constitution of Malaysia: A Contextual Analysis* (Portland, OR: Hart, 2012), pp. 9–20; Jack Jin Gary Lee, "Plural Society and the Colonial State: English Law and the Making of the Crown Colony Government in the Straits Settlements", *Asian Journal of Law and Society* 2, 2 (Nov. 2015): 229–49.
[38] Tamara Loos, *Subject Siam: Family, Law, and Colonial Morality in Thailand* (New York: Cornell University Press, 2006), pp. 44–68.

The myth that Cambodian law had been modernised rather than replaced suited the colonial administration and the Cambodian king. The French could claim to have respected the kingdom's traditions and its domestic laws. The Cambodian king also benefited, as the new laws could be presented in the light of past practices whereby powerful monarchs revised sacred legal texts.[39]

Despite their claims to have done so, and as was common in many colonies, the French did not achieve a full separation of executive and judicial functions in Cambodia. Nor did they champion judicial independence, a concept that was problematic even in France at that time. Rather, the French cultivated a Cambodian judicial corps whose members depended on colonial patronage and were unlikely ever to uphold laws or individual rights against executive (colonial) power. They invested little in legal education. Lawyers fared even worse, as the French actively impeded their ability to operate.[40] What the French called the separation of powers was more a transfer of power over judges and courts from the king to the protectorate administration.

Significantly, the indigenous jurisdiction, as it developed under the protectorate, formed the basis for Cambodia's post-colonial legal system. So during the first decades of independence, King Norodom Sihanouk, aided again by French advisers, would attribute colonial legal reforms to his royal predecessors rather than the French.[41] By contrast, in

---

[39] David Chandler, "The Tragedy of Cambodian History", in David Chandler, *Facing the Cambodian Past: Selected Essays 1971–1994* (Bangkok: Silkworm Books, 1996), pp. 295–313, see pp. 104, 295; Grégory Mikaelian, "Recherches sur l'histoire du fonctionnement politique des royautés post-angkoriennes (c.1600–c.1720). Appuyées sur l'analyse d'un corpus de décrets royaux khmers du XVIIème siècle" [Research on the History of the Political Functioning of Post-Angkorian Royalty (c.1600–c.1720). Supported by an Analysis of a Body of Khmer Royal Decrees of the 17th Century] (PhD dissertation, University of the Sorbonne, 2006), pp. 255–7.

[40] Dezalay and Garth link the formation of a vigorous semi-autonomous legal profession with litigation around trade, whereas Halliday and Karpik argue that there is a link between liberalism in post-colonial states and the emergence of an indigenous and activist bar and an impartial judiciary as a result of colonial rule. See Dezalay and Garth, *Asian Legal Revivals*, pp. 1–34; Halliday and Karpik, "Political Liberalism in the British Post-Colony", pp. 247–304.

[41] Jean Imbert, *Histoire des institutions khmères* [History of Khmer Institutions] (Phnom Penh: Entreprise Khmère de Librairie, Annales de la faculté de droit de Phnom Penh, 1961) [Annals of the Faculty of Law of Phnom Penh 1961], p. 27.

most other Asian nations, post-colonial state law was based on previously European-led court hierarchies and often on a clearer distinction between colonial and pre-colonial laws or custom.[42]

The French ruled in the name of and through the king in Cambodia. Post-independence, this could have given rise to a constitutional monarchy in which the king reigned but did not rule. Indeed, that was the vision of the men who drafted the constitution of 1947. This constitution came about because elected members of a consultative assembly outmanoeuvred the French and the conservative royal elite who had planned to impose an authoritarian royalist constitution. In response, the colonial authorities and the king's inner circle of advisers set about undermining the 1947 constitution and its democratic institutions. They maintained that such a framework for governance was unsuitable for Cambodians, whose culture and identity, they said, remained immutably linked to an absolute monarchy.

Following independence, King (later Prince) Sihanouk took advantage of the protectorate's legal and constitutional legacies, such as a weak and submissive legal profession and the notion that absolute monarchy was essential to Khmer tradition, culture and nationhood. He worked to wrest power from the democratically elected National Assembly, to manipulate elections and to take over the reins of government. Some historians claim that the protectorate failed to modernise Cambodia and to entrench a Western-style rule of state law because it did not dislodge local elites from their positions and their practices of patronage.[43] There is truth in these assessments, but it is too easy to underestimate the transformations that did take place and to dismiss the ways in which the protectorate contributed to new formulations of Cambodian law, identity and tradition. The results were indeed a fusion of Cambodian and French-derived influences and traditions, including those concerning royal power, the basis of the independent state and the authority of law.

---

[42] Dezalay and Garth, *Asian Legal Revivals*, p. 43; Lev, "Colonial Law and the Genesis of the Indonesian State", pp. 13–32; Mutaqin, "Indonesian Customary Law and European Colonialism", p. 351.

[43] Tully, *France on the Mekong*, pp. 488–9; this allegation was also made vociferously during the 1920s by French lawyer Robert Lortat-Jacob. See, for example, R.A. Lortat-Jacob, *Sauvons l'Indochine* [Save Indochina] (Paris: Éditions de "la Griffe", 1927).

Approaching Colonial Law

Good history needs landmarks if it is to be anything other than a meaningless stroll "among countless lost events".[44] Such landmarks or theoretical guideposts also help to clarify and delimit the author's position.

In this case, there are a number of challenges. How to understand and judge European colonisation and colonial law? How to analyse the transactions between Cambodians and the French? What are my own biases and those of the archival sources on which I draw? Several key works, including those discussed above, have influenced the way I have approached this study. These writings canvas a number of critical issues that can be summarised as interpretations of modes of colonialism, the influence of Cambodians' own political power, the role of sociopolitical strata and of individuals in shaping law, and the nature of materials retrieved from the archives.

Upendra Baxi proposes that there are generally three "modes" of viewing European colonisation: as an ethical enterprise; as an affair of history; and as an ensemble of practices of violence. He acknowledges that each mode, and others too, are relevant to understanding the forces that shaped colonial law and its legacies in his native Bengal.[45] I sympathise with Baxi's third mode. Colonialism ultimately depended on and imposed ethnic and religious divisions, was racist, drew arbitrary borders, was violent and exploitative, and, in many instances, distorted local economies to the detriment of colonised peoples. This is my starting point and the framework within which I interpret the colonial archive. Nevertheless, each of Baxi's modes can provide important insights into the way colonial law unfolded and operated.

Colonialism as it was practised in the late 19th and early 20th centuries is certainly an affair of history. It cannot un-happen. But it is important to acknowledge the colonial ideologies and mindsets of European superiority, economic imperatives and civilisational hierarchies that continue to affect relations, at all levels, today.

Colonial law served colonial domination, but can it also be viewed as an ethical enterprise, at least on the part of individuals involved, or in some of the changes that it imposed? In some circumstances it established

---

[44] Anne Curthoys and John Docker, *Is History Fiction?* (Sydney: University of New South Wales Press, 2006), p. 184.
[45] Baxi, "The Colonialist Heritage", p. 47.

20   *Colonial Law Making*

certain principles that, although often breached by colonial rulers, at least promised liberating and modernising improvements. Colonial education often aimed to produce reliable functionaries to serve the occupiers' administration. However, some, particularly those selected to study in Europe, imbibed and came to support the more liberal principles of Western law and democracy.

As Sally Engle Merry demonstrates, colonial law could alleviate the lot of women and other groups who had been discriminated against in pre-colonial society. Her evidence is convincing, but each colony was unique.[46] In Cambodia, aspects of women's legal and political status arguably declined under French rule, for example by the legal assumption that men were the head of the household, but on the other hand, the right of girls to education gained some ground.[47] The French formally abolished slavery, but used prison labour and required Cambodian men to perform *corvée* (a tax paid in the form of labour on government projects). They placed ethnic Vietnamese and Chinese under a different jurisdiction than ethnic Khmers, which legally entrenched racial divisions and antipathies.

One of the key factors affecting colonial law, and one of the key themes of this book, is that although formally under French domination, Cambodians were neither powerless nor passive. Thai historian Thongchai Winichakul argues that histories of external impositions can also be read as histories of localisation. People adopt and adapt the foreign, whether it be Indian transculturation, European colonisation or 21st-century globalisation.[48] I draw inspiration from Thongchai in trying to unearth the role of Cambodians, particularly elite Cambodians, in

---

[46] Sally Engle Merry, "Law and Colonialism: A Review Essay", *Law and Society Review* 25, 4 (1991): 889–922; Sally Engle Merry, "From Law and Colonialism to Law and Globalization", *Law and Social Inquiry* 28 (2003): 569–90, see 569; Sally Engle Merry, *Colonizing Hawai'i: The Cultural Power of Law* (Princeton, NJ: Princeton University Press, 2000).

[47] Trudy Jacobsen, *Lost Goddesses: The Denial of Female Power in Cambodian History* (Copenhagen: NIAS Press, 2008), pp. 163–73; Trude Jacobsen, "Divergent Perspectives on the Cambodian 'Harem' in the Reigns of Norodom (1863–1904) and Sisowath (1904–1927)", *Working Paper*, 133 (Melbourne: Melbourne University Press, 2010).

[48] Thongchai Winichakul, "Writing at the Interstices: Southeast Asian Historians and Postnational Histories in Southeast Asia", in *New Terrains in Southeast Asian History*, ed. Abu Talib Ahmad and Tan Liok Ee (Singapore: Singapore University Press, 2003), pp. 3, 13. Lauren Benton also makes this point with regards to colonial law; see, for example, Benton, *Law and Colonial Cultures*, p. 128.

shaping colonial law. Exchanges between colonial officials and the king, his ministers, provincial governors and other notables challenge the dichotomy between collaboration and resistance. At times, coloniser and colonised clashed in ways that were quite calculated. At others, they found they had common interests. Sometimes, too, they simply misinterpreted each other.

Non-elite Cambodians' voices are largely missing from the colonial archives, but they evidently had important impacts on law, for example, in the ways they persistently ignored or rejected attempts to establish a register of land titles. Cambodian peasants and French colonial officials rarely came into contact with each other. Penny Edwards points out that the Cambodian elite, particularly those who learnt to speak French, were the *gateway* between the French and the people over whom they ruled. However, that role also granted them a certain power as *gatekeepers*, controlling the information that made its way into official reports.

What can be gleaned of their interactions with the colonial apparatus from archival and other sources suggests that non-elite Cambodians experienced French power as foreign and remote, but not fundamentally new. On several occasions, the largely rural population rebelled against injustices that affected their daily lives, usually related to taxation of some form. Each time this occurred, the French were taken by surprise and left searching for explanations. Many of the means and modes of Cambodian responses to colonialism remained opaque to the French.

The personalities and ambitions of individuals, men such as King Norodom and François Baudoin, and French Prosecutor General Gabriel Michel, helped to shape the laws and courts of Cambodia's indigenous jurisdiction. These men operated within and were influenced by separate sociopolitical and professional spheres—Cambodian elite, colonial administration and colonial judiciary—but they were also driven by personal ambitions and opportunism. Moreover, clashes between the French and Cambodians over law also reflected culturally determined incomprehension similar to that which Sokhieng Au discerns in her history of the colonial health services in the protectorate. She coins the term "cultural insolubility" to describe the ways in which French and local systems of health only partially combined or overlapped.[49] Sometimes, she argues, Cambodians did not recognise colonial health services as in any

---

[49] Sokhieng Au, *Mixed Medicines: Health and Culture in French Colonial Cambodia* (Chicago: University of Chicago Press, 2011), p. 5.

way related to their wellbeing.[50] There is an echo of this mutual incomprehension in recent discussions of hybrid views of "democracy" in Cambodia today and in discussions of the impact and meaning of contemporary efforts of legal "transplantation".[51]

Law is more overtly political than health. In Cambodia, reform of the laws and the courts was more obviously linked with colonial state control than were the limited French health services. Protection talk that characterised the exchanges between the Cambodian elite and the French reflected both mutual incomprehension and conscious resistance. Elite reactions to French law were often consciously political because the elite recognised that colonial legal impositions threatened their pre-colonial power structures.

While it is impossible to know the exact motives of individuals, there are discernible patterns to the exchanges between and among the French and elite Cambodians. They each struggled, albeit from positions of unequal power, to influence justice administration. To King Norodom and the elites around him, French reforms not only threatened their obvious interests, but ruptured their cosmologies and contradicted their assumptions regarding power and law. Even those who came to accept the superiority of French legal institutions reacted to and influenced colonial legal reforms in ways that reflected their position within Cambodian society.

The French, too, approached law and legal institutions in calculated and sometimes cynical ways, but also through the lens of their professional habitus and their cultural assumptions. They interpreted notions of Cambodian kingship both through the lens of their own history of feudalism and absolute monarchy and according to the immediate exigencies of their rule. These interplays between historical circumstances and the role of individuals are richly illustrated in the Cambodia archive.

Penny Edwards' study of emergent nationalism and cultural changes during the protectorate also sheds light on the way certain French and

---

[50] Ibid., pp. 186–7.

[51] Mona Lilja, "Discourses of Hybrid Democracy: The Case of Cambodia", *Asian Journal of Political Science* 18, 3 (2010): 289–309. DOI:10.1080/02185377.2010.527220; Pip Nicholson and Simon Butt, "Official Discourses and Court Oriented Legal Reform in Vietnam", in *Law and Development and the Global Discourses of Legal Transfers,* ed. John Gillespie and Pip Nicholson (Cambridge: Cambridge University Press, 2012), pp. 202–36.

Cambodian views of Cambodian tradition and kingship influenced the myriad transactions and contests over state law.[52] Edwards focuses on the role of individual Cambodians who took on board and helped to create the protectorate's narratives of modernity, and of "Khmerness". She refers to the "symbiotic, indigenous-European cultural legacy of the French Protectorate", which helped to sculpt a "Khmer national style and character". Cambodian nationalism was forged under the protectorate "through synthesis, graft, and borrowing".[53] Modernising nationalists adapted French analyses of the need for a national "reawakening" among people who were the descendants of the glorious era of Angkor.

The modernisation narrative ran through exchanges over law between and among the French and members of the Cambodian elite, but it was often overshadowed by a protection narrative that also synthesised, grafted and borrowed. Protection encompassed myriad meanings, but in the area of law there were two dominant themes: protecting traditional Khmer law and its links with religion and the monarchy; and protecting credulous, childlike Khmer peasants from despotic rulers and external threats. Meanwhile members of the Cambodian elite adopted aspects of the modernising narrative, but they also used the language of protection and the idea of tradition to attempt to limit French encroachments on their power.

The French did not invent Cambodian traditions,[54] but they perceived them through their own lenses: drawing analogies with idealised views of their own history and culture, and interpreting Khmer tradition to justify their approaches to colonial rule. French commentators and colonial officials tended to view the Khmer kings as exotic oriental despots, but they also drew analogies with feudal European ideas of absolutist monarchs who ruled by divine right. In later years of the protectorate, when France was under Vichy rule and again after the Second World War as France's Fourth Republic struggled to hold on to its colonial possessions, the French found common cause with conservative indigenous elites against democratically minded nationalists, protesting

---

[52] Penny Edwards, *Cambodge: The Cultivation of a Nation, 1860–1945* (Bangkok: Silkworm Books, 2008).

[53] Ibid., p. 242.

[54] See Eric Hobsbawm, "Introduction: Inventing Traditions", in *The Invention of Tradition*, ed. Eric Hobsbawm and Terence Ranger (Cambridge: Cambridge University Press, 1983), pp. 1–14; and in the same volume, Terence Ranger, "The Inventions of Tradition in Colonial Africa", pp. 211–62.

that Cambodian people were unshakably attached not only to their king but to royal absolutism. After independence, King Norodom Sihanouk built on the legacy of these colonial narratives to justify his own political and constitutional ambitions.

The evidence for this story of contests and exchanges comes mainly from the National Archives of Cambodia in Phnom Penh and Les Archives Nationales d'outre mer (National Overseas Archives) in Aix-en-Provence, France. I also consulted records of the French League of the Rights of Man and Citizen in the archival collection of La Contemporaine, in the University of Paris, Nanterre. Along with most secondary sources of the period, the archives are made up of fragments of other stories, written and ordered by participants in colonisation.[55] Their contents are influenced by the agendas of those who compiled them as well as by historical chance. The archives contain only a few documents written by Cambodians, and then only elite Cambodians. Non-elite Cambodians mainly appear in the archive via colonial officials' reports, or some legal records of police or courtroom interrogations. Yet their presence looms, as the subjects of the colonial project, only ever partially known to the French.

These imperfect records inevitably affect the quality of the story. They were largely written by men whose careers rested on their ability to reassure their superiors or justify their actions. Nevertheless, the archives contain a rich lode regarding the administration of justice in the protectorate. My interpretation of these sources reflects my own experiences and inherent biases as a left-leaning Australian trained in the Anglo common law tradition, but with a long association with Cambodia. I acknowledge that my conscious and unconscious orientations influence my interpretation, but hope that I have martialled the material in ways that provide some credible insights into how colonial state law took shape in Cambodia, its nature and its consequences.

---

[55] Debates over "the archive" as a source of information about the past cover a wide spectrum. See Jacques Derrida and Eric Premowitz, "Archive Fever: A Freudian Impression", *Diacritics* 25, 4 (1995): 9–63, see 9; Carolyn Steedman, "Something She Called a Fever: Michelet, Derrida, and Dust", *The American Historical Review* 106, 4 (2001): 1159–80, pp. 1159, 1172. See also Marlene Manoff, "Theories of the Archive from across the Disciplines", *Libraries and the Academy* 4, 1 (2004): 9–25. Gayatri Chakravorty Spivak, "The Rani of Sirmur: An Essay in Reading the Archives", *History and Theory* 24, 3 (1985): 247–72, see 247.

The Course of the Story

This story starts with background sociological sketches of colonial and Cambodian society and law. Subsequent chapters follow a loosely chronological path, beginning with the struggle for jurisdiction as the French first attempted to reform Cambodian courts and legal processes, and ending with a study of the impact of the colonial legal heritage on the constitution and governance during the early years of independence (1954–68).

King Norodom lost his long battle against the French (Chapter 3). By the end of his reign, the kingdom's finances and laws were in French hands, and the king's five ministers had deserted him. Yet Norodom and the Cambodian elite had won considerable concessions and had laid the foundations for the modus vivendi between colonial administrators and colonised elites that characterised the protectorate.

After Norodom's death in 1904, France's preferred replacement, King Sisowath, proved more accommodating. The era and the fiction of codification began (Chapters 4 and 5). The French consciously started to rewrite indigenous law, but still had to move cautiously. A delicate process of negotiation, conducted through discourses of protection and modernisation, spanned almost two decades. Codification and court reform helped the French to rationalise their administration and to rein in openly recalcitrant officials. Simultaneously, contests between colonial administrators and judges contributed to efforts to completely restructure the indigenous Cambodian court hierarchy along French lines. Court reforms and a move to separate judicial and administrative functions among the Cambodian elites unsettled previous power relations and enhanced French control.

By the opening of the *Palais de Justice* in 1925, the basic architecture of the Cambodian jurisdiction was in place. The years of consolidation up to the fall of the French Third Republic in 1940 entrenched patterns of executive/royal control of seemingly modern legal institutions in Cambodia, setting the scene for what came after independence (Chapters 6 and 7). During the Second World War, the pro-Vichy colonial administration intensified previous efforts to promote a narrative that linked racially based notions of nationhood with a vision of monarchical traditions that owed much to French historical understandings.

In 1941, new legislation established the first basic constitution for Cambodia, under which the king and the *résident supérieur* ruled supreme (Chapter 8). When, during the final months of the Second World

War, occupying Japanese troops temporarily ousted the French, the young King Norodom Sihanouk reigned as undisputed head of state, although in practice under Japanese supervision. When they returned to Cambodia after Japan surrendered to the allies in 1945, the French set out to suppress emerging pro-independence currents. In the process, they helped King Sihanouk to undermine the 1947 constitution, which had aimed to establish a democratic constitutional monarchy and which might have challenged the nexus between state law and royal power.

After independence, King, and later Chief of State, Norodom Sihanouk incrementally took political power, marginalised the elected parliament and rewrote the 1947 constitution. Although formally free of French supervision, the Cambodian courts and legal professions lacked the social and political capital to play a significant role as a third arm of government. Aided by French jurists, Sihanouk perpetuated and expanded the colonial narrative that Cambodia's ancient laws had been modernised rather than replaced. In doing so, he reclaimed aspects of the jurisdictional power that the French had taken from his great grandfather, Norodom.

2

Fonctionnaires, Mandarins and Cosmologies of Law

In 1883, French administrator Jean Moura published a scathing assessment of Cambodian courts that would become a part of colonial lore, justifying colonial involvement with Cambodian justice, despite the terms of the 1863 Treaty of Protection:[1]

> The major occupation of Cambodian mandarins, of all levels of the hierarchy, is, without exception, the administration of justice. The regular income that they take from it, added to the bribes, to the valuable presents they receive or that they require, constitutes just about all their salary. They adjourn cases as long as they can, in a way that squeezes the resources of defendants or litigants ... It has to be seen with what nonchalance and what indifference these judges examine the matters that are put before them; one finds them on a sort of platform, lounging on mats, smoking their pipes, drinking tea and interrupting the debates in order to give themselves over, in loud voices, to conversations that are altogether foreign to the subject under discussion ... Finally, they finish by rendering a judgment, which the parties can, at a pinch

---

[1] For example, it was referenced by: L.P. Nicolas, "Le Cambodge" [Cambodia], in *La justice en Indochine*, Direction de l'Administration de la Justice [Justice in Indochina, Department for the Administration of Justice] (Hanoi: Imprimerie d'Extrême-Orient, 1931), pp. 113–54, see p. 116; Henri Dartiguenave, Note sur la justice Cambodgienne [Note on Cambodian Justice], 15 June 1914, NAC RSC 23803.

28   *Colonial Law Making*

> recall [*rapellent*], but with which they are generally happy, such is
> the huge respect of Khmers for a judged matter . . . [2]

Two very different conceptions of law, justice and power collided in the
French protectorate of Cambodia. One derived from local adaptations
of Theravada Buddhism, semi-divine kingship, status, patron–client relations and respect for ritual. The other derived from France's positivist
legal system, which prided itself as rational, objective and universally applicable, but that also allocated status, established hierarchies, had its
own rituals and systems of patronage, and was susceptible to corruption.
Each legal system expressed, structured and enforced a set of social and
political relations.

The Cambodian Polity in 1863

Cambodia was not necessarily a clearly defined geopolitical entity
in 1863. The Cambodian royal chronicles portrayed the kingdom as a
C-shaped walled city with gates located at the places where invading armies
had traditionally entered.[3] In this royal perspective, the king claimed
authority over all those who inhabited his realm, including the non-
Khmer ethnic minorities. From a regional perspective, Thongchai
Winichakul describes pre-colonial Cambodia as an autonomous polity,
formerly powerful and still significant, which, since the 14th century,
had paid tribute to two dominant neighbours, Siam and Annam/
Vietnam.[4] David Chandler states that the Khmer-speaking majority
often referred to themselves variously as belonging to *sruk khmer*:
sometimes this meant all people who spoke the Khmer language; it
could also signify a connection to the Cambodian king through a local
leader or *chauvai sruk* who had received a royal title or insignia.[5] Thun
Theara and Duong Keo argue that before colonisation, the term *sruk
khmer* was just one of several used to refer to Cambodia as a polity, but

---

[2] J. Moura, *Le Royaume du Cambodge* [The Kingdom of Cambodia] (Paris: Ernest
Leroux, 1883), pp. 288–90.
[3] Chandler, *History*, p. 119; Theara Thun and Duong Keo, "Ethnocentrism of
Victimhood: Tracing the Discourses of Khmer Ethnicity in Precolonial and
Colonial Cambodia", *Asian Studies Review* (forthcoming).
[4] Thongchai Winichakul, *Siam Mapped: A History of the Geo-Body of a Nation*
(Honolulu: University of Hawaii Press, 1994), pp. 88–93.
[5] Chandler, *History*, p. 119.

later, particularly under the protectorate, it became the dominant term, favoured because it linked Khmer ethnicity and nationality.[6]

During the late 18th and early 19th centuries, competition between Siam and Vietnam had weakened Cambodia. In 1794 King Rama I of Siam annexed a region centred on the town of Battambang, today in the north-west of Cambodia, and placed it under the control of a viceroy whose successors ruled there until 1907. Between 1834 and 1847 large areas of the rest of what we today call Cambodia were devastated by wars and popular unrest.[7] A more peaceful period began in 1848 when the king of Siam placed Ang Duong on the Cambodian throne.

King Ang Duong recognised Siamese suzerainty, sending two of his sons, Princes Norodom and Sisowath, to live and study in the court of King Mongkut (Rama IV r. 1851–68), but he also paid tribute to the Vietnamese emperor in Hue.[8] Late in his reign, the Cambodian king made overtures towards Emperor Napoleon III, possibly hoping that France would help him to counter the influence of one or both of his powerful neighbours. Nothing came of this initiative, but after Ang Duong died, his son Norodom signed the Treaty of Protection in 1863. In return, France supported Norodom's claim to the throne against his half-brothers, Sisowath and Sivotha. After signing the Treaty of Protection, Norodom attempted to continue his tributary relations with the court of Siam, which held part of the royal insignia necessary for his coronation. The French prevented Norodom from travelling to Bangkok in late 1863, but arranged for representatives of the Siamese king to be present at his coronation in 1864. Norodom's key rivals, Sisowath and Sivotha, took very different paths. Sisowath remained at the Cambodian court, currying favour with the French. Sivotha took to the *maquis* and attempted to wage war against the French until his death in 1891.[9]

Within *sruk khmer*, family, status and relations of obligation and protection structured social life. The king headed a small hierarchy of elites who were divided by overlapping layers of status based on lineage as well as religious and administrative functions.[10] Caste-like strata included senior members of the royal entourage, minor royals, members of

---

[6] Thun and Keo, "Ethnocentrism of Victimhood".

[7] Chandler, *History*, pp. 149–65; Winichakul, *Siam Mapped*, p. 85.

[8] Winichakul, *Siam Mapped*, p. 85.

[9] See Osborne, *French Presence*, pp. 192–9; Chandler, *History*, pp. 142–65, 171–85.

[10] Sok, *Le Cambodge*, pp. 207–22; Muller, *Colonial Cambodia's "Bad Frenchmen"*, p. 58.

the Buddhist Sangha and a small Brahminic group of baku, free commoners and slaves of various categories.[11] Families were both matrilineal and patrilineal. By marrying the daughters of powerful families, the king made and reinforced political alliances, and certain women in the royal household, including the king's mother and his senior wives, exercised considerable influence, as did his brothers and some other male relatives.[12]

In the syncretic Theravada cosmology of Khmer people, the king was the bridge between the temporal and the divine.[13] A successful king brought harmony to his realm. War and upheaval or even drought and floods could indicate poor rule within a Buddhist concept of cycles of rise and decline.[14] It is often said that the king was the owner of all the land in his domain.[15] Writing of the 17th century, Grégory Mikaelian describes a semi-contractual relationship between king and subject whereby the monarch allowed peasants a right to use the land and members of the elite rights to levy charges on the peasants.[16] Within this framework, it is important to differentiate Cambodian governance from any notion of a modern bureaucratic state. Power was highly personalised. Free men registered their allegiance to one or more powerful officials, providing services and taxes in exchange for protection and patronage. These officials, known in Khmer as *namoeun*, held power not by administering infrastructure or enforcing laws but by managing relationships and ensuring "loyalty through the distribution of sufficient rewards".[17] In the countryside, more than 50 *chauvai khet* (called provincial governors by the French) each held a specific title and exercised considerable autonomy, particularly under weak kings.[18] The governors collected taxes and raised armies as required by various patrons. Officially,

---

[11] Muller, *Colonial Cambodia's "Bad Frenchmen"*, p. 18.

[12] Jacobsen, *Lost Goddesses*, pp. 109–45.

[13] Mikaelian, "Recherches", p. 375; David Porter Chandler, "Cambodia before the French: Politics in a Tributary Kingdom, 1794–1848" (PhD dissertation, Cornell University, 1973), p. 29.

[14] Chandler, "Cambodia before the French", p. 41. Regarding cycles of rise and decline, see Anne Ruth Hansen, *How to Behave: Buddhism and Modernity in Colonial Cambodia, 1860–1930* (Hawai'i: University of Hawai'i Press, 2007), pp. 20–2.

[15] Khin Sok, *Le Cambodge*, p. 163; Virginia Thompson, *French Indo-China* (London: Octagon Books, 1968, 1937), pp. 340–1; Tully, *France on the Mekong*, pp. 142, 497.

[16] Mikaelian, "Recherches", p. 375.

[17] Edwards, *Cambodge*, p. 71; see also Khin Sok, *Le Cambodge*, p. 223.

[18] Khin Sok, *Le Cambodge*, pp. 5–7, 212–13.

Fonctionnaires, *Mandarins and Cosmologies of Law* 31

the king appointed them, but the positions could be semi-hereditary, and individuals within each province could owe fealty to different members of the royal elite.[19] The majority of free commoners were ethnic Khmer peasants who lived in sparsely populated villages centred on a Buddhist wat. They established a right to land based on use and occupation.[20] At the bottom of the social hierarchy came slaves of various categories. Slaves could be born into servitude or captured during wars or slaving expeditions.[21] Some filled special roles in pagodas and in the Royal Palace, and some were economically better off than the poorest free peasants.[22] Many became indentured through debt and could theoretically buy their freedom.[23] The French waged a protracted campaign to have King Norodom eradicate all forms of slavery, but in practice certain types of indentured labour continued into the early 20th century, particularly debt servitude.

A small Muslim population included peoples of Malay origin and ethnic Cham.[24] In the north-east of the country, linguistically and culturally separate populations of highland peoples practised swidden agriculture and did not consider themselves subjects of the Khmer king.[25] Some highland groups waged guerrilla warfare against the dual encroachment of French and Khmer power well into the 1920s and 1930s.[26] Minority ethnic Chinese and Vietnamese populations also inhabited the kingdom. It is difficult to know the sizes of these populations in 1863, particularly given the fluid geographical definition of the king's domain. Both groups increased in number during the protectorate. Chinese merchants dominated commerce, and around the king's court there was "a commercially powerful group of Sino-Khmer, which controlled

---

[19] Ibid., pp. 212–43; Forest, *Le Cambodge et la colonisation française*, pp. 17–23.

[20] Roger Kleinpeter, *Le problème foncier au Cambodge* [The Land Problem in Cambodia] (Paris: Editions Domat-Monthchrestien, 1935), pp. 17–126.

[21] Khin Sok, *Le Cambodge*, p. 229; Tully, *France on the Mekong*, pp. 42–5; Étienne Aymonier, *Le Cambodge: Le royaume actuel* [Cambodia, the Current Kingdom] (Paris: Ernest Leroux, 1900), pp. 98–102.

[22] Khin Sok, *Le Cambodge*, pp. 43–4.

[23] Ibid., p. 230. Vannary Imam, *When Elephants Fight: A Memoir* (Melbourne: Allen and Unwin, 2000), p. 5.

[24] Ernest Hoeffel, "De la condition juridique des étrangers au Cambodge" [On the Legal Status of Foreigners in Cambodia] (PhD dissertation, Charles Hiller University, Strasbourg, 1932), pp. 69–71; Chandler, *History*, pp. 120–1.

[25] Mathieu Guérin, *Paysans de la Forêt à l'Epoque Coloniale* [Peasants of the Forest in the Colonial Era] (Paris: Presses universitaires de Rennes, 2008), pp. 69–96.

[26] Ibid., pp. 94–122.

32 *Colonial Law Making*

much of the local trade".[27] In the early years of the protectorate, and later during the rubber boom of the 1920s and 1930s, the French encouraged ethnic Vietnamese to migrate to Cambodia in large numbers.[28]

Cambodian Courts and Laws

While Moura's description of Cambodian legal procedures, quoted above, was rife with Eurocentric assumptions and cultural blindness, the kingdom's legal system probably had become more corrupt and exploitative than in the past.[29] Elite Cambodians linked a sense of karmic entitlement with a very temporal approach to giving and extracting tributes, taking for granted that social relations were unequal and exploitative and that they had the right to extract income directly from the population. But as the king's realm had diminished, so too had the pool from which the elites could take their wealth, causing increased demands for tributes on individual families.

Echoing Moura's picture of a system in decay, other early French observers described a formal hierarchy of courts and procedures, but claimed it was no longer strictly operating. Based on the texts they had access to and on their conversations with senior members of the Cambodian elite, the French described a structure of courts and judges in which the king was supreme judge and lawmaker, illustrated in Figure 2.1.[30]

Numerous envoys and delegates of the king and ministers worked alongside the court hierarchy, and it seems likely that they were among the corrupt officials in search of cases to whom Moura referred. Some of these individuals paid for the right to collect certain revenues and to punish specific infractions.[31] For example, the Cambodian minister of justice could send an envoy to oversee trials for murder and theft, and the

---

[27] Muller, *Colonial Cambodia's "Bad Frenchmen"*, pp. 57–9.

[28] Forest, *Le Cambodge et la colonisation française*, pp. 442–5.

[29] Hansen, *How to Behave*, p. 54; see also Mak Phoeun, *Histoire du Cambodge de la fin du XVIe au début du XVIIIe siècle* [History of Cambodia from the End of the Sixteenth Century to the Beginning of the Eighteenth Century] (Paris: École Française d'Extrême-Orient, 1995), p. 419.

[30] Taken mainly from Leclère's descriptions; see Adhémard Leclère, *Recherches sur la législation criminelle et la procédure des Cambodgiens* [Research on the Criminal Legislation and Procedure of the Cambodians] (Paris: Challamel, 1894), pp. 56–69; also Aymonier, *Le Cambodge*, pp. 92–4.

[31] Adhémard Leclère, *Droit Cambodgien* [Cambodian Law] (Paris: Larose, 1894), pp. 128–32; Aymonier, *Le Cambodge*, p. 93. Regarding their origins and degeneration into a parasitic layer, see Mikaelian, "Recherches", pp. 19, 97, 285–7.

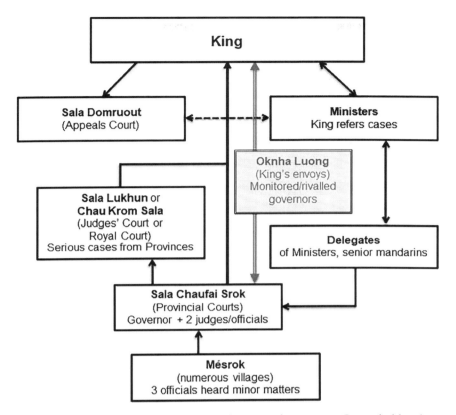

Figure 2.1: Cambodian Court Hierarchy pre-colonisation. Compiled by the author based on: Leclère, *Recherches sur la législation criminelle et la procédure des Cambodgiens*, pp. 56–69; and Forêt, *Le Cambodge*, pp. 92–4.

chief of the royal granary could sell the right to inflict punishments for agriculture-related offences. Étienne Aymonier claimed to have observed 14 such delegates operating in the small province of Bati in 1874.[32]

In theory, the king was the supreme judge and legislator, and all litigants had a right to appeal to him.[33] Three groups of officials assisted the monarch in his judicial functions. First, he could delegate a matter to his five ministers or could adjudicate in consultation with them.

---
[32] Aymonier, *Le Cambodge*, p. 93.
[33] Leclère, *Recherches sur la législation criminelle*, pp. 56–69; Aymonier, *Le Cambodge*, pp. 80–1.

Second, he could refer a case to the *Sala Domruot*, which the French described as a form of Court of Appeal.[34] French administrator and scholar Adhémard Leclère, whose translations of Khmer legal texts would become the standard reference for colonial administrators, claimed that in practice the ministers decided which cases would go before the king, and often referred them instead to the *Sala Domruot* or occasionally dealt with them directly.[35] Each of the 50-odd provincial governors presided over a local court, assisted by a judge (*sophea*) and one other official. An 1885 account from Krauchmar (on the Mekong River to the north-east of Phnom Penh, now in the province of Tboung Khmum) also refers to village-level tribunals.[36] According to this account, the *chauvai sruk*, or provincial governors, dominated the provincial courts. The *sopheas*, referred to as judges, may have had some training in the legal texts, but were subordinate to the governor. A photograph of provincial officials and French *Résident* Hertrich, taken in 1896 in the central western province of Pursat, demonstrates their relative status. The French *résident*

Figure 2.2: Provincial officials, Pursat 1896

Source: Photographer, André Salles 1896. Gallica, Bibliothèque Nationale de France (accessed 26 November 2015).

---

[34] Leclère, *Recherches sur la législation criminelle*, pp. 58–9.
[35] Ibid., p. 139.
[36] Coulgéans to Résident of Kompong Siam, 16 Oct. 1885, NAC RSC 11549; Muller, *Colonial Cambodia's "Bad Frenchmen"*, p. 107.

stands at the centre of the group, with Governor Sous standing to his left in the back row. Also standing are the governor's oldest son and Hertrich's interpreter. Judge (*sophea*) Srey is squatting second from the left in the front row, as a subordinate official.

Provincial Officials

By the time the picture in Figure 2.2 was taken, the French had control of the kingdom's revenue and had placed Cambodian officials on a state payroll. The combination of European-style jackets similar to those worn by French colonial officials and the Cambodian *sampot chang kbin* suggest that the *namoeun* were expected to be the auxiliaries of French rule. They illustrated the dual narrative of the protectorate: civilisation (Europeanisation) and protection of Khmer tradition.

Much of what we know about Cambodian laws at the time of colonisation is based on pre-colonial texts and on French accounts and translations. Cambodian linguist Saveros Pou identifies two categories of law (*cpap*) in Cambodia, those aimed at the population as a whole, which were gnomic poems circulated orally, and written texts meant as a guide for the "political layer".[37]

Influenced by Western legal thought, which prioritises written state laws over custom, and the public over the private realm, the French focused on the written texts. Grégory Mikaelian identifies three forms of such normative text in Khmer literature: a code or codes (*cpap*); a royal charter of monastic foundation; and an anthology of judicial stories.[38] These were all sacred or royal texts, intimately linked with monarchical power and available to only a small literate layer. The French referred to these texts collectively as *kram* (literally royal decrees) or codes. They saw the *kram* as encompassing texts derived from Hinduism, known in Khmer as the *Prea Thamma Sath*, and Khmer royal law. The royal law included the decisions of various kings on issues of justice, crime and punishment and rules of royal protocol. As recorded in the texts

---

[37] Saveros Pou, "La Littérature Didactique Khmère [Texte Imprimé]: Les Cpap" [Khmer Didactic Literature [Printed Text]: the Cpap], *Société Asiatique* [Asiatic Society] 269 (1981): 454–66, see 455.

[38] Mikaelian, "Recherches", p. 31. Regarding the Royal Chronicles, see, for example, David Chandler, "Cambodian Palace Chronicles (Rajabansavatar) 1927–1949: Kingship and Historiography at the End of the Colonial Era", in *Perceptions of the Past in Southeast Asia*, ed. Anthony Reid and David Marr (Singapore, Kuala Lumpur, Hong Kong: Heinemann, 1979), pp. 189–210, see p. 207.

themselves, from the late 16th century onwards, successive Cambodian kings had the codes edited, amended and recopied, signifying Buddhist cycles of renewal, restoration of order and dynastic continuity.[39]

It was arguably problematic to assume, as the French appear to have done, that the *kram*, or codes, were intended as universally applicable laws rather than, as Saveros Pou implies, guides for the educated elites and the scholars who had access to them.[40] Literacy and knowledge of the codes signified wisdom, and possession of copies or editions indicated power.[41] Some elite families who held versions of some of the codes concealed them from the French.[42]

If Moura's claim that any official could act as a judge is true, it seems likely that very few of them would have studied these rare and closely guarded texts in detail, a further indication of a system that had broken down. However, even when properly applied, Cambodian legal process at that time involved settling disputes, not applying universally applicable rules. As Pou suggests, the codes were guides for behaviour and sources of wisdom for those who ruled over others, rather than positivist norms.

Indochina and French Colonialism

Myriad reasons and contingencies led France, initially under Napoleon III and later under the sway of the *parti colonial* of the Third Republic (1870–1940), to colonise what they called *Indochine française*. France's standing in Europe had declined since the mid-1700s following defeats in the Seven Years War (1756–73), when it lost important territories in India and North America, and the defeat of Napoleon I in 1814/15. In the second half of the 19th century, France participated in the race to claim new territories in Africa, the Pacific and Asia. Some French explorers believed that Indochina could provide land or river access into southern

---

[39] Chandler, *History*, p. 164; Chandler, "Tragedy of Cambodian History", p. 104; Mikaelian, "Recherches", pp. 255–7; Hansen, *How to Behave*, pp. 50–1; Edwards, *Cambodge*, p. 107.

[40] Pou, "La Littérature Didactique", p. 455. However, see Chris Baker and Pasuk Phongpaichit, trans. and ed. *The Palace Law of Ayutthaya and the Thammasat: Law and Kinship in Siam* (Ithaca, NY: Cornell University, 2016), pp. 30–1.

[41] Edwards, *Cambodge*, p. 108.

[42] Mikaelian, "Recherches", p. 75; Edwards, *Cambodge*, p. 4. Leclère referred to the difficulty of "discovering" the texts; see, for example, Adhémard Leclère, trans., *Les Codes Cambodgiens Tome 1* [The Cambodian Codes Vol. 1.] (Paris: Ernest Leroux, 1898), p. xvi; Leclère, *Recherches sur la législation criminelle*, p. xix.

China. Others saw the region that now comprises Vietnam, Laos and Cambodia as offering strategic control over sea routes and the opportunity for trade and economic extraction.[43]

After several less successful military incursions, France occupied the southern Vietnamese town of Saigon in 1859. In 1862 the Vietnamese emperor, Tu Duc, based in Hue, ceded Saigon and three southern provinces to the French. In 1863 French naval officers established the protectorate over Cambodia and in 1867 incorporated remaining southern Vietnamese provinces into their colony of Cochin China. In 1883, the French moved north to take control of Hanoi, in the Red River delta, a region they then called Tonkin. They did not completely "pacify" Tonkin until 1896. In 1893, France forced the Siamese King Rama V to cede suzerainty over Lao territories east of the Mekong.[44]

Although it was a lesser attraction than China, Ayutthaya/Siam (Thailand) had become a focus for European colonial rivalry in mainland Southeast Asia. In the 19th century, Siamese kings were pressured to sign unequal treaties with at least 16 European countries, all of which claimed extraterritorial privileges. Successive monarchs of the Chakri dynasty bowed to European demands, but also astutely played the various European powers against each other and avoided direct colonisation.

Britain was France's most immediate rival in the region, and Siam became a geographical buffer between British-controlled Burma and the French in *Indochine française*. This rivalry may have helped the Chakri kings to evade direct colonial rule and to consolidate their hold over what would become Thailand, but they also relinquished suzerainty over considerable territory. In 1893 King Chulalongkorn (Rama V 1868–1910) recognised French claims to Lao territories east of the Mekong, and Britain took control of some of the Shan states in Burma. Between 1895 and 1909, Siam also ceded the sultanates of the Malay Peninsula to Britain, and in 1907 lost its overlordship of the Khmer-speaking regions of Battambang, Siem Reap and Sisophon, now part of Cambodia, to the French.[45]

---

[43] Brocheux and Hémery, *Indochina*, pp. 27–30; Osborne, *French Presence*, pp. 27–37; Tully, *France on the Mekong*, pp. 1–6; Stuart Michael Persell, *The French Colonial Lobby, 1889–1938* (Stanford, CA: Hoover Institution Press, 1983).

[44] Christopher Goscha, *The Penguin Modern History of Vietnam* (London: Penguin, 2008. First published Allen Lane, 2016), pp. 59–68.

[45] Regarding the north-western provinces of Cambodia, see Tully, *Cambodia under the Tricolour*, pp. 81–107; regarding British expansion in Malaysia and Burma, see

In these conditions, the French constantly worried that European rivals would use their embassies in Bangkok as a base to cultivate unrest in Cambodia. Before France and Britain signed the Entente Cordiale in 1904, and perhaps even until they fought as allies in the First World War, the French suspected Britain of having designs on its colonies. Consequently, as France strengthened its control in Cambodia, it worked to avoid giving Britain any pretext to challenge the legitimacy of its methods. In other words, the French did not want to be accused of exceeding their mandate under the 1863 Treaty of Protection. A plain reading of the treaty suggests the French did just that, but they manoeuvred as far as possible to retain some semblance of legality, usually by pressuring King Norodom to give formal assent.

As the colony of Indochina was being established, Napoleon III's reign in France ended and was replaced by the Third Republic (1871–1940). During the early decades of the republic, a debate emerged among French proponents of colonial expansion as to how best to administer overseas "possessions". The French *mission civilisatrice* had previously been based on the notion of "assimilation", whereby colonies would become part of France. They would be absorbed within the centralised systems of metropolitan administration, as was formally the case with most of Algeria. Drawing on their analyses of various parts of the British empire and of the Dutch East Indies (Indonesia), a new school of thought favoured "association". Although somewhat fluid and ill-defined, association implied that colonial rule should as far as possible be managed by cooperation with local elites, and that colonial subjects should be left to practise their own cultures, "evolving" towards European standards of civilisation at their own pace.[46] Colonial association would become official French policy by the end of the First World War, but was influential much earlier.[47]

Suwannathat-Pian, *Palace, Political Party and Power*, pp. 20–5; J.S. Furnivall, *Colonial Policy and Practice: A Comparative Study of Burma and Netherlands India* (New York: New York University Press, 1956. First published Cambridge University Press, 1948), pp. 29–39; J.M. Gullick: *Rulers and Residents: Influence and Power in the Malay States: 1870–1920* (Oxford: Oxford University Press, 1992), pp. i–vi, 1–20, 136–51.

[46] Raymond F. Betts, *Assimilation and Association in French Colonial Theory, 1890–1914* (New York: Columbia University Press, 1961), pp. 5–21.

[47] Thompson, *French Indo-China*, p. 401; Alice L. Conklin, *A Mission to Civilize: The Republican Idea of Empire in France and West Africa, 1895–1930* (Stanford, CA: Stanford University Press, 1997), pp. 6–7; Betts, *Assimilation*, pp. 129–30.

The two policies—association and assimilation—came to be linked respectively with indirectly ruled protectorates on the one hand and directly annexed colonies on the other. Although this was not strictly correct, as it confounded internal policy towards colonised peoples with the status of colonial possessions in international law, protectorates came to be linked with the policy of association.[48] Indochina became a seedbed for the policy of association and for a turn towards protectorates as the preferred form of colony. France would build on its experiences in Indochina, including in its north African protectorates of Tunisia, established in 1881, and in Morocco from 1912.

The shift in favour of indirect rule came after Cochin China was made a direct colony in 1863. Cambodia, Annam and Tonkin remained protectorates, although the French carved out directly ruled concessions over the strategically important centres of Hanoi and Haiphong in Tonkin, and Tourane (Danang) in Annam. The international legal status of Laos was mixed. Luang Prabang in the north was a protectorate, but in the south Vientiane and Champassak had been directly annexed via a treaty with Siam in 1893. This mixed status troubled French jurists and politicians, but in practice colonial administrators ruled Laos as a protectorate. The French maintained the formalities of indirect rule in all their protectorates, but to varying degrees they incrementally increased their control over each one. This mixture of regard for the form of indirect rule with actual practices of incremental control would have noticeable consequences for the administration of justice, particularly in Cambodia.

European powers regularly limited the authority of judges and courts in their colonies in ways that would not have been acceptable in the metropole, a tendency often resented by colonial judges. In Indochina, relations between the judicial and administrative arms of the colonial apparatus became particularly acrimonious after 1881, when a corps of French judges arrived to assume control of the indigenous and the French courts of Cochin China. Tension between colonial judges and administrators spread to Cambodia, with important consequences for the local courts.

A quick summary of three aspects of the French legal system and of related constitutional theory—the meaning of the separation of powers, judicial independence and the professional divisions between judges and lawyers—helps to set the scene for what took place.

Constitutional law under the French Third Republic recognised the separation of executive, legislative and judicial powers and guaranteed

---

[48] Betts, *Assimilation*, pp. 128–32.

40   *Colonial Law Making*

judicial independence. However, for those trained in modern Anglo-American common law, perhaps the most striking feature of the French legal system at that time was the relative weakness of the judicial arm of government, a legacy of the French Revolution of 1789. Before the revolution, French judges had stymied efforts to unify and reform the country's laws. Determined to stamp out such judicial interference in the national project, the revolutionaries of 1789 decreed that judges should be subject to the legislature, which expressed the will of the people. Until the late 20th century, French legal doctrine rejected any notion of judicial review of the constitutionality of legislation.[49] A judge's role was to apply rather than to interpret the law. In the 1950s, French comparative lawyer René David queried whether there was indeed a French judicial power in the meaning of a system of checks and balances as understood in US law.[50] Judges were civil servants, subject to the authority of the minister of justice, who was a member of the executive arm of government. This inevitably affected their independence. Throughout the Third Republic, the French judiciary struggled to dispel perceptions that its members were vulnerable to political interference.[51] The minister of justice had a great deal of power over appointments and promotions, although judges officially enjoyed a form of tenure or *inamovibilité*.[52] This did not sufficiently protect them from political

---

[49] Alain Laquièze, "État de Droit [Rule of Law] and National Sovereignty in France", in *The Rule of Law: History, Theory and Criticism*, ed. Pietro Costa and Danilo Zolo (Dordecht: Springer, 2007), pp. 261–91, see p. 261; Sophie Boyron, "Constitutional Law", in *Principles of French Law*, ed. John Bell, Sophie Boyron and Simon Whittaker (Oxford: Oxford University Press, 1998), pp. 47–56.

[50] René David and Henry P. de Vries, *The French Legal System: An Introduction to Civil Law Systems* (New York: Oceana, 1958), pp. 9–14, 31–3; Adhémar Esmein and Henry Nézard, *Éléments de Droit Constitutionnel Français et Comparé, Tome 1* [Elements of French Constitutional Law and Comparisons, Vol. 1] (Paris: Larose, 1921, 7th ed.), pp. 500–13.

[51] Benjamin F. Martin, *Crime and Criminal Justice under the Third Republic: The Shame of Marianne* (Baton Rouge: Louisiana State University Press, 1990), pp. 193–4; David and de Vries, *The French Legal System*, p. 19; O.S. Tyndale, "The Organization and Administration of Justice in France, with an Outline of French Procedure with Respect to the Production of Evidence", *Canadian Bar Review* (Nov. 1935): 567–83, see 567–76.

[52] Léon Duguit, *Traité de droit constitutionnel 1927–1930* [Treatise on Constitutional Law 1927–1930] (France: Ancienne Librairie Fontemoing, 1927), p. 717; Martine Fabre, "Le magistrat d'outre-mer: L'aventure de la justice" [The Overseas Judge: The Justice Adventure], in *Le juge et l'outre-mer: Les roches bleues de l'empire colonial Tome 2* [The Judge and Overseas Territory: The Blue Rocks of the Colonial Empire

pressure, and in sensitive cases many judges valued their next promotion above the letter of the law.[53]

In the colonies, powers were even less clearly separated, and French colonial judges, like their counterparts in other European colonies, were more directly subjected to the executive than their brothers in the metropole.[54] The French minister for colonies, rather than the minister of justice, had ultimate say over appointments and transfers of colonial judges, who had no right of *inamovabilité*.[55] Pressures to overlook legal principle in favour of the political exigencies were even more overt than in the metropole.

Legal historian Bernard Durand likens the colonial judges' role in steering the ship of colonial justice to that of the Greek mythical figure, Jason, and his argonauts, navigating between the colliding Cyanean Rocks. In the colonies, the rocks between which judges had to steer consisted of metropolitan legal principles on the one hand and the demands of colonial rule on the other.[56] Foreign domination and the liberating potential of Western bourgeois law were always, at best, uneasy partners.[57]

Vol. 2] ed. Bernard Durand and Martine Fabre (Lille: Centre d'histoire judiciaire éditeur, 2004), pp. 71–93, see pp. 71–3.

[53] Martin, *Crime and Criminal Justice under the Third Republic*, pp. 191–233; Tyndale, "The Organization and Administration of Justice in France", pp. 578–80; Sophie Boyron, *The Constitution of France: A Contextual Analysis* (Oxford: Hart Publishing, 2013), pp. 42–7.

[54] Bernard Durand, "Les Magistrats coloniaux entre absence et errance" [Colonial Judges: Between Absence and Wandering], in *Le juge et l'Outre-mer*, ed. Durand and Fabre, pp. 47–70, see pp. 47–8; Laurent Manière, "Deux conceptions de l'action judiciaire aux colonies. Magistrats et administrateurs en Afrique Occidentale Française (1887–1912)", [Two Conceptions of Judicial Action in the Colonies. Judges and Administrators in French West Africa (1887–1912)] *Clio@Thémis: révue électronique d'histoire du droit* 4 (2011) (accessed 31 Mar. 2014); Lee, "Plural Society and the Colonial State", p. 236.

[55] Girault, *Principes de Colonisation et de Législation Coloniale*, pp. 483–4; Durand, "Les Magistrats coloniaux", pp. 47–8.

[56] Bernard Durand, "Prolégomènes: originalités et conformités de la justice coloniale sous la Troisième République" [Prolegomena: Originalities and Conformities of Colonial Justice under the Third Republic], in *Le Juge et l'Outre-mer*, ed. Durand and Fabre (Lille: Centre d'histoire judiciaire éditeur, 2004), pp. 7–42, see p. 7; Sylvie Thénault, *Une drôle de Justice: Les magistrats dans la guerre d'Algérie* [A Strange Justice: Judges in the Algerian War] (Paris: Découverte, 2001).

[57] Lee, "Plural Society and the Colonial State"; Upendra Baxi, "Postcolonial Legality", pp. 540–55.

Administrative law also provides an example of the way colonial rule privileged the power of colonial administrators over the courts. In France, a separate system of administrative tribunals, headed by the *Conseil d'État* (Council of State), dealt with allegations of governmental illegality and excesses of power. The council played an important role during the Third Republic because the French government increasingly resorted to presidential decrees in order to bypass the unruly National Assembly. The council had the power to review many presidential decrees, but under laws inherited from Napoleon III, decrees related to colonial affairs were exempt from review.[58]

A second feature of French civil law that contrasts with Anglo common law, and which affected justice administration in Indochina, is the career divide between judge and lawyer. Whereas British judges generally start their careers as lawyers, French law students usually choose between the bar and the bench and follow different streams of study. In the inquisitorial French criminal system, prosecutors are also considered members of the judiciary. In Indochina, members of the judicial corps frequently transferred between roles as prosecutor and judge, and occasionally resigned to become lawyers, suggesting closer links between the judiciary and lawyers than in the metropole.

The Colony of Indochina: *fonctionnarisme au bon marché*

The colonies offered a refuge for many who did not share the democratic aspirations of the French Third Republic. Senior bureaucrats could enjoy an element of what Benedict Anderson calls "capitalism in feudal-aristocratic drag".[59] Glimpses of this zeitgeist of colonial privilege, its feudal overtones and its foundation in racial difference have been preserved: for example, in the archives where colonial officials routinely refer to their personal servants as "boys"; and in the fascinating film clips compiled by Rithy Pan and Raoul Jennar, where, for example, French people amuse themselves by watching a group of Cambodian children dive in the dust for tossed peanuts.[60]

---

[58] Esmein and Nézard, *Éléments de Droit Constitutionnel*, vol. 2, pp. 80–6.

[59] Benedict Anderson, *Imagined Communities: Reflections on the Origin and Spread of Nationalism* (London: Verso, 1991), p. 151.

[60] Rithy Panh, *La France est notre patrie* [France Is Our Mother Country] (Cambodia; France: Bophana Productions and Catherine Dussart Productions, released 2015).

Except during brief periods in the late 1800s and the 1920s, tight colonial budgets also constrained "civilising" impulses in Indochina, particularly away from the centres of French interest, where indirect rule allowed colonisation *au bon marché*, or on the cheap.[61] Colonial society was quarrelsome and factional, and was stratified along class and occupational lines. Colonial administrators frequently clashed with settlers and other adventurers, such as Thomas Caraman, whose career in Cambodia Gregor Muller portrays so well.[62] In these conditions, judges and lawyers often found common cause against those colonial administrators who constrained their power and overrode legal principles.

While they often competed and clashed, the administrative and judicial arms of colonial Indochina both fitted a certain bureaucratic mould, known disparagingly as *fonctionnarisme*.[63] This term, coined in reaction to the expanding apparatus of the French state at home and abroad, implied both political patronage and a certain form of bureaucratism. By the early years of the 20th century, critics in France had singled out Indochina as a den of *fonctionnarisme*,[64] the result perhaps of the relatively small number of French settlers compared with colonial officials.[65] Twenty years after the formation of the protectorate, French citizens who did not work for the apparatus comprised just 20 per cent of the 850 Europeans registered in Cambodia.[66] The proportion increased over time, but in Cambodia non-*fonctionnaires* remained a minority of the European population, particularly outside the major urban centres.[67]

France at first made Saigon its key administrative centre in Indochina, but in 1902 Hanoi became the colonial capital. The French administered Indochina as a form of colonial union in which one single French administrative corps and a single judicial corps operated

---

[61] Roderick Broadhurst, Thierry Bouhours and Brigitte Bouhours, *Violence and the Civilising Process in Cambodia* (Cambridge: Cambridge University Press, 2015), p. 99.

[62] Muller, *Colonial Cambodia's "Bad Frenchmen"*.

[63] Sager, "A Nation of Functionaries", p. 146.

[64] Ibid.

[65] Henri Brunschwig, *French Colonialism 1871–1914: Myths and Realities* (London: Pall Mall Press, 1966), p. 74; Sager, "A Nation of Functionaries", p. 156.

[66] Robert Aldrich, *Greater France: A History of French Overseas Expansion* (Basingstoke: Macmillan, 1996), p. 148. According to Aldrich, customs agents (100) were most numerous, followed by teachers (12), postal clerks (25) and judicial officials (7).

[67] In 1936, there were an estimated 2,023 French citizens living in Cambodia; see Brocheux and Hémery, *Indochina*, pp. 182–3.

across the five regions. The colonial judges presided over French Courts of First Instance in each region, and appeals courts in Saigon and Hanoi.[68] On the administrative side, some services such as cadastre, customs and excise, education, health, military and the police also came under Indochina-wide control.[69]

By 1913, the *résident supérieur* of each protectorate, and the governor in directly ruled Cochin China, had been granted considerable autonomy, including the right to levy a range of imposts on the local population. In Phnom Penh, the *résident supérieur* oversaw a "cabinet" comprising several bureaux. Budgetary constraints and bureaucratism characterised much about the protectorate, including relations with the local elite and approaches to legal reform. Bureaucratic colonialism generated its own forms of corruption, patronage and clientelism. Relatively peaceful and economically marginal, Cambodia provided scope for a man such as François Baudoin who, as *résident supérieur* from 1914 until the mid-1920s, made the protectorate his personal fief.

The lifestyles and the outlook of members of the apparatus evolved over time as relatively disciplined bureaucrats replaced the more adventurous, often aristocratic, naval officers who had claimed Cochin China and Cambodia for France. In 1887, the French government established a colonial school to train administrators and judicial officers for service in "Greater France". The social composition of colonial functionaries became more middle class. An increasing proportion were drawn from those born and raised in overseas French possessions.[70] Social mores became more conservative, or perhaps more hypocritical. For example, whereas liaisons between French officials and local women had been relatively open in the early years of occupation, the colonial apparatus of the Third Republic began actively to discourage such relations, urging

---

[68] The first French Court of Appeal was established in Saigon. Until 1919, except between 1894 and 1898, the Court of Appeal in Hanoi operated as an extension of the Court of Appeal in Saigon. They became separate courts again in 1919.

[69] See *Annuaire Général de l'Indochine* [General Directory of Indochina] for various years including 1900, 1914, 1915, 1920, 1926 (Hanoi: Imprimerie d'Extrême-Orient). For general descriptions of the governance structures of Indochina and in Cambodia, see Forest, *Le Cambodge et la colonisation française*, pp. 89–109, 191–6; Brocheux and Hémery, *Indochina*, pp. 80–115.

[70] Aldrich, *Greater France*, pp. 147, 151–2.

French women to accompany their husbands to the colony.[71] Ambitious bureaucrats henceforth risked jeopardising their careers if they lived or mixed too openly with a local partner.

Once in Indochina, French women found few professional opportunities, as the colonial bureaucracy remained overwhelmingly male. Suzanne Karpelès, who led the Buddhist Institute in Phnom Penh during the 1930s, was perhaps the only French woman to hold a position of influence in the protectorate administration.[72] Some French women worked as typists and teachers. Many others carried out charitable work, including among the numerous mixed-race children that French men continued to father, despite the supposedly restraining influence of French wives. Marguerite Duras' famous novels based on her childhood in Cambodia and Cochin China portray how difficult colonial life could be for single French women. After Duras' father died, her mother Marie Legrand/Donnadieu battled to earn a living, encountering an uncaring and often corrupt male colonial apparatus.[73]

The French colonial legal fraternity was completely male. Women gained the right to work as lawyers in 1900 in France, but not until 1939 in Indochina.[74] The French judiciary did not admit women until 1946, and only one female judge ever served in a colony.[75] Even during the First World War, when there was a dire shortage of French men to run the colonial bureaucracy, the judicial service in Indochina resisted suggestions from Paris to employ more women.[76]

Huy Kanthoul, a Cambodian politician during the 1940s and 1950s, remembered the upper echelons of the French administration as a closed society rife with jealousy and backstabbing, many of whose members had a powerful patron in Paris. According to Kanthoul every

---

[71] James Barnhart, "Violence and the Civilizing Mission: Native Justice in French Colonial Vietnam, 1858–1914" (PhD dissertation, University of Chicago, 1999), p. 434.

[72] Edwards, *Cambodge*, pp. 183–209.

[73] Marguerite Duras, *L'Amant* [The Lover] (Paris: Les éditions de Minuit, 1900); Marguerite Duras, *Un Barrage contre la pacifique* [A Wall against the Pacific] (Paris: Gallimard, 1958).

[74] Blazy, "L'Organisation judiciaire", p. 827, note 2584.

[75] Fabre, "Le magistrat d'outre-mer", pp. 75–6.

[76] Penny Edwards, "Womanizing Indochina: Fiction, Nation, and Cohabitation in Colonial Cambodia, 1890–1930", in *Domesticating the Empire: Race, Gender and Family Life in French and Dutch Colonialism*, ed. Julia Clancy-Smith and Frances Gouda (Charlottesville: University of Virginia Press, 1998), pp. 108–30, see pp. 109–113.

46   *Colonial Law Making*

résident aspired to the grade of administrator first class, which was "the trump card for acceding with a little luck and a lot of support to the post of *résident supérieur* or governor of a colony, the supreme thought of all self-respecting administrators".[77] He also recalled other less successful officials who retired in the colony in order to feed their opium habit.

The colonial judges were equally bureaucratic and as vulnerable to the temptations of colonial life as their brothers in the administration, but they had a certain esprit de corps, which would have been reinforced by their professional training and their common grievances at their lack of autonomy. There were generally three paths into the French colonial judiciary: through the judicial section of the colonial school; through direct appointment by the minister for colonies; and, after 1924, through a special exam for law graduates. At least until 1924, most were appointed by the minister for colonies.[78] The minimum educational requirement was a law degree (*licence en droit*) and some professional experience.

There was little crossover between the French judges who served in Indochina, many of whom had been born in one of France's overseas territories, and the judicial corps of the metropole.[79] Of 65 judicial officers in Cochin China and Cambodia in 1897: almost a third had been born in another French colony or overseas territory; 30 had worked, or would work, in other colonies; only 7 would ever hold a judicial position in metropolitan France, usually at the beginning of their career.[80] Forty years later, in 1937, the 113 judicial officers in Indochina had

---

[77] Kanthoul, *Mémoires*.

[78] Fabre, "Le magistrat d'outre-mer", pp. 73–4.

[79] See, for example, Agence économique des colonies françaises [French Colonial Economic Agency], *Régime législatif, administratif et judiciaire de l'Indochine* [Legislative, Administrative and Judicial Regime of Indochina] (Paris: Agence économique des colonies françaises, 1944), paras. 296, 311.

[80] For general data on French colonial judges, see the online database by Jean-Claude Farcy and Rosine Fry, *Annuaire rétrospectif de la magistrature XIXᵉ–XXᵉ siècles* [Retrospective Directory of the Judiciary 19th–20th Centuries] (Université de Bourgogne/CNRS, 2010), http://tristan.u-bourgogne.fr/AM.html (accessed 10 Mar. 2016). For information on judicial personnel in Cochin China and Cambodia in 1897, including judges of all grades, justices of the peace, prosecutors, assistant prosecutors, substitutes and *lieutenants de juge*, see *Annuaire de l'Indo-Chine Français; 1er partie: Cochinchine et Cambodge 1889–1897* [Yearbook of French Indo-China; 1st Section: Cochin China and Cambodia, 1889–1897], (Saigon: Imprimerie coloniale, 1890), pp. 166–73.

similar backgrounds.[81] Seventy-one had served or would serve in other French overseas possessions.[82] Forty-four were born in a French colony or overseas territory, including 11 in Indochina itself. Only 18 would ever hold a judicial appointment in France, mostly following the Second World War.

Indochina appears to have been a popular posting for colonial judges, as over a third (24) of those listed in 1897 would never serve in another colony. A further 16 remained in Indochina for 20 or more years and another 6 for over a decade.[83] In 1937, of the 113 listed judicial officers, 93 spent more than 10 years in the colony and 66 remained for 20 or more years.[84]

One judicial official who spent his entire career in Indochina was Gabriel Michel, who reappears later in this book because he locked horns with *Résident Supérieur* François Baudoin over who should run the French courts in rural Cambodia. Michel worked in Indochina for 34 years. He was born in the French colony of Réunion in 1862 and arrived to take up a junior position in the courts of Saigon in 1883. Among other postings, Michel headed the French court of Phnom Penh from late 1889 to mid-1893.[85] He rose through the ranks to become the prosecutor general of Indochina, the most senior judicial officer in the colony, in 1909. In 1917 Governor General Sarraut forced Michel to retire, alleging that the prosecutor general headed a clique of obstructive, self-interested and possibly corrupt judicial officials.[86] Sarraut was not the only person to complain about the judges of Indochina. There were no doubt many conscientious judges, but François Romerio, who himself served as a judge in Indochina from 1934 to 1941, readily acknowledged that a number of his colleagues had succumbed to alcohol, opium and corruption.[87]

---

[81] *Annuaire Administratif de l'Indochine* [Administrative Yearbook of Indochina] (Hanoi: Imprimerie d'Extrême-Orient, 1937), pp. 152–68.

[82] Farcy and Fry, *Annuaire rétrospectif.*

[83] Ibid.

[84] *Annuaire Administratif de l'Indochine*, pp. 52–68.

[85] Farcy and Fry, *Annuaire rétrospectif.*

[86] Sarraut to Minister of Colonies, 25 Oct. 1917, CAOM GGI 65618.

[87] François Romerio, *Le Métier de magistrat, entretiens avec Robert Hervet* [The Judicial Profession, Interview with Robert Hervet] (Paris: Editions France-Empire, 1977), p. 64.

48 *Colonial Law Making*

French lawyers in Indochina, known as *avocats défenseurs* (defence lawyers), sat outside the colonial bureaucracy and had less formal influence than the judiciary. There were also fewer lawyers than judges. Nineteen had registered to work in the courts of Cochin China and Cambodia in 1897. By 1939 there were just over 60.[88] Two of the 19 lawyers listed in 1897 had previously held junior judicial positions, including one whose appointment as a judge had been revoked.[89] *Avocats défenseurs* registered with the courts, as approved by the prosecutor general of Indochina. They could be de-registered if they broke the law but also if they failed to show due respect for the laws. Every five years the governor general of Indochina decided how many *avocats défenseurs* could register in the jurisdiction.[90]

Robert Lortat-Jacob, who became a thorn in the side of the Cambodian protectorate administration during the 1920s, started his career in the colony as a junior judge in 1916. He resigned in 1919 and later became a vocal member of the bar.[91] He and several other lawyers joined the local chapter of the *Ligue des droits de l'homme et citoyen* (League of the Rights of Man and Citizen), which was formed in France after the wrongful conviction of Alfred Dreyfus for treason in 1895 scandalised and divided French society.[92] Lawyers had formed chapters of the League in Indochina as early as 1903, protesting against restrictions on their rights to practise and later on the decision that certain reforms to French criminal procedure enacted in France did not apply in Indochina.[93] During the 1920s, Robert Lortat-Jacob used the League's

---

[88] *Annuaire de L'Indochine Française: Cochinchine et Cambodge 1897*, pp. 160–3, 178–9. For a list of *avocats défenseurs* registered with the Court of Appeal in Saigon in 1931–32, see CAOM GGI, 65742.

[89] *Annuaire de L'Indochine Française: Saigon et Cambodge 1897*, pp. 179–8. Also Farcy and Fry.

[90] (Presidential) Decree of 5 November 1888, arts. 2, 6, 7. *Annuaire de L'Indochine Française: Saigon et Cambodge 1897*, pp. 160–3.

[91] Farcy and Fry, *Annuaire rétrospectif.*

[92] Charles Sowerwine, *France Since 1870: Culture, Society and the Making of the Republic* (Basingstoke: Palgrave Macmillan, 2009), pp. 64–9, 79–81.

[93] See Vice President of the Tonkin branch of the League for the Rights of Man and Citizen to Governor General, 19 Aug. 1906, and attached motion objecting to restrictions on the rights of lawyers in Tonkin, passed on 11 July 1903, CAOM GGI 4556.

networks in the French media and National Assembly to circulate his virulent criticisms of the protectorate administration.[94]

The Opening Acts

Two very different legal and social cosmologies met, combined and competed to form state law in the French protectorate of Cambodia. It would be easy to see the Cambodian elites' transactions with colonial power as corrupt and motivated merely by a desire to cling to old privileges. But their sense of entitlement was as deeply rooted in karma, status, law, patronage and royal power as was that of the French officials in notions of progress and of civilisational and racial superiority. French colonial law was part of the *mission civilisatrice*, championing ideals of universality and impartiality, but, as the following chapters show, colonial legal practice often sacrificed legal principles to the exigencies of domination, geopolitics and the professional ambitions of judicial and administrative *fonctionnaires*.

The first phase of the struggles and exchanges that shaped colonial state law in Cambodia started in the 1860s and culminated in 1897. During these decades, the Cambodian elite, led by King Norodom, openly contested France's expanding mandate. On their part, French officials judged Cambodian legal procedures to be corrupt and often barbaric. They therefore assumed the right to intervene in and to try to control the kingdom's courts, despite the terms of the 1863 Treaty of Protection. The French interpreted the treaty as having established different jurisdictions, the limits of which they proceeded to redefine in order to limit King Norodom's judicial power and to divide the population along ethnic lines. These moves by the French to take control of law were part of a broader process by which they also usurped other aspects of the king's administration. One colonial official would later describe this period as the transition from an external to an internal protectorate. Norodom's ultimately unsuccessful defiance nonetheless taught the French that there were limits beyond which they could not push the Cambodian elites, who retained considerable sway over the population. These early decades therefore laid the basis for the modus vivendi between colonial power and local elites that would define the protectorate, including its key legal institutions.

---

[94] See, for example: Judicial Adviser to Governor General, 16 Mar. 1927; Résident Supérieur Aristide Le Fol to Governor General, Sept. 1927, NAC RSC 36097.

3

The Jurisdictional Dispossession of King Norodom

In 1898, the year after King Norodom had finally conceded temporal authority to the French, he wrote to protest their dismissal of Cambodian Minister of Justice Ouk, a Norodom loyalist.[1] The king's letter, translated by Milton Osborne, is a poignant statement of the various humiliations inflicted on him by the French, not least of which were jurisdictional reforms:

> His Majesty loves the French Government very much and has always conformed to its desires . . . It asked him for all the country's taxes; it asked him for control over the Chinese and Annamites, who have always been under royal authority, so that they could submit to French tribunals; . . . It is desirable that the French Government also love His Majesty, who asked to have the Khmer Kingdom placed under French protection . . . From the point of view of Cambodian law, the master of the kingdom must have authority over the Cambodians, the inhabitants.[2]

Much of what David Chandler has called Norodom's long "tug-of-war" with the French, from 1863, when he signed the Treaty of Protection, until his death in 1904, has been well told.[3] Norodom resisted as best he

---

[1] Osborne, *French Presence*, pp. 242–3, also endnotes 43 and 44 at p. 345.
[2] Taken from the text as translated and quoted by Osborne, *French Presence*, p. 243. Osborne's source is: Cambodian National Archives, uncatalogued archives Box C. 6 No. 165: personal dossier of Nguon, containing a letter from King Norodom to the Résident Supérieur, Phnom Penh, 18 Nov. 1898.
[3] Chandler, *History*, p. 179.

The Jurisdictional Dispossession of King Norodom   51

could when his new protectors began incrementally to usurp his temporal powers, particularly the power to collect revenue.[4] The concurrent competition for control of law and jurisdiction has been less thoroughly examined. Three themes emerge: first, the ways in which the French used their extraterritorial rights under the treaty to create jurisdictions that extended their rule; second, contests often focused on competing narratives of protection; third, these early decades of struggle laid the foundations for the modus vivendi between the French and the Cambodian elite that would define the protectorate for the rest of its existence.

France moved to exert stronger control in Cambodia within a broader process of taking hold of Indochina and influenced by increasingly intense colonial expansion and competition in nearby countries. Britain and France, had defeated China in the second Opium War (1856–60), signalling a period of European dominance in Southeast Asia. Britain annexed Upper Burma in 1885 and exiled King Thibaw, causing a war of resistance that lasted until the early 1890s. The British also established protectorates in the Malay Peninsula and then in 1895 incorporated Selangor, Perak, Negeri Sembilan and Pahang into the Federated Malay States (FMS). While each FMS member state was a separate protectorate and retained its own ruler, the British gradually integrated their administration of the FMS with that of the directly ruled Straits Settlements centred on Singapore. Japan and the United States also entered the competition for markets and colonies in East and Southeast Asia during these decades.[5]

After making themselves the protectors of Cambodia, it took the French more than 20 years to "pacify" all the territories they called French Indochina. The main events in this process of conquest took place in Vietnam. By 1867 the French had incorporated the remaining provinces of Cochin China into the directly ruled colony they had established five years earlier. From 1873 until at least 1887, the French fought successive wars of pacification in the northern and central Vietnamese regions, Tonkin and Annam. When they sacked the imperial capital at Hue in 1885 and exiled the Nguyen Emperor Ham Nghi, some among

---

[4] For general accounts of these years, see Osborne, *French Presence*, pp. 175–258; Chandler, *History*, pp. 171–80; Forest, *Le Cambodge et la colonisation française*, pp. 59–76.

[5] Goscha, *Modern History of Vietnam*, pp. 96–8; Paul D. Hutchcroft, "Colonial Masters, National Politics, and Provincial Lords: Central Authority and Local Autonomy in the American Philippines, 1900–1913", *Journal of Asian Studies* 59, 2 (2000): 277–306.

the French wanted to abolish the dynasty and directly annex the territory, as they had Cochin China.[6] Instead, the French collaborated with members of the Nguyen court to make Ham Nghi's brother, Dong Khanh, the nominal emperor of the French protectorates of Annam and Tonkin.

By then, the French had realised that indirect colonial rule was less expensive, and more easily facilitated cooperation from sections of the indigenous elite. They doubtless wished to avoid a repeat of the administrative void that had occurred when the Confucian elites had fled Cochin China to avoid French rule.[7] Moreover, if France had directly annexed Tonkin, they would have breached an earlier treaty with China, which recognised Tonkin as a protectorate.[8] In Annam, the French would work to maintain and modify pre-existing administrative hierarchies, but they made Tonkin a direct colony in all but name, possibly because its population proved more restive, and its location on the border with China made it more vulnerable. They would also take direct control of most of the local courts and legal processes of Tonkin.[9]

In the territories that would become Laos, the French began to clash with Siam for influence over the princedoms of Vientiane, Champassak and Luang Prabang. Tensions between France and Siam climaxed when the French sent troops into central and southern Laos and in 1893 sailed gunboats up the Chao Phraya River to threaten the Siamese royal palace in Bangkok. King Rama V (Chulalongkorn) then signed a treaty recognising French claims to Lao territories on the left bank of the Mekong. Unlike Cambodia, France's Lao possessions were not a coherent political entity, as Luang Prabang in the north was a protectorate, while Vientiane and other territories further south had been directly annexed.[10] However, the French would attempt to administer the territories as one unit, for example, by establishing a single "indigenous"

---

[6] Robert Aldrich, *Banished Potentates: Dethroning and Exiling Indigenous Monarchs under British and French Colonial Rule, 1815–1955* (Manchester: Manchester University Press, 2018), p. 129.

[7] Milton E. Osborne, "The Debate on a Legal Code for Colonial Cochin China", *Journal of South-east Asian History* 10, 2 (1969): 224–35.

[8] Goscha, *Modern History of Vietnam*, pp. 60–8, 80–1. Aldrich, *Banished Potentates*, pp. 124–9.

[9] Habert, "Le Tonkin", pp. 175–210.

[10] Martin Stuart-Fox, "The French in Laos, 1887–1945", *Modern Asian Studies* 29, 1 (1995): 111–39, see 120.

jurisdiction.[11] The French declared the Union of Indochina, comprising Cochin China, Annam, Tonkin and Cambodia, in 1887. They added Laos and the leased territory of Guangzhouwan (Kouang-Tchéou-Wan) in southern China in 1898.[12] Civilian administrators began to replace naval officers, and after 1888 successive civilian governors general ruled over Indochina, with far-reaching powers that were sometimes compared to those of the British viceroys in India.[13] Paul Doumer, a future French president, became governor general in 1897 and over a five-year term created a centralised French administration across all five regions, working to make Indochina a paying concern, largely through monopolies and taxation, to which Cambodians would contribute disproportionately.[14]

Given their preoccupations elsewhere in Indochina, French inroads into Cambodian power were sporadic and opportunistic and made with an eye to colonial competition. Nevertheless, early representatives posted to Phnom Penh seemingly inevitably became embroiled in local affairs, not least because they had to try to keep order among the French soldiers and adventurers who had begun to arrive in the protectorate.[15] They soon also began to take an interest in local law and justice.

Extraterritoriality, Protection and Jurisdiction

The French would frequently claim that the 1863 Treaty of Protection established three jurisdictions in Cambodia: one to deal with French citizens; one to deal with "mixed" cases that involved French citizens and Cambodians; and finally Cambodia's own indigenous jurisdiction. Yet Article 7 of the Treaty of Protection simply stated that the French *résident* would deal with disputes between French citizens and Cambodians or other foreigners. Similarly, Cambodians would go to the French *résident* if they had complaints against any French citizen, but if an agreement could not be reached, the *résident* would decide the matter

---

[11] Cressent, "Administration mixte: le Laos", pp. 82–112.

[12] Brocheux and Hémery, *Indochina*, pp. 17–69.

[13] G. Mariol and H. François, *Législation Coloniale* [Colonial Legislation] (Paris: Les Manuels Coloniaux, Librairie La Rose, 1929), p. 149; Brocheux and Hémery, *Indochina*, pp. 80–1.

[14] Goscha, *Modern History of Vietnam*, p. 91. Regarding Cambodia's contribution to the budget of Indochina, see Forest, *Le Cambodge et la colonisation française*, pp. 224–32.

[15] Muller, *Colonial Cambodia's "Bad Frenchmen"*, pp. 54–6.

54   *Colonial Law Making*

jointly with an authorised Cambodian official. Article 7 then specifically prohibited the French from interfering in domestic legal matters:

> The French *résident* will abstain from any intervention in cases between Cambodians; for their side the French will depend, for all difficulties that may arise between them, on the French jurisdiction, and the Cambodian authority will not intervene in any case, including matters that may arise between French people and European foreigners which will be judged by the French *résident*.

Article 7 was substantively similar to articles VIII and IX of the Treaty of Amity, Commerce and Navigation, concluded between Napoleon III and King Rama IV (Mongkut) of Siam in 1856, under which France established consular courts that formally dealt only with French citizens.[16] Both treaties granted extraterritorial rights to French people, making them subject to French, not Siamese or Cambodian authority. In Siam, as in Cambodia, the consul would try to mediate any mixed French–Siamese disputes and would involve local authorities only if he could not attain an amicable settlement.

Like it did in Cambodia, France expanded its consular jurisdiction in Siam well beyond the treaty's apparent intent, but unlike in Cambodia, France's extraterritorial rights existed alongside those of the many other European powers that had signed similarly worded treaties.[17]

In Siam the consular courts established by numerous foreign powers, particularly the British and the French, began to hear cases that involved their protégés and subjects from other colonies and protectorates. So, for example, the French consular court claimed jurisdiction over Vietnamese and Cambodians living in Bangkok.[18] Opportunistic

---

[16] Treaty of Amity, Commerce and Protection between France and Cambodia (Treaty of Protection), 11 Aug. 1863 in Parry, *Consolidated Treaty Series: 1648–1919*, vol. 128, p. 143; Treaty of Friendship, Commerce and Navigation, concluded 15 Aug. 1856 between France and Siam, in Parry, *Consolidated Treaty Series*, vol. 115, p. 391.

[17] The United States, France, Denmark, the Hanseatic Republic, Portugal, the Netherlands, Prussia, the Grand Duchies of Mecklenburg, Sweden, Norway, Belgium, Italy, Austria–Hungary and Spain, and later Japan and Russia, all signed treaties that granted their nationals extraterritorial rights in Siam. See Loos, *Subject Siam*, pp. 42–3; Eldon R. James, "Jurisdiction over Foreigners in Siam", *The American Journal of International Law* 16, 4 (1922): 585–603, see 591.

[18] James, "Jurisdiction over Foreigners in Siam", p. 591; Loos, *Subject Siam*, pp. 42–3; Hong Lysa, "Extraterritoriality in Bangkok in the Reign of King Chulalongkorn, 1868–1910: The Cacophonies of Semi-Colonial Cosmopolitanism", *Itinerario:*

The Jurisdictional Dispossession of King Norodom

Chinese entrepreneurs also registered as British or French protégés, thereby escaping Siamese domestic law. Some of these Chinese business men acted as middlemen between foreign powers and the Siamese monarchy, and consequently entrenched their political and economic influence in Siam/Thailand.[19]

In Cambodia, the 1863 Treaty of Protection had granted France the right to control Cambodia's international relations and to exclude other foreign powers (art. 4). On this basis, but arguably in breach of the treaty, the French would transform the consular court into a court of first instance in the French jurisdiction of Cochin China. The French used the notion of extraterritoriality to place the sizeable populations of ethnic Vietnamese and Chinese living in Cambodia under the French jurisdiction. However, to achieve these outcomes, they had to move cautiously, to avoid international criticism, but also to overcome Cambodian resistance.

Colonial protectorates established a form of dual sovereignty that helped to shape the contests between coloniser and colonised. The legal complications of dual sovereignty came to the fore in Cambodia when, in 1874, the French attempted to arbitrate Thomas Caraman's claim of debt against King Norodom.[20] To the chagrin of the colonial authorities, Caraman, an unscrupulous French entrepreneur, had signed a contract with Norodom to import and supply a range of luxury goods.[21] When Norodom refused to pay for an apparently grossly overpriced gilded screen, French officials in Phnom Penh and Saigon tried in vain to negotiate a solution.[22] Finally, they allowed Caraman to invoke the dispute procedures of the contract. Prosecutor François Augier travelled to Phnom Penh from Saigon to act as the French representative in a joint Cambodian–French arbitration. King Norodom appointed a member of his court to represent him on the tribunal.[23] After Augier had worked

---

Journal of Imperial and Global Interactions 27, 2 (2003): 125–46, see 128–34; Trais Pearson, *Sovereign Necropolis: The Politics of Death in Semi-Colonial Siam* (Ithaca, NY: Cornell University Press, 2020), pp. 58–69; Wasana Wongsurawat, *The Crown and the Capitalists: The Ethnic Chinese and the Founding of the Thai Nation* (Seattle: University of Washington Press, 2019).

[19] Wongsurawat, *The Crown and the Capitalists,* pp. 90–8.

[20] Muller, *Colonial Cambodia's "Bad Frenchmen"*, p. 124.

[21] Ibid., p. 97.

[22] Moura to Governor of Cochin China, 14 June 1874, CAOM GGI 11829.

[23] Muller, *Colonial Cambodia's "Bad Frenchmen"*, p. 101; Moura to Governor of Cochin China, 26 May 1874, CAOM GGI 11829.

for several weeks having relevant documents prepared and translated, the joint commission began proceedings. However, when Augier asked the Cambodian member of the tribunal how he thought the panel should proceed, Norodom's representative announced that his role was to inform other members about Cambodian "customs", according to which a royal subject could never judge his king's legal obligations.[24] The conflict resolution clause of the contract was therefore unenforceable and the tribunal dissolved.

The immediate outcome of the Caraman case proved that, 11 years after signing the 1863 treaty, Norodom still had the power to reject French jurisdiction over his actions. Subsequently, the French managed to prevent such cases from arising by restricting access to the king. However, the position of the sovereign and other members of the royal family remained problematic. At first, the protectorate authorities decreed that future complaints brought by a European against the Cambodian government would be judged by the *Conseil Privé* in Saigon, which was the local equivalent of a French administrative court.[25] This measure re-elevated Norodom to the status of government representative rather than private protégé, but it nevertheless subjected him to French jurisdiction in disputes with any French citizen. In criminal matters, a Royal Ordinance of 1911 largely excused members of the royal family and other senior dignitaries from having to appear in person before a French court in criminal matters, but they were still technically subject to its decisions.[26]

Regardless of the formalities of dual sovereignty, the actual balance of power incrementally shifted in favour of the French. As part of this process, they gradually expanded the jurisdiction of their courts, and also began to interfere in the indigenous courts, in direct breach of the 1863

---

[24] Augier and Moura to Governor of Cochin China, 10 Dec. 1874, CAOM GGI 11829.

[25] "Convention of 18 December 1881: Moving to the Conseil Privé of Cochin China, the Responsibility to Judge Litigious Matters between the Cambodian Government and Litigants Who Fall under the French Court", *Annuaire de l'Indo-Chine Française: Cochinchine et Cambodge 1889–97* (Hanoi: Imprimerie d'Extrême-Orient, 1890), p. 582. Francesca Bignami, "Comparative Administrative Law", in *The Cambridge Companion to Comparative Law*, ed. Mauro Bussani and Ugo Mettei (Cambridge: Cambridge University Press, 2012), pp. 145–70, see pp. 148–9.

[26] Royal Ordinance 13 Oct. 1912. A draft, written by the Prosecutor General of Indochina in 1911, is contained at the National Archives of Cambodia, NAC RSC 36976.

The Jurisdictional Dispossession of King Norodom   57

treaty. In doing so, they claimed they needed to protect Cambodians from a corrupt and, in many ways, barbaric indigenous legal system.

Protecting Cambodians from Barbarism and Corruption

Jean Moura, who published his scathing assessment of Cambodian judges in 1883, quoted in the previous chapter, served two terms as head of the protectorate between 1868 and 1881.[27] Moura developed a rapport with Norodom while also skilfully extracting concessions from the king in return for services such as suppressing armed challenges to his reign.[28]

In 1873, a talented military officer, archaeologist and explorer, Étienne Aymonier, joined Moura in Phnom Penh. Fluent in Khmer, Aymonier assumed special responsibility for indigenous affairs. In 1874, the same year Augier attempted to arbitrate King Norodom's debts to Caraman, Aymonier wrote a confidential report on Cambodia. He painted a picture of a vulnerable population with little redress against the avarice of individual officials, especially since the French had started to suppress internal rebellions, which had, he said, been the people's only means of reining in their rulers.[29]

Aymonier described Cambodian legal processes as "brigandage decorated with the name of justice".[30] As Moura would do in his 1883 publication, Aymonier decried the lack of separation of judicial and administrative functions, and the tendency for officials of all kinds to assume the role of judge as a means of enrichment. Among the examples of corruption that Aymonier cited were that of the senior judge, (*pongsa akreéch*), who reportedly took people into custody and tortured them until they agreed to pay a penalty. Another local official had profited by selling a young woman into slavery because she had become pregnant

---

[27] The title of the most senior French representative in Cambodia changed. Until 1884 the incumbent was known simply as the representative. From 1884 to 1889, the title became *résident général* and after that, *résident supérieur*; see Tully, *France on the Mekong*, p. 116, note 25.

[28] Osborne, *French Presence*, pp. 189–205.

[29] Étienne Aymonier, "Confidential Report on Cambodia", 1874. Forwarded by Governor of Cochin China to French Minister for the Navy, 5 Sept. 1874. CAOM FM AF C13, dossier A30 (22).

[30] Ibid.

58 *Colonial Law Making*

out of wedlock.[31] Aymonier was also dismayed that Cambodians seemed to expect him to act in the same way as their local patrons. For example: one litigant offered him a reward if he would change the outcome of a court case; another supplicant asked him to "take" a girl to save her from being bound to serve one of the royal princesses.[32]

Despite his distaste for the idea, Aymonier may have reinforced local perceptions that his methods were indeed similar to those of Cambodian officials. He encouraged Cambodian litigants to write to him if they were dissatisfied with the outcome of a court case. At times, he and Moura would recommend specific judgements, and by the late 1870s they were inundated with requests to deal with such matters.[33] As well as directly contravening the 1863 treaty, Aymonier and Moura unwittingly presented themselves as potential patrons who could, at times, offer an alternative source of protection.

French commentators considered the Cambodian codes to be antiquated and in places barbaric. Few could resist mentioning the forms of prescribed torture in the *Law on Criminals* (*Kram Chôr*). This *kram* describes 21 methods of execution for defendants found guilty of serious offences.[34] For example:

> The executioners, after having inflicted large wounds to the head of the patient [sic], from which blood flows, place him on a bar of burning red iron and leave him there until all the flesh is consumed and there is nothing left but bare bones; They skin the head, so as to make the skin fall over and cover the face; They pour oil into the mouth of the guilty party, which is held open with a gag, and set the oil alight with a wick; They crack the mouth on both sides, up to the ears, and leave it gaping with a gag until the patient expires; They wrap the ten fingers of the hands with a cloth soaked in oil and set it alight.[35]

---

[31] Aymonier, "Confidential Report on Cambodia", 1874, CAOM FM AF C13, dossier A30 (22).

[32] Ibid.

[33] Muller, *Colonial Cambodia's "Bad Frenchmen"*, pp. 120–1.

[34] Leclère, *Codes Cambodgiens*, vol. 2, pp. 287–312; see also Cordier's translation, *Cochinchine française: les codes cambodgiens [Traduits par Mr Cordier]* [French Cochin China: The Cambodian Codes (Translated by Monseigneur Cordier)] (Paris: Imprimerie Nationale, 1881), pp. 5–13.

[35] Code Pénal, Titre III Krâm Chôr, III (a) 1–6, in Leclère, *Codes Cambodgiens*, vol. 2, pp. 292–3.

As the *Law on Criminals* explains, King Preas Chey Chestha had in 1621 reduced the punishments, which he considered too harsh.[36] Moreover, in 1860, King Ang Duong had decreed that most corporal punishments could be replaced with financial penalties.[37] Aymonier argued, though, that as long as they remained in the texts, a cruel sovereign could reintroduce these "numerous terrible and varied punishments, traces of primitive barbarism".[38] This made sense if the *kram* were read as codes, like those of France, rather than historical records of the wisdom and continuity of royal power, and as guides to behaviour. Less spectacular forms of torture and injustices *were* common practice in Cambodia, and Aymonier and Moura may have linked these to the "barbarities" of the past.[39]

In Cochin China in 1880, Governor Le Myre de Vilers had finally decided to replace the Vietnamese Code Gia Long, with a modified French Penal Code. He and Aymonier discussed a similar idea for Cambodia.[40] However, the decision had been contentious even in directly annexed Cochin China, where a vocal minority argued the *indigène* should continue to be ruled by their own laws.[41] In the Cambodian protectorate, such a move was still untenable, and the more cautious Moura had already advised against it.[42] Instead, Moura and Aymonier focused on reforming legal procedure in the Cambodian jurisdiction.

In 1877, Aymonier and Moura persuaded Norodom to issue a Royal Ordinance that regulated the provincial courts headed by the governor of each province and established a Court of Appeal in Phnom Penh. Henceforth only designated officials had judicial powers, and court-imposed costs and fines were to be paid to the royal treasury.[43]

---

[36] Code Pénal, *Titre* III *Krâm Chôr*, II, in Leclère, *Codes Cambodgiens*, vol. 2, pp. 295–6.

[37] Code Pénal, *Titre* III *Krâm Chôr*, III *Préambule*, in Leclère, *Codes Cambodgiens*, vol. 2, pp. 296–7.

[38] Aymonier, *Le Cambodge*, p. 87.

[39] Leclère, *Recherches sur la législation criminelle*, pp. 112–32; see also Moura to Governor of Cochin China, Mar. 1878 (day not recorded), CAOM GGI 10284.

[40] Le Myre de Vilers to Aymonier, 22 Sept. 1880, CAOM GGI 10231.

[41] Osborne, "Debate on a Legal Code"; Barnhart, "Violence and the Civilizing Mission", pp. 348–415.

[42] Le Myre de Vilers to Aymonier, 22 Sept. 1880, CAOM GGI 10231; Moura to Governor Cochin China, 3 July 1878, CAOM GGI 10284.

[43] Royal Ordinance 15 Jan. 1877, arts. 2, 3, 6, 7, 8, CAOM GGI 12033. Also quoted by Maxime Léger, "L'organisation judiciaire du Cambodge et son

60   *Colonial Law Making*

The two colonial reformers also attempted to establish the link between judicial procedure and legal codes. Even though they considered sections of Cambodia's legal texts to be barbaric and outdated, Aymonier and Moura assisted Norodom to complete a new compilation of the legal texts in 1881.

While publishing a new edition of the *kram* was traditionally a sign of royal power, the French ensured Norodom's texts carried a colonial imprimatur. First, they had some French text included in the royal seal that authenticated each volume.[44] Secondly, in a sharp break with tradition, they paid to print 65 copies of each volume and distributed a set to each of the 56 provincial governors.[45] Norodom's father, King Ang Duong, had introduced aspects of Siamese law into the codes, and it is possible the French and King Norodom were also inspired by recent events in Siam, where King Mongkut had, for the first time, allowed a two-volume edition of the royal Three Seals Code to be printed and circulated. Previously, there had been just three copies of the Three Seals Code—one for the royal bed chamber, one for the royal library and one for senior judges.[46]

The new edition of the Cambodian *kram* also included an admonition that all legal procedures should be based on the laws contained therein, and that a judgement was valid only if the presiding judge referred to a copy of the laws that carried the royal seals.[47] In other words,

---

évolution depuis le traité du Protectorat (1863) jusqu'à la promulgation de la nouvelle Constitution du Royaume Khmer (6 mai 1947)" [The legal and Judicial Organisation of Cambodia and its Evolution Since the Treaty of the Protectorate (1863) up to the Promulgation of the New Cambodian Royal Constitution (6 May, 1947)], in *Recueil général de jurisprudence, de doctrine et de législation coloniales et maritimes* [General Collection of Colonial and Maritime Jurisprudence, Doctrine and Legislation], ed. D. Penant (Paris: Marchal & Billard, 1950), pp. 47, 50.

[44] Leclère, *Codes Cambodgiens*, vol. 1, "Grand Préamble", para (2) and (4), p. 5.

[45] Leclère, *Codes Cambodgiens*, vol. 1, p. xi.

[46] Regarding Ang Duong, see Mikaelian, "Recherches", p. 54. Regarding King Mongkut's decision to allow copies of the Three Seals Code to be printed and circulated, see Tamara Loos, "Gender Adjudicated: Translating Modern Legal Subjects in Siam" (PhD dissertation, Cornell University, 1999), pp. 44–6.

[47] Leclère adds a footnote here saying, "that means they will have to appeal", Leclère, *Codes Cambodgiens*, vol. 1, p. 6, note 3. The 1805 version of the Three Seals Code carried a similar admonition. Baker and Phongpaichit, *Palace Law*, p. 2.

only those officials who had access to one of the 65 newly printed editions of the laws could act as a judge. Even after the new edition of the *kram* was distributed, implementation remained haphazard at best. In 1905, the colonial authorities discovered that the court of Kompong Som had been missing one volume of the *kram* for over six years.[48]

Even though Cambodian officials often did not comply with these early efforts at reform, French intervention had begun to subvert the role and the meaning of Cambodian law. They started to extract the *kram* from the Cambodian world view that gave life and meaning to them, transforming them into defective and outdated codes that warranted further revision.[49] Concurrently with these early forays into the indigenous jurisdiction, the French set about expanding and transforming their own jurisdiction.

Transforming Consular Jurisdictions

Based on the provisions in Article 7 of the 1863 treaty, the French decided there should be a "mixed" court to judge cases involving French citizens and Cambodians. The 1873 Royal Ordinance to formalise the mixed court specified that it had jurisdiction over matters involving all Europeans, not just French citizens.[50] However, King Norodom inserted a clause stating that all "Asiatics" came under the Cambodian jurisdiction.[51]

The mixed court was arguably a means of implementing provisions in Article 7 of the Treaty of Protection, but the protectorate administration appeared to directly breach Article 7 when it established a regular

---

[48] Tit, Governor of Kompong Som, to Résident of Kampot, 4 Dec. 1905 (trans.); and Tet, former Governor of Kompong Som, to Résident of Kampot, 5 Sept. 1905 (trans.), NAC RSC 14680.

[49] See David Engel's discussion of local meaning and legal transplants in Thailand, David M. Engel, "Litigation across Space and Time: Courts, Conflict, and Social Change", *Law and Society Review* 24, 2 (1990): 333–44.

[50] Royal Ordinances of 1 April 1873. Regarding the legal attributions with regard to Europeans admitted to reside in Cambodia, CAOM Fonds Ministériels, Ancien Fonds (FM AF), 250-0-01 (10) Carton 250—CAOM FM AF 250-0-01 (10) Carton 250. See also Blazy, "L'Organisation judiciaire", p. 48.

[51] Royal Ordinances of 1 April 1873; Hoeffel, *De la condition juridique des étrangers*, p. 48, note 8.

62   *Colonial Law Making*

French court, in Phnom Penh in 1880.[52] Instead of a consular court, as envisaged in the treaty, the new court was part of the Indochina-wide French jurisdiction.

Worried that France's colonial rivals would object that a French court breached the 1863 treaty, Governor Le Myre de Vilers needed Norodom's consent.[53] He instructed Aymonier, then acting *résident supérieur*, to find an opportune moment to have Norodom endorse a statement that accorded French and European litigants "the guarantees resulting from the procedure of . . . the Court of Saigon".[54] As reassurance for Norodom and for France's international critics, the statement denied any intention of altering the existing laws regarding "cases where Cambodian litigants are parties".[55] Nevertheless, that is exactly what happened when, the following year, a French presidential decree to establish the new court in Phnom Penh gave it jurisdiction over *subjects* as well as citizens of any European or American power.[56] This contravened the spirit of the statement Norodom had endorsed and overrode his claim to jurisdiction over all the "Asiatics" in his realm. It also retrospectively sanctioned the protectorate's practice of including resident Indians and Filipino Tagals in the French jurisdiction.[57] More significantly for Norodom, as French subjects, Vietnamese from Cochin China, and possibly even protégés from Annam and Tonkin, now technically came under the French jurisdiction. Aymonier counselled against immediately implementing this aspect of the decree, which he thought the king would not accept.[58] Several years later, his

---

[52] Le Myre de Vilers (Governor of Cochin China) to the Minister of Marines and Colonies, 17 Apr. 1879, CAOM FM AF 250-0-01 (10) Carton 250.

[53] Le Myre de Vilers to Minister of Colonies, 17 Apr. 1879, CAOM FM AF 250-0-01(10).

[54] Declaration between France and Cambodia relative to the Trial of Causes between Europeans, 17 Nov. 1880 (Declaration of 17 November 1880), ConTS 189, p. 157, reproduced from De Clercq, *Recueil des Traités de la France* [Collection of Treaties of France], vol. 15, p. 618. Regarding the need to find an opportune moment, see Le Myre de Vilers to Aymonier, 24 July 1880, CAOM GGI 12297.

[55] Declaration of 17 November 1880, preamble, 157 ConTS p. 189.

[56] Decree issued by the President of the Republic, 24 Feb. 1881, art. 1, in Hoeffel, "De la condition juridique", p. 50.

[57] Muller, *Colonial Cambodia's "Bad Frenchmen"*, pp. 115–18; L.P. Nicolas, "L'Organisation de la Justice Cambodgienne" [The Organisation of Cambodian Justice], *La Révue indochinoise juridique et économique* [Indochinese Legal and Economic Review] 21 (1943): 1–68, see 15.

[58] Aymonier to Governor of Cochin China, 10 Sept. 1880, CAOM GGI 12297.

and Le Myre de Vilers' successors would learn the wisdom of such caution.

Résident Supérieur Augustin Julien Fourès, who replaced Aymonier in 1881, complained that Norodom continued to avoid many of his demands. Aymonier, a student of Cambodian language and customs, had acted as the French judge in the mixed court and claimed he was generally able to prevail over the Cambodian judge. Fourès, however, complained bitterly that the Cambodian judge of the mixed court too readily deferred to the king.[59]

Fourès and Charles Thomson, who had become governor of Cochin China in 1881, were increasingly frustrated by the king's intransigence, especially his reluctance to cede control of the country's revenues and to abolish slavery. In 1884, Thomson decided to force Norodom's hand. Under threat of arms, he compelled Norodom to sign a convention which ceded almost all his powers to the French.[60] Article 1 of the 1884 Convention authorised the French to make any "administrative, judicial, financial and commercial reforms" they deemed necessary.[61] Eight French *résidents* were to be deployed around the country "in order to ensure, in concert with the Cambodian authorities, that justice is rendered in an equitable manner, [and] that the products of taxes be used for grand works of public utility".[62]

In the following months, the French moved quickly to overhaul the administration of the protectorate. They launched a series of public works and took over the administration of Phnom Penh.[63] They also began to

---

[59] Fourès to Governor of Cochin China, 26 Sept. 1884, CAOM GGI 11816.

[60] Convention between France and Cambodia for the Regulation of their respective Relations (hereafter 1884 Convention), signed at Phnom Penh, 17 June 1884, 164 ConTS, p. 99. For an account of the manner in which Norodom was forced to sign this treaty, see Osborne, *French Presence*, pp. 209–11; Tully, *France on the Mekong*, pp. 74–5; Paul Collard, *Cambodge et Cambodgiens: métamorphose du Royaume Khmèr par une méthode française de protectorat* [Cambodia and the Cambodians: The Metamorphosis of the Khmer Kingdom by the Method of the French Protectorate] (Paris: Société d'éditions géographiques, maritimes et coloniales, 1925), pp. 109–11.

[61] 1884 Convention, arts. 1 and 3.

[62] "Proclamation of Governor Thomson to the Cambodian people", 18 June 1884, reproduced in Georges Taboulet, *La geste française en Indochine: Histoire par les textes de la France en Indochine des Origines à 1914* [The French Gesture in Indochina: A History by Texts of France in Indochina from its Origins to 1914] (Paris: Adrien-Maisonneuve, 1956), p. 672.

[63] Muller, *Colonial Cambodia's "Bad Frenchmen"*, pp. 189–90.

reorganise the Cambodian jurisdiction. Indigenous courts were to be jointly presided over by French and Cambodian judges, similar to the mixed court in Phnom Penh.[64] Like the mixed court, these new courts were to rule according to "equity", although they were to respect Cambodian law as far as possible and to draw inspiration from French law. It seems likely that Thomson intended to abolish the Cambodian jurisdiction completely, and to absorb the kingdom into Cochin China, but he had underestimated the Cambodian reaction.[65]

The Convention of 1884 struck at the power of the Cambodian elite, including the provincial governors, many of whose functions were to be usurped or supervised by the French *résidents*.[66] From early 1885, rebellion spread across most of the country and within months reached the outskirts of Phnom Penh. Armed bands of Cambodians waged guerrilla warfare against French-related institutions and settlements. Though he was careful to deny it, Norodom probably gave at least tacit support to some of the rebels. The colonial troops fought the rebellion ruthlessly, and at times employed their own forms of barbarity. They did not militarily defeat the rebels, and hostilities ceased only when Norodom called on his subjects to lay down their arms in 1886.[67]

In return for the king's assistance, the French agreed to postpone implementing some aspects of the 1884 Convention, and over the following year they quietly mothballed other measures, including much of their planned court reform. In view of events in the neighbouring protectorates of Annam and Tonkin, where rebellion also broke out in 1885, Norodom played a cunning role, avoiding the fate of the 14-year-old Nguyen Emperor Ham Nghi, who, willingly or not, was implicated as a leader of the uprising and exiled to Algeria.[68] Norodom would also have been aware that the British had deposed and deported

---

[64] Blazy, "L'Organisation judiciaire", p. 375. Also Marquant, Résident of Kampot, to the Résident Général, 25 Oct. 1885, in which the logistics of implementing the reforms are discussed, NAC RSC 1752.

[65] Tully, *France on the Mekong*, p. 76; Brocheux and Hémery, *Indochina*, p. 45; Imbert, *Histoire des institutions khmères*, p. 78.

[66] 1884 Convention, art. 3 and 4; Chandler, *History*, p. 176.

[67] This summary of the rebellion draws on: Collard, *Cambodge et Cambodgiens*, pp. 112–28; Tully, *France on the Mekong*, pp. 83–95; Muller, *Colonial Cambodia's "Bad Frenchmen"*, pp. 204–10; Chandler, *History*, pp. 177–8; Osborne, *French Presence*, pp. 214–17.

[68] Robert Aldrich, *Banished Potentates*, pp. 121–32.

Figure 3.1: King Norodom
Source: Die Katholicischen Missionen https://commons.wikimedia.org/wiki/File:Norodom-I.jpg (accessed 4 September 2023).

66 *Colonial Law Making*

the Burmese King Thibaw in 1885 and were waging war to annex the area they called Upper Burma.

Although they would continue to whittle away the king's power, the protectorate administrators reverted to a more cautious approach and abandoned hopes of merging Cambodia with Cochin China or of abolishing the Cambodian courts.[69] Even so, through the 1884 Convention the French had granted themselves legal authority to move beyond the 1863 Treaty of Protection, and retrospectively laid to rest questions about the legality of past and future judicial and legal reforms.[70]

In the settlement of 1886, the French agreed to reduce from eight to four the number of *résidents* to be stationed around the country.[71] One of the early *résidents* was Adhémard Leclère, posted to the southern region of Kampot. Leclère would come to be recognised as the leading French authority on Cambodian law. His interest may have been sparked when the colonial authorities encouraged *résidents* to study local customs in order to better understand how to implement the terms of the 1884 Convention.[72] In 1898, Leclère published translations of the Cambodian *kram*, including some that were previously unknown to Europeans.[73]

Leclère was a dedicated colonial official and a sincere believer in the *mission civilisatrice*, but he also held firmly to the theory that Cambodian law should be left intact except where it was repugnant to European notions of civilisation.[74] Ironically, his translations furthered the process of changing Cambodian law. He embedded categories such as public, private, procedural, criminal and civil, and presented the texts like French codes, with numbered articles and divisions. He also reportedly made significant translation errors.[75]

Despite the setback the French had suffered as a result of the 1885–86 rebellion, they saw the 1884 Convention as having authorised

---

[69] Osborne, *French Presence*, pp. 224–7.

[70] Au Chhieng, *Fondement du deuxième traité de Protectorat français sur le Cambodge*, [The Basis of the Second Treaty of the French Protectorate over Cambodia] Introduced and edited by Grégory Mikaelian (forthcoming) (Paris: Association Péninsule, Cahiers de Péninsule, Vol. 14, Aug. 2023).

[71] Kompong Svay, Kampot, Pursat and Kratie; Tully, *France on the Mekong*, p. 92.

[72] Mikaelian, *Un partageux au Cambodge*, pp. 58–9.

[73] Leclère, *Codes Cambodgiens*, vol. 1, p. xvi.

[74] Leclère, *Recherches sur la législation criminelle*, pp. 121–7.

[75] Mikaelian, "Recherches", p. 72. L.F., "Indochine [Note Bibliographique]", [Indochina (Bibliographic Note)] *Bulletin de l'École Française d'Extrême-Orient* 3, 1 (1903): 328.

them to continue to intervene in the Cambodian courts, and the new *résidents* did this within their assigned rural regions.[76] In the meantime, the judicial and administrative arms of the colonial apparatus had begun to clash over who should control the French and mixed jurisdictions. Aymonier and Le Myre de Vilers had wanted a French court in Phnom Penh, but they had opposed the judges of the Saigon Court of Appeal, and the French minister for colonies, who suggested that the personnel of the new court should also preside in the mixed jurisdiction.[77] Aymonier and Le Myre de Vilers may have been concerned over how Norodom would react to such a move, but by the mid-1880s they would also have been influenced by the deepening animosity between French judges and colonial administrators in Cochin China. Le Myre de Viler's 1881 decision to replace the Vietnamese courts in Cochin China with French courts run by French judges had caused the colonial administration considerable logistical and financial difficulties.[78] The first cohort of French judges who arrived in Cochin China were ill prepared and quickly raised the ire of French administrators, who claimed the new judges did not understand the particular contextual requirements.[79]

While tensions between the administrative and judicial wings of colonial power were common in many colonies, and would simmer throughout Indochina, relations in Cochin China became intensely and sometimes publicly hostile. One high point came in 1905 at a meeting of senior colonial officials when the governor of Cochin China, Rodier, disparaged the local French judiciary and called for the Vietnamese courts and judges to be reinstated in Cochin China.[80] His remarks circulated widely in Saigon, outraging the prosecutor general and other judges.

Leaving aside questions of their reported lack of expertise and experience, it was inevitable that judges fresh from France or another colony would struggle to administer Vietnamese law. They would not have been familiar with the Code Gia Long, which applied in all civil matters. They relied largely on interpreters who consequently were able to manipulate

---

[76] See Leclère's account of a case in which he intervened, Leclère, *Recherches sur la législation criminelle*, pp. 128–30.

[77] Blazy, "L'Organisation judiciaire", pp. 364–5; Résident Supérieur to Prosecutor General in Saigon, 5 Sept. 1897, NAC RSC 9906.

[78] Barnhart, "Violence and the Civilizing Mission", pp. 459–84.

[79] Ibid.

[80] Governor General to the Minister of Colonies, 4 Oct. 1905, CAOM, FM NF 11 52(1).

68   *Colonial Law Making*

cases to their own advantage. The judges also subjected their compatriots in the colonial administration to scrutiny and challenged the legality of some of their actions, particularly as relations between the two groups deteriorated.[81]

In Cambodia, this friction began to play out in the mixed jurisdiction. To the chagrin of the French judiciary, the *résident supérieur* had insisted that he or his delegate, not the French judge in Phnom Penh, whose caseload was not initially very heavy, should preside in the mixed court.[82] The judiciary pointed to a needless breach of the principle of the separation of powers,[83] but the administrators were determined to keep control of the mixed courts, whose cases often touched on sensitive matters such as relations with the king.[84] Nevertheless, they too were frustrated that Norodom could still influence the Cambodian co-judges who sat alongside them in the mixed courts.[85]

Following the 1885–86 rebellion, the protectorate administrators found a way to solve both of these problems. They simply moved the mixed courts out of Phnom Penh to the seats of the newly deployed *résidents*.[86] Only appeals from these local mixed courts were to be heard in Phnom Penh, by a commission that included the *résident supérieur* and Cambodian officials. In 1891, Norodom, who was by then old and frail, signed an ordinance that retrospectively confirmed these basic

---

[81] Barnhart, "Violence and the Civilizing Mission", pp. 459–97, 514–18; J. Joleaud-Barral, *La Colonisation française en Annam et au Tonkin* [The French Colonisation of Annam and Tonkin] (Paris: Librairie Plon, 1899), pp. 183–8.

[82] Blazy, "L'Organisation judiciaire", pp. 388–90. At pp. 381–2, Blazy states that in 1884 the French court was not very busy, hearing only 59 cases, and in the following two years, 101 and 144 respectively; see also Résident Supérieur to Prosecutor General in Saigon, 5 Sept. 1897, NAC RSC 9906; Report of the Prosecutor of Phnom Penh on the judicial organisation of Cambodia, 12 Sept. 1886, CAOM GGI 12030.

[83] Report of the Prosecutor of Phnom Penh on the judicial organisation of Cambodia, 12 Sept. 1886, CAOM GGI 12030.

[84] Blazy, "L'Organisation judiciaire", p. 388. The *résident* of Kampot made it clear he did not want to relinquish his judicial powers; see Marquant to the Résident Général, 25 Oct. 1885, NAC RSC 1752.

[85] Résident Supérieur Fourès to Governor Cochin China, 22 Feb. 1884, CAOM GGI 12310.

[86] Report of the Prosecutor of Phnom Penh on the judicial organisation of Cambodia, 12 Sept. 1886, CAOM GGI 12030; Prosecutor General to Governor of Cochin China, 13 Sept. 1886, NAC RSC 11543.

arrangements.[87] The French judges were infuriated not only because they had failed to expand their role in the protectorate, but also because the new mixed courts consumed scarce financial resources.[88]

The judges found a champion in Etienne Camille Lafarge, who became prosecutor general of Indochina in late 1895, two months after arriving in the colony from a posting in Guadeloupe. He argued that Article 7 of the Treaty of Protection was based on the principle that Cambodians and the French were each entitled to their "natural judge".[89] He then went on to state that the rights of the protector must take precedence over those of the protected, so any matter involving a French or European party should fall only within the French jurisdiction, regardless of the nationality of the other parties, thus making the mixed courts superfluous. Having reinterpreted the 1863 Treaty of Protection and the very concept of protection, Lafarge brushed aside concerns that Norodom would not consent to such an arrangement. Ignoring political realities, he emphasised that the Convention of 1884 had bound the king to accept any measures with regard to justice that the French considered necessary.[90] Lafarge's view held sway in 1897, when Norodom finally conceded the running of his government to the French.

In the aftermath of the 1885–86 rebellion, the French also attempted several times to further expand the French jurisdiction's coverage of "foreign Asiatics". Norodom responded by going on the offensive. Most notably, the king issued another ordinance that asserted his authority over immigration of foreign Asians.[91] Norodom specifically claimed control over all ethnic Vietnamese, Siamese, Laotians, Indians, Arabs and Chinese, and thus attempted to delegitimise claims that European colonial subjects and protégés should come under French jurisdiction.

In 1895, the metropole countered Norodom's manoeuvre and issued a decree that moved all "foreign Asiatics", including all ethnic Vietnamese, to the French jurisdiction.[92] However, the colonial

---

[87] Blazy, "L'Organisation judiciaire", p. 390.

[88] Report of the Prosecutor of Phnom Penh on the judicial organisation of Cambodia, 12 Sept. 1886, CAOM GGI 12030; Prosecutor General to Governor of Cochin China, 13 Sept. 1886, NAC RSC 11543.

[89] C. Lafarge, Report to the Governor General on French Justice in Cambodia, 17 Feb. 1897, CAOM GGI 8495, cited in Blazy, "L'Organisation judiciaire", p. 393.

[90] Ibid.

[91] Hoeffel, "De la condition juridique", p. 57.

[92] Ibid., pp. 60–1.

70   *Colonial Law Making*

administration did not fully implement this decree as they were still wary of pushing Norodom and the senior elites too far.[93] This issue was not finally settled until 1897, when the Cambodian ministers agreed to acknowledge French authority ahead of that of their king.[94]

Ending the King's Jurisdiction and Limiting French Judges

In January 1897, Norodom fell ill and was confined to bed. Using the false pretext that the king was dying, *Résident Supérieur* de Vernéville persuaded the Cambodian ministers to meet with him and to make decisions in Norodom's absence.[95] On 4 March, the five ministers, claiming to act in the name of the king, issued amendments to several aspects of judicial procedure.[96] One article of their ordinance implied that the king and members of the royal family were subject to the courts.[97] This shocking act of *lèse majesté* was a sign that the ministers had switched allegiance, sensing that the king had finally lost his battle with the French.[98]

In the following months, the French negotiated a new dispensation with Norodom that formally left the king and his successors with only a ceremonial role.[99] Henceforth, his five ministers would meet as a council "away from the presence of the king, under the presidency of the *Résident Supérieur*".[100] Norodom had finally relinquished any direct role in government. He continued to sign Royal Ordinances presented to him by the Council of Ministers but, in order for these to come into effect, they had to be counter-signed by the *résident supérieur*.[101]

---

[93] Ibid.

[94] Osborne, *French Presence*, pp. 237–40.

[95] Tully, *France on the Mekong*, p. 108; Osborne, *French Presence*, pp. 237–8.

[96] Untitled Ordinance 4 March 1897, NAC RSC 32941.

[97] Ibid., art. 6.

[98] Osborne, *French Presence*, pp. 247–51.

[99] Osborne, *French Presence*, pp. 236–40; Tully, *France on the Mekong*, p. 109.

[100] Untitled Ordinance 4 Mar. 1897, art. 1, NAC RSC 32941.

[101] Royal Ordinance of 11 July 1897, art. 2, in Gabriel Michel, *Code Judiciaire de l'Indo-Chine: lois, décrets et arrêtés concernant le service judiciaire et applicables par Les cours et les tribunaux de l'Indo-Chine 1904–1913* [Judicial Code of Indo-China: Laws, Decrees and *arrêtés* Concerning the Judicial Service and Applicable by the Courts and Tribunals of Indo-China 1904–1913] (Hanoi: Imprimèrie d'extrême orient, 1914), p. 840, NAC Doc, 537.

King Norodom, also lost nearly all formal judicial power, even in the indigenous jurisdiction. A newly constituted Court of Appeal put an end to any residual right Cambodians may have had to appeal directly to the king in legal matters.[102] The king's sole remaining judicial role was to grant mercy for those condemned to death, and even this was subject to a report from the minister of justice, now supervised by the *résident supérieur*.[103] Nevertheless, even though exercised under supervision, the king's authority over life and death was symbolically important, as was the fact that laws continued to be issued in his name.

The mixed jurisdiction was abolished and all ethnic Vietnamese and Chinese inhabitants were classified as foreigners who came under the purview of the French court.[104] Thereafter, French law would apply in cases that involved a European, an American or a French citizen.[105] For all ethnic Vietnamese residing in the protectorate and any "Asiatic" who was not the subject of a Western power other than France, the *Annamite* laws of Cochin China applied, being the modified French Penal Code of 1880, and aspects of the Code Gia Long in private law matters.[106] Henceforth, French courts in Cambodia would, as they did in Cochin China, apply two different sets of laws, according to the ethnicity of litigants.[107]

Although the colonial judiciary may have expected that their role in Cambodia would expand as a result of these reforms, they were sadly disappointed. In Cambodia, unlike Cochin China, the indigenous courts survived, with jurisdiction limited to cases that solely involved litigants considered to be ethnic Khmers. Moreover, instead of establishing

---

[102] Royal Ordinance of 11 July 1897, art. 5.

[103] Ibid., art. 6.

[104] Royal Ordinance of 11 July 1897, art. 7 in ibid., Arrêté on Suppression of the Commission of Appeal and the mixed courts, attribution of the competence to the Court of First Instance of matters previously submitted to the mixed jurisdiction, 13 Aug. 1897, in *Recueil de législation et jurisprudence colonials* [Collection of Colonial Legislation and Jurisprudence], ed. Dareste, P. and Appert (Paris: Challamel, 1898), p. 12.

[105] Arrêté on Suppression of the Commission of Appeal, art. 8, in ibid.

[106] Ibid., art. 9.

[107] Decree of 6 May 1898, Regarding the reorganisation of justice services in Cambodia (Decree of 6 May 1898), art. 2, in Dareste, *Recueil de legislation 1989*, pp. 131–2. Blazy notes that the Royal Ordinance of 11 July 1897 was affirmed the next month by an *arrêté* of the governor general, see Blazy, "L'Organisation judiciaire", pp. 398–9.

72   *Colonial Law Making*

regional French Courts of First Instance to take on the work of the French jurisdiction, which had expanded to include all matters that had previously been dealt with in the "mixed jurisdiction" as well as cases between French citizens, the colonial administration granted judicial powers to the *résidents*. The French court of Phnom Penh remained the only judge-run court in the protectorate.

The question of the king's power, and the colonial judiciary's discontent at being excluded from rural Cambodia, would influence the future of colonial justice as, after 1897, the French quickly legislated to further expand their mandate and their control beyond Phnom Penh. Two innovations, the judicial power of the *résidents* and an administrative code called the *indigénat*, entrenched French rule in the countryside. Both illustrated the instrumental bias of colonial law.

Summary Justice and the Judicial Power of *résidents*

A French presidential decree of 6 May 1898 expanded the French jurisdiction in Cambodia and sanctioned the decision to place it in the hands of the *résidents*, at least outside of Phnom Penh.[108] The *résidents* were vested with the powers of "justices of the peace with extended competence" (*Justices de la paix de compétence étendues*).[109] Their *tribunaux résidentiels* would become more important in Cambodia than elsewhere in Indochina because of their jurisdiction over the sizeable ethnic Vietnamese and Chinese minorities. By placing the rural courts in the hands of *résidents*, rather than judges, the French government breached the principle of the separation of powers, and incensed the colonial judiciary.

The decree of 6 May also introduced the *Indigénat* to Cambodia and gave the *résidents* another means of disciplining their local constituents, including ethnic Khmers.[110] The French had initiated such

---

[108] By 1901, there were nine *résidents* stationed in: Kampot, Kompong Chhnang, Kompong Speu, Kompong Thom, Kratie, Prey Veng, Pursat, Svay Rieng and Takeo, see *Annuaire Général de l'Indochine Français* (1900), pp. 413–29; there had been four in 1890, see *Annuaire de l'Indo-Chine Française* (1890), pp. 616–17.

[109] Decree of 6 May 1898, art. 4, in *Recueil de législation*, ed. Dareste and Appert, pp. 131–2. Regarding the courts of Cochin China, see Garrigues, "à Administration unique: La Cochinchine" [Unique Administration: Cochin China], p. 53.

[110] Decree of 6 May 1898, art. 7, in *Recueil de législation*, ed. Dareste and Appert, pp. 131–2.

a code of summary administrative justice in Algeria, but in Indochina some commentators claimed it embodied vestiges of pre-colonial *Annamite* law.[111] The *Indigénat* gave *résidents* the power to punish certain prescribed offences with up to eight days' detention or a maximum fine of 50 francs without recourse to the courts.[112] The *résident supérieur* could order the internment of people other than French citizens and could sequester their belongings.[113]

Some of the offences that the *résidents* could punish included disorderly behaviour (*tapage*); receipt of stolen cattle; giving shelter to people who had no identity papers; failure to notify a birth or a death; refusal to cooperate with local or French officials; and late payment of taxes.[114] They could also penalise disrespect towards the administration and individual administrators.[115]

The *Indigénat* highlighted the fundamental insecurity of colonial rule, which could be unsettled by apparently disrespectful villagers. It flouted the separation of powers and punished certain acts that were not illegal in France, and was therefore highly controversial.[116] It remained in force in Cambodia until at least 1912.[117] The *Indigénat* was an extreme example of the pre-modern methods that permeated colonial law and that, even though they were sometimes justified by reference to indigenous law, originated with the French.[118]

---

[111] René Pommier, "Le régime de l'indigénat en Indo-Chine" [The Regime of the Indigenant in Indo-China] (PhD dissertation, University of Paris, Faculté de droit, 1907), p. 17; see also Barnhart, "Violence and the Civilizing Mission", pp. 502–86.

[112] Pommier, "Le régime de l'indigénat", p. 26. In 1899, the estimated annual salary of a Cambodian minister was 1,800 French piastres; for a low-level provincial secretary, it was 16 piastres per month. The piastre hovered at just below three francs during that year. In other words, a fine of 50 francs would have been worth slightly more than the monthly salary of a provincial secretary; Brocheux and Hémery, *Indochina*, p. 139.

[113] Barnhart, "Violence and the Civilizing Mission", p. 508.

[114] Pommier, "Le régime de l'Indigénat", pp. 58–9.

[115] Ibid.

[116] Ibid., pp. 7, 58–9; disrespect to authorities is number 12 on the list.

[117] *Résident Supérieur* Outrey to Governor General, 22 Oct. 1912, CAOM GGI 65346.

[118] Emmanuelle Saada, "The Empire of Law: Dignity, Prestige, and Domination in the 'Colonial Situation'", *French Politics, Culture & Society* 20, 2 (2002): 98–120.

74   *Colonial Law Making*

Royal Power: Eclipsed but Not Extinguished

In 1897, Norodom's 30-year struggle had apparently ended in defeat, and French control was complete. Legally, Norodom's situation now resembled that of the rulers of those five Malay sultanates that were were pushed into a federation under the British in 1895. Like Norodom, their role had largely been reduced to rubber stamping legislation initiated by the colonial power, represented in each state by a resident.[119] On the other hand, in some respects, Norodom's position, and that of his successors, was closer to that of the rulers of the Unfederated Malay States (UMS), which became British protectorates after 1909. A British adviser (instead of resident) in the UMS also exerted de facto control, but the UMS rulers arguably retained more social and political power than their counterparts in the FMS.[120]

In Cambodia, and in both the Federated and Unfederated Malay States, local sovereigns maintained varying degrees of state-sanctioned religious authority. In theory, the Malay rulers retained considerable authority in religious (Islamic) affairs, including much family law, although this was restricted in the Federated states.[121] The Cambodian king's religious authority was less directly connected to state law, but French authority in the eyes of the Cambodian people, and internationally, rested on their claim to rule in the name of the king. After Norodom's death, the French helped to create, and actively reinforced, the monarchy's symbolic and ritual role as well as the king's semi-divine status.[122]

One significant difference with the Malay protectorates was that a distinct indigenous (Khmer) jurisdiction had been preserved in Cambodia. The judicial system in the Federated and (at a slower pace) in the Unfederated Malay States came into the hands of British administrators and judges. Except in some areas of Islamic law, British-dominated courts incrementally and selectively absorbed *adat* into locally applied English common law.[123] This jurisdictional melding contrasted with France's attempts to maintain strict demarcations between ethnically

---

[119] Suwannathat-Pian, *Palace, Political Party and Power*, p. 30; Gullick, *Rulers and Residents*, p. 4.
[120] Suwannathat-Pian, *Palace, Political Party and Power*, pp. 82–6.
[121] Ibid.
[122] Osborne, *French Presence*, pp. 272–3.
[123] Tan Sri James Foong, *The Malaysian Judiciary: A Record* (Selangor Darul Ehsan, Malaysia: LexisNexis, 2017, 3rd ed.), pp. 17–45.

determined jurisdictions, especially in its colonial protectorates.[124] In Morocco, most of which became a French protectorate in 1912, colonial administrators sought to impose strict, and arguably artificial, boundaries between Islamic law, which applied to the majority Arab population and remained under the authority of the sultan, and the laws and customs of Berber peoples.[125] Like King Norodom, successive Moroccan sultans struggled to maintain judicial authority over all the inhabitants of their realms as the French incrementally imposed jurisdictions that appeared to transgress their respective treaties of protection.

King Norodom engaged flexibly with colonial law. At times he played by its rules, appealing to the limits that the Treaty of Protection placed on the French. At other times, he retreated behind the shield of Cambodian law and tradition or simply refused to implement agreed reforms. Members of the Cambodian elite would employ similar tactics, in more muted forms, over the following decades.

Throughout Norodom's tug of war with the French, different narratives of protection and of the protectorate took hold. By 1897 Cambodia had been transformed from an external to an internal protectorate, which involved increasingly direct control.[126] Cynically, we might say that the Treaty of Protection provided a fig leaf for French expansionist ambitions on the one hand and for Norodom's desire to hold on to power on the other. Yet the sometimes competing, and sometimes opportunistic, narratives of protection helped to shape the colonial regime. For example, Aymonier and Moura appear to have genuinely believed in their mission to protect Cambodians from what they perceived to be barbarous and unjust practices. Norodom and the Cambodian elite attempted to protect their realm, and their powers, from changes that for

---

[124] Lekéal, "La Place de la justice française", pp. 43–63; Sana Ben Achour, "Juges et magistrats tunisiens dans l'ordre colonial" [Tunisian Judges and Magistrates in the Colonial Order], in *La Justice française et le droit pendant le protectorate en Tunisie*, ed. Nada Auzary-Schmaltz (Rabat: Institut de recherché sur le Maghreb contemporain, 2007), pp. 153–73; Messaoudi, "Grandeur et limites", pp. 146–55; Katherine E. Hoffman, "Berber Law by French Means: Customary Courts in the Moroccan Hinterlands, 1930–1956", *Comparative Studies in Society and History* 52, 4 (2010): 851–80.

[125] Guerin, "Racial myth", pp. 361–80.

[126] Hoeffel, "De la condition juridique", p. 43.

76 *Colonial Law Making*

them constituted a "moral rupture" by claiming to be protecting tradition and culture.[127]

The need to be seen to comply with the Treaty of Protection affected the pace and nature of French impositions and forced the colonial authorities to work hard to win Norodom's formal consent to changes that greatly reduced his power. Over the 20 years following Norodom's death in 1904, with Sisowath on the throne, the French felt more confident to push reforms. Yet they continued to work within political parameters, and with the jurisdictions, that had been established during Norodom's reign.

---

[127] Paul Mus, *Le destin de l'Union Française: de l'Indochine à l'Afrique* [The Destiny of the French Union: From Indochina to Africa] (France: Laudun L'Ardois, 1954), p. 53.

4

Codification Begins

Three years before he died, King Norodom signed the 1901 Royal Ordinance creating a joint Cambodian–French commission to elaborate a code of Cambodian laws. The preamble to the Ordinance stated "there is a reason to revise the texts of the laws currently in force, reconciling current needs with the traditions of Our Kingdom". According to the preamble, the "old texts" were incomplete, not easily comprehensible and sometimes contradictory, and they imposed inappropriate penalties. Procedures were long and costly, obliging "the population to undergo lengthy absences that are too onerous for their resources".[1]

It would take another ten years to finalise and enact the first "revised" laws. In 1911, King Sisowath and *Résident Supérieur* Outrey signed into law: a Criminal Code; a Code of Criminal Investigation and Judicial Organisation; and the first section of a Civil Code that purported to establish the *état civil*, the system designed to record the civil status of Cambodians, their births, deaths and marriages.[2] The three codes came into effect in 1912. While it might seem reasonable that it would take many years to rewrite the laws of a country, colonial rulers often moved more rapidly, and generally with less outward regard for the opinions of local elites. In neighbouring Laos, one French expert and the local colonial administration took less than four years to draft three

---

[1] Preamble and art. 1, Royal Ordinance of 11 Aug. 1901, NAC RSC 30549.
[2] Criminal Code and Code of Criminal Investigation and Judicial Organisation (Kingdom of Cambodia, 1911), NAC Box 423; Civil Code (Kingdom of Cambodia, 1911), NAC RSC 30549.

78 *Colonial Law Making*

new codes.[3] The drafting process took so long in Cambodia partly because of a constant turnover of French personnel, but also because it was a highly sensitive process that could, if imposed too quickly, have sparked widespread unrest and even revolt, as had happened in 1885–86. The French had to tread carefully, even after the more pliable King Sisowath, whom they hand-picked, ascended the throne following Norodom's death in 1904.

The 1911 codes were an important milestone in a process by which the French transformed the Cambodian jurisdiction. They established new Courts of First Instance and completed the separation of judicial and administrative functions. Alain Forest has described what took place during those years as a "slow gestation of 'independent' justice".[4] The process was indeed slow compared with the wholesale reforms that the protectorate had attempted to impose after Governor Charles Thomson forced King Norodom to sign the 1884 Convention. This chapter considers the first phase of that "gestation" up to 1915. By then, the 1911 codes had been in force for three years, and considerable teething problems had become apparent, leading several French officials to lobby for further changes, particularly of Cambodian personnel, but also for more direct French participation in the indigenous courts.

King Sisowath's ascension in 1904 coincided with an era of stable leadership in the protectorate administration. Whereas from mid-1897, after the French took full control of the Cambodian government, until December 1905 there had been eight different *résidents supérieurs*, over the following nine years there would be just two, Louis Paul Luce (1906–11) and Ernest Outrey (1911–14). Towards the end of 1914, the year the First World War broke out in Europe, François Baudoin took up the position of *résident supérieur*. Baudoin would dominate the protectorate until the mid-1920s, including when he acted as provisional governor general of Indochina from 1920 to 1924. His predecessors Luce and Outrey had begun to consolidate a colonial state apparatus, and Baudoin continued the process, albeit in more difficult circumstances as the war in Europe drained the colonies of funds and French personnel.

King Sisowath was far more cooperative than his half-brother Norodom had been, complying with most French demands. French prestige in Cambodia received a considerable boost in 1907 when Siam

---

[3] Cressent, "Administration mixte: le Laos", p. 86.
[4] Forest, *Le Cambodge et la colonisation française*, p. 107; Nicolas "Cambodge", pp. 118–21.

agreed to relinquish sovereignty over three provinces in what is now the north-west of Cambodia centred on the town of Battambang.[5] Yet the Cambodian elite, and even King Sisowath, were not always happy with French reforms. Moreover, Sisowath's coronation had upset some royals, particularly members of the Norodom branch of the family.[6] Although the five Cambodian ministers had formally switched their allegiance to the French in 1897, neither they nor other members of the elite had relinquished their traditional ties of patronage and protection. Some elites still had the power to defy the French openly, often using the courts and legal processes to protect their personal interests.

A number of legal disputes from the early 1900s, discussed in the first section of this chapter, illustrate the still unruly relations between the French administration and the Cambodian elites, particularly those in and around the capital, Phnom Penh. These cases demonstrate that the law courts in Phnom Penh remained instruments of elite personalised power and traditional patronage. The new codes of 1911, and the process of drafting them, took place against this backdrop of unruly elites. The codes started to restructure the courts and to reform legal procedures in ways that aimed to lessen the local elites' ability to influence cases and openly to defy the colonial authorities. The drafting process reflected the delicate, albeit unequal, relations between the protectorate authorities and the Cambodian elite. The new Criminal Code replaced and redefined offences, but it did reflect some aspects of pre-existing law and the ambiguity of Cambodian sovereignty under the protectorate. The Code of Criminal Investigation and Judicial Organisation began to separate judicial and administrative roles, starting with the courts in Phnom Penh, and it established a new Court of Cassation, but it left the provincial courts in the hands of the Cambodian provincial governors.

Many factors influenced colonial law during these early years of codification, including economic, political and personal factors. Exchanges over writing and implementing the reforms demonstrate that even after the French had in reality seized direct control of Cambodia, their rule rested on the foundations, and the narrative, of indirect rule and protection, affecting the way the colonial state unfolded.

---

[5] Tully, *Cambodia under the Tricolour*, pp. 81–2.
[6] Norodom and Sisowath were half-brothers, sons of King Ang Duong.

Figure 4.1: François Baudoin, early 1920s when he was acting Governor General of Indochina Baudoin
Source: National Archives of Cambodia, 0674.

Figure 4.2: King Sisowath

Source: Bibliothèque Nationale de France, Gallica (undated) https://gallica.bnf.fr/ark:/12148/btv1b101119307?rk=21459;2# (accessed 4 September 2023).

The Phnom Penh Courts, the Elite, and the *résident supérieur*

The fate of one man, Oung, reveals something of the residual power of elites with royal connections to flout French authority during the early years of the 20th century.[7] In 1909, Oung was the governor of a province close to Phnom Penh in which the protectorate administration had become embroiled in a complex dispute over some rice fields. The area fell within the purview of the French *résident* of a region called Kandal, Monsieur G. Jeannerat. The two Cambodian parties to the dispute were members of the elite. On one side was *Oknha* Nhem[8] and on the other were the descendants and clients of a deceased official and former judge, referred to as *Moha Vinichay* Sot.[9] Both parties claimed to own the land. In 1883, the Phnom Penh court (*sala lukhun*) had granted the land to Nhem's father, Op, but a year later the decision had been overturned and Op had been murdered.[10] According to *Résident* Jeannerat, for over 20 years Nhem had been attempting to appeal the matter but had been stymied by his opponent's connections in the palace.[11] Jeannerat claimed that the Council of Ministers had refused to hear the matter, despite having been authorised to act as a Court of Cassation and to discipline Cambodian officials.[12] It was only after the French authorities pressured them to do so, in 1908, that the ministers issued a judgement in favour of Nhem.[13]

Governor Oung's troubles began when *Résident* Jeannerat ordered him to see that the disputed land was handed to Nhem, in accord with the ministers' judgement. The people who were occupying the land were related to Sot, whose descendants claimed the land was theirs. They reacted violently when asked to vacate the land, and reportedly attempted

---

[7] Personnel Dossier of Oung, NAC RSC 20644.

[8] *Oknha* was (and still is) an honorific title for senior members of the elite.

[9] See Royal Ordinance of 14 Aug. 1908, NAC RSC 20644. The title *Moha Vinichay* roughly translates as Senior Judge.

[10] Jeannerat to Résident Supérieur, 8 July 1908, NAC RSC 20644. Jeannerat claimed the decision had been reversed by the *san prea aya*, an official who examined appeals to decide if they should go before the king, see Leclère, *Recherches sur la législation criminelle*, p. 139.

[11] Jeannerat to Résident Supérieur, 8 July 1908; Jeannerat to Résident Supérieur, 7 Jan. 1909, NAC RSC 20644.

[12] Nicolas dates the cassation powers to 26 June 1903; see Nicolas, "Le Cambodge", p. 120.

[13] Royal Ordinance of 14 Aug. 1908, NAC RSC 20644.

to burn down the house of the claimant, Nhem.[14] To make matters more complex, Governor Oung's second-in-command, a man named Khut, was allied with the recalcitrant occupants, and his wife was the sister-in-law of the Cambodian minister of defence, which may explain why the Council of Ministers had not ruled on the case until forced to do so by the French. After Governor Oung attempted to enforce the order in favour of Nhem, his assistant, Khut, accused him of corruption.[15] Oung made counter-accusations against Khut, and the Council of Ministers suspended both men.[16] This infuriated *Résident* Jeannerat, who claimed that his planned programme of road building could not proceed without Oung's help.[17] Jeannerat argued that the suspensions were illegal, asserted Oung's innocence, and accused the Council of Ministers of favouring Khut.[18] Khut then wrote to the *résident supérieur*, accusing Jeannerat of bias against him.[19] The Council of Ministers insisted their decision to suspend the two men conformed to procedures that had been sanctioned by the *résident supérieur*.[20] Oung's career was ruined. There was an attempt on his life in 1910;[21] he was transferred to another province and in 1911 was suspended for "*outrage*" (contempt of court) against the Council of Ministers, despite a plea for leniency from King Sisowath.[22] That year, a French official wrote on Oung's file that he was "a very good official whom I regret having lost due to intrigue in the palace".[23]

As Oung's case shows, members of the royal court and the Council of Ministers continued to operate in a sphere that lay at least partially beyond the reach of the colonial authorities.[24] Some Cambodians turned

---

[14] Jeannerat to Résident Supérieur, 7 Jan. 1909, NAC RSC 20644.

[15] Oung to Jeannerat (trans.), 4 Jan. 1909, NAC RSC 20644.

[16] Jeannerat to Résident Supérieur, 8 Mar. 1909, NAC RSC 20644.

[17] Ibid.

[18] Jeannerat to Résident Supérieur, 27 Mar. 1909, NAC RSC 20644.

[19] Khut to Résident Supérieur, 8 Apr. 1909, NAC RSC 20644.

[20] Cambodian Minister of Interior to Résident Supérieur (trans.), 12 Mar. 1909, NAC RSC 20644.

[21] Résident of Kandal to Résident Supérieur, 20 July 1910, NAC RSC 20644.

[22] See extract of minutes of the 154th meeting of the Council of Ministers, 19 Aug. 1911, item 1, NAC RSC 20644.

[23] Résident of Kandal to Résident Supérieur, 20 July 1910, NAC RSC 20644; see also Résident of Prey Veng, monthly report, Aug. 1911, CAOM RSC 237.

[24] See also Résident of Prey Veng, monthly report, Feb. 1911, in which he complains about the tardiness of the council in disciplining local officials, CAOM RSC 237.

84   *Colonial Law Making*

to the *résident supérieur* as their only possible recourse in disputes with powerful Cambodians, particularly those from the palace.[25] Archival dossiers from 1901, 1903 and 1908 contain reports on numerous such cases in the indigenous jurisdiction in which the French authorities intervened. One matter concerned a woman called Ruoi, and her nine-year-old son, who had been bound to serve Princess Khan Char in order to work off a debt.[26] Debt bondage was common and still legal in Cambodia, although the French had tried to regulate it.[27] In breach of palace rules, Khan Char had repeatedly ordered Ruoi to smuggle alcohol into the royal compound for her, and Ruoi had been caught and beaten by the palace guards. Rather than risk another beating, Ruoi had left the palace to try to raise money so she could buy her freedom. When she failed to do so, the princess had Ruoi and her son imprisoned in the palace. Ruoi's husband implored the *résident supérieur* for help.[28] Unfortunately the dossier does not record what happened next, which suggests that the French did not feel they could intervene against Princess Khan Char.[29]

Royals and other elites also used the courts to punish their enemies. A man named Ouk wrote to the *résident supérieur* to say that he had borrowed 60 piastres from Queen Khun Than, who had been the first wife of King Norodom. Ouk agreed to repay his debt in instalments.[30] Khun Than had passed the debt to a princess, who demanded the Phnom Penh court order Ouk to repay the entire amount immediately, or place him in debtors'

---

[25] See complaints of Neang Ruong, 19 Feb. 1903 and 29 July 1903, Council of Ministers to Résident Supérieur, 18 Apr. 1903; Neang Tinlap Apr. 1903 and Chea 18 Jan. 1903, NAC RSC 37283; see also complaint of Chou Ouk, 18 July 1901, NAC RSC 12596. Regarding Aymonier's interventions in the 1870s, see Muller, *Colonial Cambodia's "Bad Frenchmen"*, pp. 119–21; Aymonier's Confidential Report on Cambodia, 1874, CAOM FM AF C13, dossier A30 (22).

[26] Complaint by Ruoi against Princess Khan Char of the palace of His Majesty the King, 29 July 1903, NAC RSC 37283. For a discussion of French attempts to lessen the influence of the women of the palace, see Jacobsen, *Lost Goddesses*, pp. 152–60.

[27] Debt bondage was not abolished when other forms of slavery were declared illegal by the French in 1884, and it remained widespread during these years, see Forest, *Le Cambodge et la colonisation française*, pp. 337–57.

[28] Complaint from Ruoi, 29 July 1903, NAC RSC 37283. There is no information in the file on the outcome of the case; there is a handwritten instruction, in the margin of the complaint, to refer the matter to a palace official.

[29] Regarding cuts to the king's entourage, see Forest, *Le Cambodge et la colonisation française*, pp. 75–9.

[30] Chou Ouk to Résident Supérieur, 18 July 1901 (trans.), NAC RSC 12596.

custody.[31] The *résident supérieur* wrote to the court suggesting its judges should negotiate with the princess to allow Ouk to repay in instalments, but the president of the court replied that he could not defy the princess.[32]

A curious matter from 1908 suggests that the Cambodian courts were unwilling or unable to rule against royals and other senior members of the elite, but may also at times have tried to alleviate the conditions of some of their victims.[33] A woman called Kun wrote that her elderly parents had been held in debtors' custody for eight years by the Cambodian court.[34] Two previous judges had taken pity on her parents and allowed them certain privileges. Kun asked the French authorities to ensure that the new judges would continue this kindness. After learning of Kun's request to the French authorities, one of the unnamed creditors demanded that the Cambodian court arrest her.[35] The *résident supérieur* passed the matter to the Cambodian minister for justice, who, rather than providing details on the actions he had taken, reported merely that he had asked the new judges to regularise cases of debt in which the former judges had colluded with the creditors.[36]

Members of the elite, royals and officials who held the title of *oknha* also used the courts to settle disputes among themselves, sometimes appealing to the *résident supérieur* when things did not go their way. In these cases, the complainant usually alleged malpractice by judges.[37] The

---

[31] Imprisonment for debt was still legal under Cambodian and French law, see Nicolas, "Le Cambodge", pp. 147–8.

[32] Draft letter Résident Supérieur to President of the *sala lukhun*, 30 July 1901; President of *sala lukhun* to Résident Supérieur, 2 Aug. 1901, NAC RSC 12596; see also the case of Chea, who was being held illegally in debtors' prison, NAC RSC 37283.

[33] Neang Kun to Prosecutor of the French court of Phnom Penh (trans.), 12 Oct. 1908, NAC RSC 12596; see also the complaint of Neai Oknha Chum to Résident Supérieur, 27 July 1903, in which he states that the judges of the Court of Appeal were afraid to rule in his case against the head of the palace guard and his wife, NAC RSC 37283.

[34] Neang Kun to Prosecutor of the French court of Phnom Penh, 12 Oct. 1908, NAC RSC 12596.

[35] Ibid.

[36] Cambodian Minister of Justice to Résident Supérieur (trans.), 19 Aug. 1908, NAC RSC 12596.

[37] In NAC RSC 37283, see dispute between Neai Oknha Chhun and Oknha Sophea Thippeday, former Vice President of *sala lukhun*, 1903; complaint of Oknha Chhum against the President of the second chamber of the *sala outor,* Jan. 1903; complaint of Oknha Phumin Bin against the Council of Ministers, 7 Aug. 1903; complaints against the *sala lukhun* by Neang Roung, 19 Feb. and

86   *Colonial Law Making*

Council of Ministers had the formal power to deal with such complaints, but, as in the land dispute between Nhem and the family of Sot discussed above, they often failed to respond until prompted to do so by the *résident supérieur*. One official, Neai Oknha Chhum, alleged that the president of the Civil Chamber of the Court of Appeal had ruled on a criminal matter after having presided in the original case when he worked in a lower court.[38] Further, Chhum alleged that in the lower court the same judge had allowed other court officials to post bail for the defendant, Um, who had then robbed Chhum's house and run off with two of his female servants.[39] Instructed by the *résident supérieur* to investigate their colleague in the Court of Appeal, the Council of Ministers determined only that the judge had erred in allowing the court personnel to post surety for the defendant and should possibly be fined.[40]

The *résident supérieur* had become the only hope for some individuals in disputes with members of the royal family and the Council of Ministers. They approached him as a possible alternative source of power, patronage and protection. As one man begged: "you who are the protector of Cambodia, [should] be willing to accord me your high protection".[41] However, even the chief colonial administrator could not always force local elites to comply with his directions.

It is easy to condemn the instances of cruelty in some of these cases and to understand that the *résident supérieur* would want to see the courts act more independently of outside influence. However, when it suited them, the French undermined their own attempts to impose respect for rule-bound legal procedures.[42] For example, in 1898 a female member of the entourage of Cambodian Prime Minister Um alleged that he had tortured and attempted to rape her.[43] Senior French

---

7 Oct. 1903; and dispute between the heirs of ex-prime minister Um 1903. In NAC RSC 10042, see Council of Ministers to RSC regarding complaint by Cha Meas against the court of Longvek, 9 July 1903.

[38] Complaint of Oknha Chhum against the President of the second chamber of the *sala outor*, Jan. 1903, Résident Supérieur, NAC 37283.

[39] A 1902 Royal Ordinance had established a court of appeal (*sala outour*) in Phnom Penh, divided into criminal and civil sections. See Nicolas, "Cambodge", pp. 119–120.

[40] Council of Ministers to Résident Supérieur (trans.), 19 Mar. 1903, RSC, NAC 37283.

[41] Complaint by Oknha Phumin Bin against the Council of Ministers, 7 Aug. 1903, RSC, NAC 37283.

[42] Forest, *Le Cambodge et la colonisation française*, p. 82.

[43] See Prosecutor General Edgard Assaud to Governor General, 18 July 1898, and complaint of Neang Cotine, 27 June 1898, CAOM GGI 22702 (thanks to Dr Matthieu Guérin for copies of these documents).

judicial officers and *Résident Supérieur* Ducos colluded to grant Um's request that the matter be heard by the Cambodian courts, despite the woman's claim to be "half-Chinese" and therefore subject to the French jurisdiction.[44] By contrast, they dealt harshly with less accommodating officials. As Milton Osborne recounts, in 1901 they dismissed Judge Alexis Louis Chhun on charges of corruption, largely because the dissident Prince Yukanthor, who was banished by the French, had praised Chhun.[45]

The courts of the Cambodian jurisdiction operated to enforce hierarchical, traditional patronage-based social relations. This was a system that the French would struggle to dismantle, but at times, as in Um's case, would also exploit. Nevertheless, their desire for more control over these unruly members of the elite reinforced their determination to reform Cambodian law by codifying it. They embarked on a process that, on the pretext of modernising the *kram*, replaced them with a simple set of codes that drew heavily on French law. They also remodelled the courts of the indigenous Cambodian jurisdiction, particularly those in Phnom Penh.

The 1911 Codes

From the 1880s to the 1920s, the colonial authorities negotiated and imposed reforms to the indigenous jurisdictions in Tonkin (1917), Laos (1905–08) and Cambodia (1911–15).[46] Two aspects of the Cambodian codes set them apart from those of Tonkin and Laos. First is the length of time it took to draft them. Second, despite the elaborate process of consultation, spanning more than 10 years, the new codes, particularly the Criminal Code, borrowed more extensively and more directly from French metropolitan law than in any of the other Indochinese protectorates. Drafting commissions were also established in Tonkin, but undertook a less radical rewriting of the pre-existing law—the Vietnamese Code Gia Long—than occurred in Cambodia.[47] In Laos, a single French jurist drafted a new set of codes in less than four years, and claimed to

---

[44] Prosecutor General to Governor General, 18 July 1898, CAOM GGI 22702.

[45] Osborne, *French Presence*, pp. 245–7. Regarding Prince Yukanthor, see, for example, Tully, *France on the Mekong*, pp. 110–14.

[46] Habert, "Le Tonkin", p. 184, Cressent, "Administration Mixte: Le Laos", p. 86, Nicolas, "Le Cambodge", p. 123; M.B. Hooker, *A Concise Legal History of South-East Asia* (Oxford: Clarendon Press, 1978), pp. 154–75.

[47] Blazy, "L'Organisation judiciaire", p. 713.

88   *Colonial Law Making*

have thoroughly synthesised what he took to be local laws and customs with French principles and substance.[48]

The different approach in Cambodia reflected both its history and the particular distribution of power between the colonial authorities and the local elites upon which they rested. By establishing joint drafting commissions, the French warded off critics who claimed they were expanding the protectorate mandate and sustained the argument they were modernising rather than replacing pre-existing Cambodian law. At the same time, the commissions preserved the king's dignity and gained royal authority and elite consent for the new codes.[49] A few Cambodians who had made their careers in service to the colonial authorities also played a key role in drafting and translating the codes. Among them were Penn and Keth. In 1905, the two men had established a Society for Mutual Education, which helped Cambodians to learn French in order to win higher office in the protectorate. Both started their careers as interpreters and went on to become senior judges in the reformed courts. Penn became the minister for justice in 1933 and retired in 1943.[50]

Superficially, the drafting commissions in Cambodia and in Tonkin resembled those established by King Chulalongkorn in Siam, but, politically, they had opposite effects.[51] In Cambodia, French judges and officials chaired the commissions, and the new codes strengthened French control of law. In Siam, King Chulalongkorn and trusted family members oversaw each drafting committee, ensuring the interests of his dynasty would be protected and even strengthened.[52] Moreover, the Siamese codes would help to end the extraterritorial rights of foreigners.[53] Yet there were some parallels between the French-controlled process in Cambodia and the Siamese reforms, because, although the 1911 Cambodian codes further curtailed the Cambodian elite's temporal powers, they also enshrined the monarchy in state law as the source of and authority for the new codes.

It is difficult to tell how much input the Cambodian members really had to the drafting process. The French judge who presided over the

---

[48] Ibid., p. 708.

[49] Minutes (*procès verbal*) of a meeting in the hall of the Hotel of the Council of Ministers in Phnom Penh, 23, 25, 27, 28 and 30 Jan. and 1 Feb. 1909 (trans.), NAC RSC 30546.

[50] NAC RSC 36305, 19286; Edwards, *Cambodge*, p. 85, note 129.

[51] Loos, *Subject Siam*, pp. 43–8.

[52] Ibid., pp. 47–51.

[53] Ibid.; Hong, "Extraterritoriality".

sub-commission responsible for the Cambodian Criminal Code claimed that the work was done by Cambodian members of the commission, left to meet on their own. However, of 283 articles in the 1911 Criminal Code, 258 reproduced French law.[54] By contrast, the codes of Laos in 1908 and Tonkin in 1917 focused more on compiling and reorganising existing laws, with some additions from the French, particularly in procedural law.[55]

According to the report by the French jurist who participated in drafting the Criminal Code, most instances in which old Cambodian law was reflected in the new code concerned the severity of sentences. For example, assassination of senior royals was punished more severely than the murder of more distant relatives of the king.[56] Another concession, made in response to a request from a senior Buddhist monk, allowed for a ceremony to be performed in order to release the souls of felons who had been executed.[57]

Some sections of the Criminal Code that did draw on the *kram* dealt with "certain offences and misdemeanours committed to the prejudice of His Majesty".[58] These clauses embedded the sovereign as a sacred head of state and laid the basis for post-independence *lèse majesté* laws. For example, it was an offence to pass in front of the throne, to cross the royal chamber, to lie or sit on the king's bed or to touch the head of a royal.[59]

The Criminal Code also adapted clauses from the French Penal Code (arts. 86–90), enacted by Napoleon Bonaparte, that punished certain subversive activities, including disrespect to the king and the Buddhist clergy,[60] as well as crimes against the external security of

---

[54] Nicolas, "Le Cambodge", p. 143.

[55] Cressent, "Administration mixte: Le Laos", pp. 86–9; Blazy, "L'Organisation judiciaire", pp. 713–14.

[56] Criminal Code 1911, art. 40.

[57] The Criminal Code stipulated that the body of the deceased should be delivered to his or her family for the ceremony of *Bon Loeuk Khmoch*; Criminal Code 1911, art. 11.

[58] Criminal Code 1911, arts. 112–17.

[59] Criminal Code 1911, art. 117. See *Kram Tumrong Sakh* (Law on Protocol), in Leclère, *Codes Cambodgiens*, vol. I, pp. 117, 223–32.

[60] Ibid., arts. 67–85. The 1810 French Penal Code included a similar section regarding plots against the then emperor (Napoleon Bonaparte) and his family; Penal Code (France), 1810, arts. 86–90. English translation transcribed by Tom Holmberg, available at https://www.napoleon-series.org/research/government/france/penalcode/c_penalcode3b.html (accessed 8 June 2023).

90   *Colonial Law Making*

the kingdom (arts. 74–82).[61] The *kram* certainly covered such topics,[62] so it may have appeared politic in 1911 to include them as evidence that the *kram* were being modernised rather than replaced. Moreover, the French may not have wanted to confront Sisowath with the fact that they, not the king, held sway over such high matters of state, particularly subversion. Thirteen years later, a revised Criminal Code omitted these clauses, suggesting the French by then felt more confident of their power.

Although it was ambivalent with regards to sovereignty, the Criminal Code started to reposition the king in relation to the colonial state. Crimes of *lèse majesté* would henceforth be defined and administered through the state, under the code, rather than by royal prerogative. Nonetheless, the code embedded the king as the head of state, and as the source of state laws.

The 1911 codes imposed a modified French format on the laws of the Cambodian jurisdiction and built on some reforms that had already been decreed, such as regulation of complaints against judges, costs and procedures for appeals, the use of case registers and specified roles for officials in the provincial courts.[63] The Criminal Code and the Code of Criminal Procedure and Judicial Organisation were divided into numbered "books" (*livres*), titles (*titres*) and articles. Penal offences were divided into three categories according to their gravity: *crime* (felony), *délit* (less serious crime or misdemeanour) and *contravention de simple police* (petty offence).[64] In sentencing defendants, Cambodian judges now had to apply specific regulations regarding mitigation and aggravation.[65] Another notable change introduced limits on debt-related detention, which, if applied, would have benefited some of the victims in the cases discussed above.[66]

---

[61] Criminal Code 1911, arts. 74–82. Roughly equivalent provisions in the 1810 French Code came under a separate heading, "Of Crimes tending to disturb the State by Civil War, Illegal Employment of the Armed Forces, Public Devastation and Pillage", Penal Code (France), 1810, arts. 91–102.

[62] Leclère, *Codes Cambodgiens*, vol. 2, p. 289, translating Code Pénal, *Titre* III *Krâm Chôr*, II 1.

[63] Royal Ordinance No. 27, 4 Mar. 1897; Royal Ordinance No. 2, 7 Feb. 1902, NAC RSC 33034.

[64] Criminal Code 1911, art. 1.

[65] Ibid., arts. 43–56.

[66] Criminal Code (Kingdom of Cambodia), 1911, art. 40; see also Prosecutor of the Phnom Penh court to *Résident Supérieur*, 30 Sept. 1911, CAOM GGI 65576.

The Code of Criminal Investigation and Judicial Organisation began to reorganise the court structure and moved further towards separating judicial and administrative functions. These were important reforms that exemplified the limits and the expansion of French control in 1911. In Phnom Penh, the Council of Ministers lost its power of cassation, which it had held since 1903, to a new Court of Cassation (*sala vinichhay*) led by two permanent judges.[67] The Court of Appeal (*sala outor*) and the Phnom Penh Court of First Instance (*sala lukhun*) were also to be staffed by full-time judges. The Criminal Code prohibited judges from interfering in administrative matters and administrative personnel from interfering in judicial matters.[68] These moves towards what the French would call the separation of powers significantly curtailed the judicial role of some Cambodian elites, particularly members of the Council of Ministers. The reforms were far less significant beyond Phnom Penh where each governor still acted as president of the local provincial court.

Implementation of the new criminal procedures and court structures did not run smoothly, even in the capital, the centre of the protectorate administration and the seat of royal power. The French placed the blame almost entirely at the feet of the Cambodian elite. The dedicated judicial officials in the senior courts largely failed to meet French expectations, even though they theoretically now had to pass an exam to be admitted to their jobs. Henri Dartiguenave, a judge of the French Court of Appeal of Indochina, claimed that Cambodian "mandarins" were unfit to apply the new codes. They were "out of their depth" and "paralysed by secular procedure".[69] Dartiguenave wrote that the codes required a new kind of judge, sufficiently educated and remunerated to be able to apply the new laws properly, something that could be achieved only if they were tutored by French judges.[70]

The 1911 codes had therefore begun to transform Cambodian law into a domain of French knowledge, shared perhaps by one or two of the most senior Cambodian judges, such as Keth, who knew French and had worked for the protectorate administration. But even he did not have the full trust of the colonial judiciary. In reality, the French had made

---

[67] Code of Criminal Investigation and Judicial Organisation 1911, art. 185.
[68] Code of Criminal Investigation and Judicial Organisation, art. 130; Criminal Code, arts. 84–5.
[69] Note on Cambodian Justice, 15 June 1914, NAC RSC 23803.
[70] Ibid.

insufficient efforts to help the majority of Cambodian judges to learn how to apply the new laws. A short-lived school of law was established in 1911, but in 1914 it was absorbed into the *École des kromokars* (school for officials), which offered basic courses for Cambodian administrators and judges.[71] There, using interpreters, officials of the French court of Phnom Penh taught courses in Cambodian law.[72] Regardless of the "mentality" of Cambodian mandarins, most must have been impossibly under-trained to administer new concepts in the codes, such as the degree to which mitigating circumstances should affect sentencing.[73]

Just how ill prepared Cambodian judges and court officials were became apparent in 1914, when 16 applicants sat tests to qualify for positions in the Court of Cassation. Henri Morché, the prosecutor of the French court in Phnom Penh, headed the selection committee, which also included Keth, by then a judge in the Court of Cassation.[74] Reporting on the test results, Morché wrote that in penal law "only three candidates understood the question and treated it in a satisfactory fashion. Two others seem to have understood it but gave an imprecise answer. Finally, the 11 other candidates submitted copy that was very mediocre or completely worthless".[75]

Comprehension of the 1911 *état civil*, discussed below, was even worse, according to Morché. He found only two answers acceptable, stating that the remaining 14 were all "of the same worthlessness". He reported that most candidates lacked an elementary knowledge of the law and demonstrated a "complete absence of reasoning".[76] If this was the level of candidates for the highest court, those working in the lower courts would have had even poorer understanding of the new laws.

Why, then, impose laws that the responsible judicial officials did not understand? As with the early codifications in Tonkin and Laos, it is likely the French were the main beneficiaries of the 1911 codes.[77] Protectorate authorities now had a set of laws and structures they could

---

[71] Forest, *Le Cambodge et la colonisation française*, p. 102.

[72] Extracts from recommendations made by the prosecutor of the French court of Phnom Penh in 1913, reproduced in Note on Cambodian justice, 15 June 1914, NAC RSC 23803. Regarding Morché, see RSC to Governor General, 2 Mar. 1915, CAOM GGI 65576.

[73] Criminal Code 1911, arts. 43–56.

[74] Minutes of recruiting committee, 4 Dec. 1914, NAC RSC 12715.

[75] Morché to Résident Supérieur, 21 Nov. 1914, NAC RSC 12715.

[76] Ibid.

[77] Blazy, "L'Organisation judiciaire", p. 726.

understand and try to enforce. The Criminal Code and the Code of Criminal Investigation and Judicial Organisation focused on control and administration of the courts and crime, important underpinnings of the colonial state.

Civil Code: Land and Lists

The colonial power, and potential French investors, also stood to gain administratively and economically from a civil code that would register the population and regulate some aspects of private property, including property in land. Although one of the joint drafting commissions had spent considerable time working on a lengthy civil code, only the first "book" on the *état civil* was promulgated in 1911.[78]

In 1913, the governor general of Indochina was on the point of signing the rest of the code into law when a telegram from Paris instructed him not to go ahead because it did not comply with the recommendations of Monsieur A. Boudillon, adviser to the French government on colonial land titling systems.[79]

The main challenge for the French was that rural Cambodians had consistently resisted changes to the rules by which they recognised a right to land. The protectorate administration had been focusing on the "problem of land ownership" since the late 19th century.[80] In 1908 and again in 1911, the French tried in vain to have Cambodians register their land holdings with local commune chiefs. These efforts had failed, partly due to the inhabitants' indifference and suspicion for colonial registers and to the inability of the commune chiefs to keep the rolls. Cambodian farmers simply continued to observe their long-established practice whereby land rights lay with those who used and occupied the land over a certain time.[81]

---

[78] Civil Code 1911, NAC RSC 30549.

[79] Résident Supérieur to Governor General, 13 Apr. 1915, CAOM GGI 65576. For examples of Boudillon's work, see A. Boudillon, *Le régime de la propriété foncière en Indochine* [The System of Real Property in Indochina] (Paris: Émile Larose, 1915); A. Boudillon, *La question foncière et l'organsiation du livre foncier en Afrique Occidentale française* [The Question of Real Property and the Organisation of Land Registers in French West Africa] (Paris: Challamel, 1911).

[80] Kleinpeter, *Le problème foncier.*

[81] Hel Chamroeun, "Introduction to the Land Law of Cambodia" in *Introduction to Cambodian Law*, ed. Hor Peng, Kong Phallack, Jörg Menzel, (Phnom Penh: Konrad Adenauer Foundation, 2012), pp. 313–34, see pp. 313–6.

94 *Colonial Law Making*

Boudillon had recommended that all of Indochina be subject to one set of land laws and one system of registration. He argued for a system based on that of Cochin China, but conceded that it should be introduced gradually to Cambodia, starting with a centralised register of land held by constituents of the French jurisdiction. The French authorities in the protectorate opposed this measure. They had previously introduced a system for granting land concessions to French citizens and since 1908 had been trying to impose the commune-level system of registration on the majority Khmer population.[82] They argued Boudillon's suggestion would add a third layer of complexity. Moreover, they were concerned that the new register, which was to be located in Phnom Penh, would create opportunities for unscrupulous elements to cheat innocent Cambodians. It took over five years to reach a compromise, which was incorporated into the 1920 Civil Code.[83] Even then, the law merely foreshadowed a future system of land registration while continuing to recognise a right of possession that could be established by proving prior occupation, or that there was no legal reason why they could not own it.[84]

The French had a strong interest in fostering French investment in Cambodia. A register of land titles would have allowed land to become a tradeable commodity and a means of raising capital, encouraging more colonial landholdings.[85] However, they encountered a barrier in the "mentality" of Cambodians, who, justifiably, associated colonial lists and rolls with taxation.[86] They did not willingly accept the French notion that unused land, of which there was still then a plentiful supply, belonged to the state and could not be freely acquired through use and occupation.[87] During the 1920s and 1930s, the French would continue to struggle to impose a cadastral register, although they were more successful after 1933, when they began to use aerial photography to map land use, and the amount of free land had diminished.[88] Still, as late as

---

[82] Ibid., pp. 189–91.

[83] Civil Code (Protectorate of Cambodia), 1920.

[84] Ibid., arts. 644, 690, 723.

[85] Kleinpeter, *Le problème foncier au Cambodge*, p. 13.

[86] Ibid., p. 204.

[87] The French had gradually imposed this concept of public or crown land, beginning in the 19th century when they had assumed the right to make concessions of certain tracts of land and had restricted access to forests, see Kleinpeter, *Le problème foncier au Cambodge*, p. 194.

[88] See Kleinpeter's summary of progress by Jan. 1937, Kleinpeter, *Le problème foncier au Cambodge*, p. 259.

1938, French jurist Maxime Léger wrote: "It is not a secret that if the Cambodian has a profound feeling of proprietorship over his movable possessions, it is not the same for his immovable goods. In the matter of land, the concept of possession triumphs over that of property."[89]

The Cambodian and to a lesser extent the French jurisdiction continued to be plagued by cases arising from these different conceptions of real property, and later by the opportunities for corruption that land titling presented. In their roles as overseers of the local Cambodian jurisdiction, and as judges in the French jurisdiction, French *résidents* had to address many disputes over land. For example, records from Kompong Cham during the early 1930s show the *résident* variously rebuking two commune chiefs for illegally selling concessions in state-owned forests, dealing with petitions from market gardeners who claimed the right to cultivate an island that had recently appeared in the Mekong River, and advising the local Cambodian court on how to deal with other intractable cases.[90]

In the years following its promulgation in 1911, the new *état civil* also proved difficult to enforce, and would not be fully effective until the mid-1920s.[91] The law devolved responsibilities for the new registries of births, deaths and marriages to the heads of communes and provinces.[92] Some of the barriers to implementation were similar to those encountered with regard to land law; Cambodians remained suspicious of official registers, and commune officials lacked the capacity, resources and possibly the will to administer them.

Whereas in France the *état civil* had been, at least partly, a means of abolishing differential status based on birth or privilege, the Cambodian code actually enforced status. For example, palace officials kept a special register of royals.[93] The code also reinforced the divide between Europeans and "others". A seeming anomaly of the code was that it provided for separate registers for ethnic Chinese and Vietnamese who

---

[89] Maxime Léger, "Rapport de Présentation" [Presentation Report], introducing the Code of Civil Procedure (Protectorate of Cambodia), 25 Mar. 1938, NAC RSC 4569.

[90] In NAC RSC 16204, see, for example: Résident Kompong Cham to governors of Tboung-Khmum and Kompong Cham districts, 4 Apr. 1930 (draft); the case of Kim, Yut and Leap, 1936; and complaint of 250 inhabitants from Kompong Cham, 28 May 1927.

[91] Kleinpeter, *Le problème foncier au Cambodge*, p. 189.

[92] Civil Code 1911, NAC RSC 30549.

[93] Ibid., arts. 16, 17.

96   *Colonial Law Making*

in other respects were not subject to indigenous law.[94] In this respect the code transgressed the otherwise strict division between those considered to be Khmer and those classified as Chinese and Vietnamese, but maintained the gulf between Europeans and "others". Ultimately, the French also treated the Chinese and Vietnamese as *indigènes*, subject to colonial taxes, although answerable to different courts than ethnic Khmers.

The applicants for positions in the Court of Cassation in 1914 appeared to prosecutor Morché to be even less well versed in the *état civil* than in the Criminal Code. Nevertheless, the test answers indicate that the candidates were aware their society was starting to be regulated in new ways, that this was generally related to French control and that the changes were not always clear or welcome. At least one candidate appears to have confused the register of births, deaths and marriages, with registers of land titles.[95] Some candidates were aware that the new code affected the legal position of women, but not that it changed their status or social mores. When asked why nuptials should be preceded by eight days' public notice, one lower-ranked candidate wrote that it was to ensure the bride-to-be did not love anyone else, and another claimed it was in order to avoid giving a girl to someone she was not destined to marry. Six candidates also mentioned the use of the civil rolls to protect the interests of women and children in divorce proceedings.[96]

The Codes and Contests over Power

In his report for the 1931 colonial exhibition in Paris, jurist Raoul Nicolas echoed Judge Dartiguenave, blaming the "ignorance of the judges" and the "confusion of powers" for problems in implementing the 1911 codes.[97] However, he also claimed that the royal government had jealously guarded "the vestiges of its judicial power", suggesting the Council of Ministers and other Cambodian officials in Phnom Penh had undermined the new laws and courts. King Sisowath and the Council of Ministers certainly showed their unease over the new reforms when it

---

[94] Ibid., art. 11. This provision appears to ignore the fact that these groups were not subject to Cambodian law.
[95] Royal Ordinance (Cambodia), 28 Jan. 1908, establishing land registers, NAC RSC 26315; see also Boudillon, *Le régime de la propriété foncière en Indochine*, p. 299.
[96] Ibid.
[97] Nicolas, "Le Cambodge", p. 126.

came to appointing a new head of the Court of Cassation (*sala vinichhay*) in 1914, when the first president of the court, Prince Maghavan, died.

Résident Supérieur Baudoin apparently proposed to appoint a French judge to replace Prince Maghavan, arguing that not even the "most deserving and educated of Cambodians"[98] could fill the position: first because the new codes were so "strongly impregnated with the spirit of our . . . institutions"; and secondly because the cassation process should produce jurisprudence which would, presumably, guide the lower courts. According to Baudoin, the Council of Ministers objected to his proposal, arguing that to appoint a French judge would be an affront to tradition and to the principle of the protectorate.[99] It would have been a rare event for the Cambodian ministers to oppose so openly a proposal by Baudoin, who chaired their meetings. Given the *résident supérieur*'s penchant for control, it seems surprising that he was apparently swayed by the ministers in this case. It is likely that Baudoin also did not want the colonial judiciary, whom he was campaigning to exclude from the French jurisdiction in rural Cambodia, to take control of the indigenous courts.

Outside Phnom Penh, *résidents* still presided in the French courts, acting as justices of the peace with expanded competence. Although the prosecutor general of Indochina monitored their judicial work, the *résidents* answered to Baudoin. Similar *tribunaux résidentiels* operated in other protectorates of Indochina, but "*la justice résidentielle*" was more important in Cambodia than elsewhere because a larger percentage of the population fell within its jurisdiction.[100] The ethnic Vietnamese and Chinese residents, who had been transferred from the indigenous Cambodian jurisdiction to a special sub-jurisdiction of the French courts, together comprised approximately 15 per cent of the Cambodian population in 1914.[101] The *résidents* found that the bulk of their judicial work involved that sub-jurisdiction, administering *Annamite* law to ethnic Vietnamese and Chinese. Some of these rural courts were quite busy and involved quite complex cases, for example disputes among Chinese merchants.[102] The colonial judiciary based in

---

[98] Baudoin to Governor General, 25 Nov. 1914, NAC RSC 7758.

[99] Ibid.

[100] Résident Supérieur Richomme to Governor General, 24 Oct. 1935, NAC RSC 35864.

[101] The 1914 figures are taken from estimates in *Annuaire Général de L'Indochine* (1914), pp. 514–24.

[102] See, for example, Prosecutor General to Director of Administration of Justice, 1 June 1929, CAOM GGI 65840.

98   *Colonial Law Making*

Saigon had long lobbied for them to be replaced by regular courts run by career judges.

When Baudoin arrived in Cambodia in 1914, he found that Prosecutor General Gabriel Michel had manoeuvred to abolish some of the courts of the *résidents* by expanding the reach of the French court of Phnom Penh.[103] Furious, Baudoin launched a fevered campaign to reverse the changes and also to prevent any new, judge-run French courts from being established in Cambodia.[104] Ironically, given the 1911 codes had started to separate judicial and administrative tasks in the Cambodian courts, Baudoin argued that the mentality of the *indigène* (in this case ethnic Vietnamese and Chinese) was not yet adapted to the concept of the separation of powers. Tellingly, he wrote that administrator-run courts better suited the "principle of domination".[105] Baudoin eventually won his battle with Michel in the aftermath of the anti-tax protests of early 1916, discussed in the next chapter, but in 1914 he was on the back foot and the dispute was intense. It is therefore not surprising that Baudoin gave way when the Cambodian ministers objected to having a French judge head the Court of Cassation. That would have meant handing control of the Cambodian jurisdiction to the colonial judiciary, headed by Gabriel Michel himself.

Whatever his motivations, Baudoin's respect for Cambodian tradition had its limits, as he then proposed to appoint the loyal Cambodian, Judge Keth, to the position, raising the ire of King Sisowath, who wrote a rare letter of complaint. The king claimed that Baudoin's predecessor, Outrey, had promised the head of the Court of Cassation would be a prince.[106] Outrey had kept his word and had earlier appointed Prince Maghavan, a son of King Norodom, who died in 1914. But Keth was not a prince. Echoing Norodom's lament of 1898 after the dismissal of Judge Ouk, Sisowath wrote that "the highest jurisdiction of

---

[103] For more detail of this dispute, see Sally Low, "Les Tribunaux Residentiels: Disputed Jurisdictions in the Protectorate of Cambodia", *French Colonial History* 16 (2016): 73–102.

[104] Baudoin to the Governor General (draft), 4 Aug. 1915, NAC RSC 9912. In NAC RSC 9912, see Baudoin to the Governor General, Telegram No. 11, 9 Apr. 1915; Baudoin to the Governor General (draft), 26 Feb. 1915; Baudoin to the Governor General (draft), 28 May 1915; Baudoin to the Governor General (draft), 23 Nov. 1914; Note aimed at establishing the illegality of the *arrêté* of 31 Mar. 1915 attached to Baudoin's letter to M.D. Penant, 7 Apr. 1916.

[105] Baudoin to Governor General, 26 Feb. 1915, NAC RSC 9912.

[106] Sisowath to Résident Supérieur (trans.), 17 June 1914, NAC, RSC 12715.

Codification Begins 99

the Kingdom has always been presided over by a Prince" and urged Baudoin to respect that tradition.[107] In this instance, Baudoin did not back down, but he made a tactical retreat. Keth went on to head the Court of Cassation, but he operated under the title of "provisional" president for several years, likely as a sop to the king.[108] Baudoin ultimately had his way, but the incident demonstrates that he had to tread carefully and that King Sisowath, his close advisors, and possibly also the Council of Ministers were deeply unhappy with aspects of the new codes.

While Baudoin may have been wary of handing the Cambodian jurisdiction to the French judiciary, he still wanted a French official to watch over Keth and the other Cambodian judges.[109] In 1915, he succeeded in having a French delegate appointed to work alongside the Cambodian minister of justice, but answering to the *résident supérieur*. This compromise may also have suited the king and the ministers, as it maintained the façade of Cambodian control. As we shall see, in the early 1920s the position of delegate would be replaced by a judicial adviser (*conseilleur juriste*), a French judge. However, the adviser was seconded from the judicial apparatus and also answered directly to Baudoin. In this respect, the Cambodian jurisdiction resembled that of Annam, where the *résident supérieur* or his delegate also oversaw the higher courts of the indigenous jurisdiction, while the *résidents* monitored the lower instance courts in their regions.[110]

Significance of the 1911 Codes

By 1915, with a French delegate working alongside the Cambodian minister for justice and overseeing the courts, it would have been more difficult, although likely not impossible, for a princess of the palace to issue orders to the Phnom Penh court, as Princess Khan Char had earlier done. In such circumstances too, the new Court of Cassation, led by Judge Keth, would have been unlikely to prevaricate over Nhem's land

---

[107] Ibid.

[108] See, for example, Arrété (decree) 549 of the Résident Supérieur, 24 Oct. 1919, NAC RSC 30544; see also in NAC RSC 12715: Le Gallen to Cambodian Minister of Justice, 27 Oct. 1914; and Keth to the Minister of Justice, 17 Feb. 1914.

[109] Baudoin to Governor General, 25 Nov. 1914, NAC RSC 7758.

[110] A. Bonhomme, "L'Annam" [Annam], in Direction de L'Administration de la Justice, *La justice en Indochine* (for the Exposition Coloniale Internationale, Paris 1931: Indochine Française) (Hanoi: Imprimerie d'Extrême-Orient, 1931), pp. 155–74, 163–5.

claim in the way the Council of Ministers had in 1909. With the 1911 codes, the French took an important step towards control of the Cambodian courts, extracting the power of cassation from the Council of Ministers and further limiting the influence of unruly members of the elite. Rewriting Cambodian law was therefore a highly politicised process that required a cautious mixture of negotiation and coercion because neither the ministers nor the usually compliant Sisowath acquiesced willingly to aspects of the reforms.

The 1911 codes also represented an accommodation between the French and the Cambodian elite. The protectorate had given rise, during these years, to shifting patterns of political compromise and dependence, and the codes thus made concessions to what the French understood to be Cambodian tradition. Judge Keth's 1914 appointment to the Court of Cassation severed the connection between judicial and royal power, yet the Criminal Code recognised the king's sovereignty. It enshrined respect for the monarch and the Buddhist clergy in ways that identified them with the emerging colonial state. Non-elite Cambodians influenced these outcomes, as clients to their Cambodian patrons and as landholders who guarded established patterns of ownership. Yet when persecuted by a powerful Cambodian, some appealed to the French as an alternative source of power.

The codes were an effort to create social change from above, and to stimulate French investment and commerce, making it easier for a market in land to develop. Rather than bringing about changes in the behaviour of many Cambodian officials, however, the new laws set standards which they were mostly not able to meet, particularly given the inadequate training that was on offer. Their subsequent failure to conform adequately to French standards would in turn lead to further reform and French intervention.

Intermingled with these contests between the colonial administration and the Cambodian elite, their interests coincided against those of the colonial judiciary to help preserve the *tribunaux résidentiels* and to avoid having a French judge head the indigenous court of cassation. Over the coming years, Baudoin, in alliance with the Cambodian elite, would continue this campaign against the French judges. Championing the concept that "Khmer should judge Khmer", he minimised the influence of his enemies in the colonial judiciary, cemented his own power and claimed to be supporting the principles of the protectorate. This tactic served him well as his administration began the next stage of reform of the Cambodian jurisdiction, focusing on the 53 provincial courts, between the years 1915 and 1922.

5

Rural Jurisdictions and the 1916 Affair

In December 1915, groups of rural Cambodians began to travel to Phnom Penh, petitioning King Sisowath to redress their grievances against a complex array of taxes and *corvée*, whereby men were forced to work for the state for a certain number of days each year. The resulting demonstrations, which continued throughout January, were one aspect of what came to be known as the 1916 Affair.[1] The first delegation of peasants returned home dissatisfied and drew up a set of demands that began to circulate across the provinces and seem to have inspired more protests.[2] Estimates of the total numbers who travelled at different times to Phnom Penh vary from 40,000 to 100,000.[3] In most parts of the country, people also began to withhold their taxes and their labour,[4] and there were violent confrontations in some areas between angry farmers and the local Cambodian officials who collected the taxes. One Cambodian official and an unknown number of protesters were killed.[5]

---

[1] Tully, *Cambodia under the Tricolour*, pp. 184–206; Milton E. Osborne, "Peasant Politics in Cambodia: the 1916 Affair", *Modern Asian Studies* 12, 2 (1978): 117–243; Forest, *Le Cambodge et la colonisation française*, pp. 412–31.

[2] Tully, *Cambodia under the Tricolour*, pp. 184–92; Tully, *France on the Mekong*, pp. 178–9.

[3] Chandler, *History of Cambodia*, p. 188; Forest, *Le Cambodge et la colonisation française*, p. 415.

[4] Tully, *France on the Mekong*, pp. 178–83.

[5] Ibid., p. 183; Forest, *Le Cambodge et la colonisation française*, pp. 418–20.

102   *Colonial Law Making*

In the main, the protesters did not attack French officials, but they potentially threatened some outposts of the administration.

Résident Supérieur Baudoin attempted to downplay what he came to refer to as the "effervescence",[6] but the 1916 Affair deeply unsettled the French. Localised protests against taxes had been common in previous years, but the colonial administration were shocked when the petitioners started travelling to Phnom Penh.[7] In particular, they were at a loss as to how an initiative that started in just one district spread across the country. Their suspicions fell on a range of "outsiders", including dissident factions within the royal family, some of whom lived in Bangkok, and itinerant Buddhist monks, but the protectorate authorities failed to identify convincingly any single organising force.[8]

As had been the case with the 1885–86 rebellion, the French needed the king's help to restore order, demonstrating both the power that rural Cambodians invested in their king and his role in legitimising the protectorate. King Sisowath toured the country, and on 4 February promised an amnesty to those who had not committed any criminal offence, provided they ceased their protests and civil disobedience immediately.[9]

The inability of the French to understand how the unrest spread revealed the fragility of their control, which relied on, but was also threatened by, the ongoing ties between the king, the Cambodian elites and the population. In the midst of the crisis, before he had regained his composure, *Résident Supérieur* Baudoin suggested that even certain members of the Cambodian Council of Ministers might have been involved. He instructed each minister to use his patronage networks to find the ringleaders.[10] He threatened that the leaders of the rebellion would be treated with degrees of severity in proportion to their social ranking.[11]

The 1916 Affair had a significant impact on justice administration, as it facilitated further reforms in the Cambodian jurisdiction,

---

[6] Résident Supérieur to all Résidents, chiefs of regions in Cambodia, Circular No. 22, 4 Mar. 1916, NAC RSC 16031.

[7] Tully, *France on the Mekong*, pp. 169–72.

[8] Ibid., pp. 180–2.

[9] Ministerial Circular from Minsters of Interior and of Justice to all governors, 4 Mar. 1916 (trans.), NAC RSC 16031.

[10] Minutes of the 239th session of the Council of Ministers (Item two), 1 Jan. 1916, NAC RSC 24419.

[11] Ibid.

and consolidated the provincial, administrator-run courts in the French jurisdiction. Baudoin used the unrest to tighten his grip over both jurisdictions, strengthening his own control and that of the colonial administration. After 1916, the protectorate administration's contradictory policies on the separation of powers in each jurisdiction ensured that the Cambodian codes and courts, not those of the French, would eventually form the basis of the kingdom's justice system.

By way of background, the first part of this chapter considers the unsettling effect of the French presence on rural society, including the immediate impact on Cambodians of France's participation in the First World War. The second section examines the interdependence of the French *résidents* and the Cambodian governors in rural areas. The governors' standing had declined under French rule, but they still held considerable sway as gatekeepers between the *résidents* and the people, not least as heads of their local courts. The third part focuses on a trial in the Cambodian jurisdiction in the aftermath of the 1916 Affair, examining the impossible tasks facing the Cambodian judges in the criminal Court of First Instance and the influence of French interests on the indigenous Court of Appeal in Phnom Penh. The fourth part illustrates the contrasting impacts of the 1916 Affair on the rural Cambodian and French courts.

Unsettled Relations in the Countryside

For many rural Cambodians, taxes and *corvée* characterised French rule.[12] By 1911, men who could not buy their way out of *corvée* were obliged to supply up to 90 days of labour on colonial public works each year.[13] Most Cambodians were subject to a head tax as well as taxes on their crops and produce, on basic goods, imports and exports, and some government services.[14] The French regulated the fishing industry and the opium trade through a system of licences, and even fishing boat engines attracted a levy.[15] In addition to *corvée*, from the late 1880s each village had to supply its quota of "volunteers" to serve in the indigenous

---

[12] Forest, *Le Cambodge et la colonisation française*, p. 191.

[13] Tully, *France on the Mekong*, p. 171.

[14] Ibid., p. 170; Forest, *Le Cambodge et la colonisation française*, pp. 198–212.

[15] Osborne, *The French Presence*, p. 207.

104   *Colonial Law Making*

militia for two years, under the command of a French gendarme or military officer.[16]

Historians differ on the degree to which these imposts were harsher than the gifts and services required of non-elite Cambodians by their patrons in pre-colonial times. What cannot be disputed is that the population deeply resented the taxes and associated them with the French administration.[17] As early as 1874, the French explorer and administrator Étienne Aymonier had heard that Cambodians assumed increased taxes were the price King Norodom had had to pay for French protection.[18] Cambodian officials were generally responsible for collecting and enforcing these imposts, and administering the civil rolls and land titles of which so many locals remained highly suspicious.

Colonial demands on non-elite Cambodians intensified during the First World War. Desperate to increase their revenue to contribute to the war effort in Europe, the French raised existing taxes and invented new ones. Cambodian men faced pressure to "volunteer" for the war effort. Only about 2,000 Cambodians went overseas, either to fight or to work in French factories, suggesting that most felt no urge to uproot their lives in order to support their protectors.[19]

At the same time, French rule had begun to loosen relations between the people and the provincial governors, and disturbed local hierarchies. Aiming to further undermine the power of the Cambodian governors, the colonial power had introduced a new administrative division in 1908, the commune, to be headed by a locally elected council.[20] Cambodian officials had been placed on the French payroll and became part of the nascent state bureaucracy.[21] For example, Huy Kanthoul, a future prime minister of independent Cambodia, remembered a

---

[16] Broadhurst, Bouhours and Bouhours, *Violence and the Civilising Process in Cambodia*, pp. 12–95.

[17] Tully, *France on the Mekong*, pp. 169, 172.

[18] Étienne Aymonier, Confidential Report on Cambodia, 1874, CAOM FM AF C13, dossier A30 (22).

[19] Tully, *Cambodia under the Tricolour*, p. 170.

[20] Osborne, "Peasant Politics in Cambodia", p. 240; see Forest's discussion of the early years of the commune, in Forest, *Le Cambodge et la colonisation française*, pp. 117–26; Margaret Slocomb, *An Economic History of Cambodia in the Twentieth Century* (Singapore: NUS Press, 2010), p. 41.

[21] Forest, *Le Cambodge et la colonisation française*, p. 102.

childhood journey taken in 1915 when his father transferred from Baray province in the region of Kompong Thom to take up a post in Kompong Speu in the "mysterious west".[22]

Résidents and Governors

There were nine French *résidents* in Cambodia in 1915 and a further 10 lesser delegations and French administrative posts scattered across the country.[23] Each *résident* headed a region, or *circonscription*, which incorporated several Cambodian *khet*, or provinces. The *résident* of Kompong Thom was in charge of five *khet*, while *Résident* Bellan in Prey Veng (including Svay Rieng in the far south-east) oversaw eight. Officially, the *résidents* had become the central point of authority through whom all government business was required to flow,[24] and in this sense had usurped much of the Cambodian governors' previous power. Whereas during Norodom's time the governors considered themselves the social equal of any French official and often directly approached the *résident supérieur*, by 1912, when the new Cambodian codes came into effect, they had been incorporated into a centralised hierarchy with set tasks about which they reported to the *résident*.[25] Yet although he formally controlled them, the *résident* would have been helpless without the governors and other local officials; if the governor did not perform, the province, including its court, became dysfunctional.[26]

The French presence had lessened the governors' autonomy, but these important Cambodian officials adapted to their new situation. The protectorate administration created a "hybrid bureaucracy" in which

---

[22] Kanthoul, *Mémoires*, pp. 19–25; see various minutes of the meetings of the Council of Ministers that discussed appointments and transfers, for example, Item 3, 29 Apr. 2015, NAC RSC 24386.

[23] *Annuaire Général de l'Indochine* (1915) (Hanoi: Imprimerie d'Extrême-Orient), p. 275. Residential regions in 1915 were: Battambang, Kampot, Kompong Speu, Kompong Cham, Kompong Chhnang, Kompong Thom, Prey Veng, Stung Treng and Takeo. Delegations and posts included: Siem Reap, Koh Kong, Kompong Trach, Kratie, Mera, Pursat, Banam, Svay Rieng, Maloupoumok (Veun Say) and Mélouprey (Chéom Ksan).

[24] Forest, *Le Cambodge et la colonisation française*, pp. 89–106, see p. 93.

[25] Ibid., pp. 103–5.

[26] See, for example, Pursat, Quarterly Political Report to 1 Jul. 1919, NAC RSC 5118; see also Report from Prey Veng, Feb. 1911, CAOM RSC 237.

106   *Colonial Law Making*

centralised colonial state structures were administered by Cambodian mandarins who remained immersed in personalised relations of power.[27] They operated across two distinct systems of authority.

One report on banditry in Prey Veng, located to the east and southeast of Phnom Penh, illustrates the governors' position as gatekeepers between the protectorate and its protégés. In 1918, *Oknha* Var, governor of Baphnom province, reported to the *résident* of Prey Veng *circonscription*, Charles Roux-Serret, that two local gangs had raided and robbed several houses.[28] *Résident Supérieur* Baudoin asked for more information from *Résident* Roux-Serret, who passed the request on to Governor Var.[29] Several weeks later, Var wrote to say that he and his officials had searched for the miscreants but to no avail. He followed with a general reflection on the nature of banditry and why it had not been eradicated:

> In general, the *malfaiteurs* who have committed, from time to time, theft or pillage in villages, hide in the unimportant remote hamlets. They want to eat, like everyone, but they also have bad intentions . . . When they want to go and rob and pillage in some village or province, they have gathered in one place. There are even some who, before leaving, have notified the commune authorities of their absence. But we cannot find the proof to be able to take them. In my opinion, I estimate that in order to repress acts of theft and pillage, it would be necessary for all the provincial functionaries and communal authorities to execute the [royal ordinances against banditry].[30]

Governor Var lectured *Résident* Roux-Serret on the basic facts of rural life, which lay beyond French control, and the *résident* had to take it on trust that Var had conducted a proper search for the miscreants. Governor Var offered no solutions to the problem that Cambodian officials in his province were not implementing the colonial regulations

---

[27] Forest, *Le Cambodge et la colonisation française*, p. 110.

[28] Governor of Baphnom to Roux-Serret, 12 Mar. 1918 (trans.), NAC RSC 15952.

[29] Baudoin to Roux-Serret, 14 Mar. 1918, NAC RSC 15952.

[30] Governor of Baphnom to Roux-Serret, 2 Apr. 1918 (trans.), NAC RSC 15952. The Royal Ordinances he refers to would include the 1911 Penal Code, which does not specifically refer to banditry but covers it, for example, in art. 241 (armed robbery), art. 75 (leading, directing or supplying armed gangs, which was considered a crime against state security) and arts. 139–44 (rebellion or armed defiance of government authorities). NAC Doc, Box 423.

against banditry. In another instance, Cambodian officials directly challenged the authority of the then *résident* of Prey Veng by going over his head. In this case, the governor of Lovea Em province, Khoun Thonn, and the chief of the local Chinese community, Kouy Lim, accused each other of various abuses of power.[31] Khoun Thonn had received no satisfaction from the *résident*, so he encouraged two members of the Chinese community to complain about Kouy Lim directly to the French court of Phnom Penh.[32] Khoun Thonn no doubt knew that this would cast doubt on the *résident*'s ability to govern his *circonscription*.

In addition to ensuring revenue flows and maintaining the peace, local issues of law and justice constituted an important part of the duties of each *résident*. As justices of the peace with expanded competence, they presided in the local French courts, dealing mainly with the sub-jurisdiction covering ethnic Vietnamese and Chinese. With this workload, they often found it difficult also to monitor all the Cambodian provincial courts within their *circonscription*.[33]

On the other hand, the Cambodian provincial governors must have found it difficult to comply with the new laws enacted in the 1911 codes. The governors remained in control of their provincial courts, but the Code of Criminal Investigation and Judicial Organisation did impose important procedural demands on them. The code required that governors be aided by two other officials, usually called *sophea*, while another official, the *yokebat* or *yoskbat*, acted as the court clerk (*greffier*).[34] The Cambodian minister of justice, advised by the French delegate who now worked alongside him, nominated one *sophea* to act as the *juge d'instruction*, or investigating judge.[35] He and the *yokebat* (court clerk) were expected to prioritise court matters over their other work.[36] In this way, in theory, some specialisation of roles had been imposed.

---

[31] In NAC RSC 12503, see Prosecutor Phnom Penh Court to Résident Supérieur, 25 Mar., 1916; Desenlis to Résident of Prey Veng, 10 Nov. 1916; Résident Prey Veng to Baudoin, 12 Nov. 1916.

[32] Ibid.

[33] See, for example, handwritten note, undated (1917), NAC RSC 9361.

[34] Code of Criminal Investigation and Judicial Organisation, (1911), art. 19.

[35] Ibid., arts. 20–5.

[36] See Circular to all Résidents from Résident Supérieur Outrey, 14 Nov. 1912, NAC RSC 12713.

As well as providing the governors with a formal judicial position description, these procedural innovations challenged existing hierarchies among the provincial elites. For example, the new procedures altered the balance of power between the governor and the designated *sophea*, who now combined the roles of co-adjudicating judge, investigating judge and prosecutor.[37] The governor was the court president, but under the new code he also performed the task of judicial police and, in theory, could be directed to undertake a criminal investigation by the *sophea*, acting as the investigating judge.[38] It is difficult to imagine that the governors would have been motivated to comply with these new procedures unless closely monitored by the relevant *résident*.

The 1911 codes therefore demanded that the governors adopt new ways of thinking about law and about managing their provinces. The French expected each governor to become "a man of dossiers" reporting to the *résident*.[39] For example, the governor had to ensure that his court kept multiple registers: of complaints; of hearings; of judgements; of custodial sentences; of committals; and of defendants who had fled.[40] Some governors found this difficult to do, or simply chose not to comply. *Résident* Bellan in Prey Veng, for example, discovered in 1913 that one governor had been registering judgements only when one of the parties wanted to appeal.[41]

Many Cambodian provincial officials lacked the capacity or the training to implement the new codes or to fulfil other tasks demanded of them, as one example illustrates. In 1917, the Cambodian minister of justice reprimanded the governor of Baray province because his court had dealt incorrectly with a defendant who had re-offended while serving

---

[37] Code of Criminal Investigation and Judicial Organisation (Kingdom of Cambodia, 1911), art. 20.

[38] Ibid., arts. 18, 23.

[39] Forest, *Le Cambodge et la colonisation française*, p. 104. Each provincial court was required to keep a register of complaints, a court roll, a record of defendants placed under restraint, a register of committals and a list of defendants who had fled; each commune chief also had to record those he had condemned to short periods of detention; see report on the province of Kien Svay in Report on the Functioning of Provincial Judicial Services in Kandal, 24 Dec. 1912, NAC RC 12713.

[40] See report on the province of Kien Svay, in Report on the Functioning of Provincial Judicial Services in Kandal, 24 Dec. 1912, NAC RC 12713.

[41] Bellan to the Résident Supérieur, 17 Jan. 1913, NAC RSC 12713.

a suspended sentence.[42] The provincial court had merely enforced the suspended sentence rather than add a punishment for the new infraction. Further, the judges had failed to cite the relevant section of the 1911 Criminal Code and had erred in awarding costs.[43] The Cambodian governors also sometimes had to conduct preliminary investigations or to enforce civil judgements in the French jurisdiction, following procedures that were not always clearly explained in Khmer.[44] They had many other non-judicial duties, and some complained that they did not have time to oversee their courts.[45]

As early as 1912, the Cambodian minister of justice and some *résidents* warned Baudoin that governors were overwhelmed by the range of tasks now expected of them.[46] If the Cambodian governors had difficulty complying with the new codes, the commune chiefs found it almost impossible. Although many commune chiefs were barely literate, they had been made responsible for recording, judging and punishing petty offences that incurred penalties of up to five days in prison or a maximum fine of six piastres.[47] One unfortunate man reportedly reimbursed all the fines he had levied on his constituents rather than provide a written report to his governor.[48]

The People, the Courts and the Right of Appeal

The 1911 codes were a milestone in the process of transforming, or, as many French officials would have said, rationalising the Cambodian jurisdiction. The codes purported to capture the governors' judicial roles within

---

[42] Minister of Justice to Governor of Baray Province (trans.), 26 June 1917, NAC RSC 9361.

[43] Ibid.

[44] See, for example: Résident of Kandal to Baudoin, 21 Sept. 1917, NAC RSC 14678; List of Cambodian Assessors for the French Court, 1919, NAC RSC 12503; Bellan, to Baudoin, 25 Sept. 1915, NAC RSC 9914; Council of Ministers Circular, 3 Oct. 1913, instructing governors as to when and how they could make initial arrests in cases that fell within the French jurisdiction (trans.), NAC RSC 20912.

[45] *Oknha* Pusnoulok Chum to Ministers of the Interior and Justice, 7 Sept. 1912 (trans.), NAC RSC 12713.

[46] Ministers of the Interior and of Justice to Résident Supérieur, 9 Sept. 1912 (trans.), NAC RSC 12713; Reports from Kandal and Kompong Chhnang in 1913, NAC RSC 12713.

[47] Code of Criminal Investigation and Judicial Organisation (Kingdom of Cambodia, 1911), arts. 80–2.

[48] Forest, *Le Cambodge et la colonisation française*, p. 125.

110   *Colonial Law Making*

the confines of a rudimentary state bureaucracy, though with only partial success. However, the codes, and the new courts, also began to reclassify matters of vital interest to lives of ordinary people. In particular, they began to prioritise civil disputes according to their monetary value.

In Cambodia and across Indochina, colonial judges and administrators alike regarded the locals as too litigious and too prone to lodging hopeless appeals over matters that the French considered trivial. In 1915, the Civil Chamber of the Court of Appeal for the Cambodian jurisdiction in Phnom Penh registered 396 new cases in which litigants came to the court to settle disputes over such issues as: their rice fields, gardens, residential plots, rights of way and water (usually ponds); debts, livestock and commercial transactions and inheritances; use of abusive or insulting language (*propos injurieux* and *insultes*); matrimonial issues (usually divorce, or complaints that a woman had deserted the conjugal home); and illicit sexual relations, including adultery.[49]

At the beginning of 1915, the Court of Appeal had registered a backlog of 407 civil cases, including 14 matters dating back to 1907.[50] That same year, the *résident supérieur* and the Cambodian Council of Ministers agreed to impose minimum monetary values of 400 piastres for land disputes and 200 piastres for other matters to be brought before the court. These were large sums given the estimated "average individual fortune" of Cambodians was 200 piastres. They further agreed there should be a charge of 20 piastres for each appeal and a fine of 30 piastres if the appeal was abusive, the test for this being if the appeal lost. Losing parties in the Court of Cassation would forfeit 100 piastres.[51]

These arbitrary values, imposed on disputes that were often very important to each party, reflect the colonial attempt to have Cambodian law transition from something that could potentially deal with all aspects of daily life, to a system in which the public and the private were

---

[49] Figures compiled from monthly reports for 1915, NAC RSC 14070.

[50] By the beginning of 1915, the Court of Appeal had a backlog of 481 penal and 407 civil cases. There were also 441 outstanding matters before the Court of Cassation. The oldest matters before the Penal Chamber of the Court of Appeal dated from 1912 (38 cases). The Civil Chamber listed 14 cases that had been on its books since 1907 and 105 from 1914. Figures compiled from monthly reports for 1915, NAC RSC 14070.

[51] Item 2, Council of Ministers 206th meeting, 29 Apr. 1915, NAC RSC 24386. Regarding the wealth of Cambodians, Baudoin was quoting from a report of the commission charged with drafting a new Civil Code for Cambodia.

separate, and contract rather than status was the subject of law.[52] There is no record of what monetary value the ministers or Baudoin would have placed on the consequences of a woman leaving her husband, or committing adultery, or the loss of standing that someone might suffer if they were insulted in public. They no doubt considered such matters should not reach the higher courts at all. Yet it is easy to imagine that in small rural communities such issues could affect the livelihood and the status of individuals in important ways. In effect, the higher courts were no longer meant to deal with certain matters that were important in the daily lives of rural people; they were being restructured to facilitate and to protect commercial relations and to support a monetised market economy.

Even after the next round of colonial reforms further transformed their courts, Cambodians continued to resist colonial ideas of what matters were and were not worth appealing. To Cambodians versed in notions of personalised power and patronage, it must have made sense to take matters as high up the court hierarchy as they could. It was a matter of mutual incomprehension, a clash between economic efficiency and speedy resolution of cases on the one hand, and the right to be heard, or to try one's luck regarding disputes of personal importance, on the other.

A Trial in the Cambodian Jurisdiction: The Aftermath of 1916

There were evident dualities of meaning in the records of one criminal trial following the 1916 protests. After most of the unrest had died down, *Résident Supérieur* Baudoin blamed corrupt local Cambodian officials rather than unpopular colonial taxes for the people's anger.[53] Once the instigators of the 1916 Affair had been selected and tried, many provincial officials were also charged or dismissed.[54] In the meantime, the Cambodian governors faced an impossible task as they were

---

[52] Henry Sumner Maine, *Ancient Law: Its Connection with the Early History of Society and Its Relation to Modern Ideas* (London: John Murray, 1920, 4th ed.), p. 174.

[53] Tully, *France on the Mekong*, pp. 184–6; Forest, *Le Cambodge et la colonisation française*, pp. 422–7. Tully notes that low-level unrest continued for several years, see Tully, *Cambodia under the Tricolour*, p. 198, note 188.

[54] Tully, *France on the Mekong*, pp. 184–5; Forest, *Le Cambodge et la colonisation française*, p. 423.

112   *Colonial Law Making*

expected to apply the 1911 codes to try offenders who had, in many cases, targeted them personally.

In March 1916, the Cambodian minister of justice instructed provincial governors to arraign people in their provinces who had continued to protest after King Sisowath's 4 February amnesty, or who they suspected had committed other felonies or misdemeanours as part of the unrest. The minister urged governors to conduct investigations and trials rapidly, "with all the rigour of the law".[55] They were to impose stern but impartial punishments, taking account of extenuating circumstances, a concept prescribed by Article 54 of the 1911 Criminal Code. *Résident Supérieur* Baudoin sent the minister's circular to all *résidents*, instructing them to monitor its execution.[56]

Following the minister of justice's instructions, criminal courts around the country tried 560 people, found 375 guilty, imposed 13 death sentences and acquitted 183 defendants.[57] As prescribed by the 1911 codes, five judges presided in felony trials in the Cambodian jurisdiction. The bench comprised the governor and two *sophea* from the province where the alleged crime took place and two other Cambodian officials, one of whom was nominated by the *résident*.[58] French commentators criticised many of these 1916 trials for imposing excessively harsh sentences and failing to follow prescribed procedure.[59] The Cambodian minister of justice subsequently appealed most of the verdicts in the Court of Appeal, which commuted all 13 death sentences but also overturned 92 of the 183 acquittals.[60]

It is hardly surprising that the provincial courts failed in these trials to comply with the procedures laid down by the 1911 codes, which many of the governors had found difficult to follow at the best of times. The governors were under pressure to restore calm and to punish the

---

[55] Circular No. 22, 2 Mar. 1916, NAC RSC 16031.

[56] Ibid.

[57] Forest, *Le Cambodge et la colonisation française*, p. 420, referencing Rapport du Résident Supérieur, 2nd Trimestre, 1916, AOM, Aix 2FF. The report is also available in CAOM RSC 430.

[58] Code of Criminal Investigation and Judicial Organisation (Kingdom of Cambodia, 1911), arts. 143–57.

[59] Tully, *Cambodia under the Tricolour*, p. 194.

[60] Forest, *Le Cambodge et la colonisation française*, p. 420; Forest claims 13 death sentences were commuted by the Court of Appeal; see Code of Criminal Investigation and Judicial Organisation (Kingdom of Cambodia, 1911), art. 172, which granted the minister the right to appeal cases.

ringleaders and were at the same time embroiled in the cases as victims and targets of the discontent, as presidents of the courts and as officials whose authority had been directly challenged.

One of the regions most affected by the unrest was the *circonscription* of the *résident* of Prey Veng. Its provincial courts prosecuted 143 people, more than any other region.[61] Unrest continued in Prey Veng well after King Sisowath called for calm on 4 February. On 12 February, in Peareang province in Prey Veng, a crowd of around 2,000 demonstrators attacked the governor's headquarters in an attempt to release four prisoners. From within the governor's premises, members of the indigenous guard fired on the protesters, killing eight people. A French-language record of the subsequent trial of 16 men accused of taking part in and organising the attack has survived in the Cambodian archives.[62]

On 13 March, just six weeks after the king's proclamation, and a month after the attack and shootings at the Peareang *sala khet*, the provincial criminal court of the Cambodian jurisdiction sentenced 15 of the men.[63] They had been accused of having formed a band led by Khieu, the self-styled king of the group, and Toung, who allegedly called himself the minister of the navy.[64] The provincial court's judgement portrayed the defendants, led by Khieu and Toung, as having incited rebellion after Sisowath's 4 February amnesty. The judgement referred to a series of incidents, rather than presenting one coherent narrative, and cited instances of anti-French sentiment. For example, the court found that one of Khieu's co-accused claimed to have cast a spell over an axe that would allow him to "defend himself and to make war against 100 European militia".[65] Others were accused of having raised money in order to bribe the French to deliver the governor of Peareang into their hands. The same governor presided over the trial.

---

[61] Forest, *Le Cambodge et la colonisation française*, pp. 417–20.

[62] NAC RSC 16032.

[63] Balat of Peareang, office of judicial police, vs. Chap, Kep, Ma, Kan, Nhem, Preap, Chan, Pau, Toung, Ros, Oum, Ouk, Ngin, Min, Khieu, Yon. Kingdom of Cambodia, Criminal Court of the province of Peareang, Judgment No. 13, 13 Mar. 1916 (trans.) (hereafter Balat of Peareang Vs 16), NAC RSC 16032.

[64] Ibid. The title of minister of navy possibly referred to river transport rather than seagoing warfare, as the accused were allegedly organising boats to take protesters from Peareang to Phnom Penh.

[65] Ibid.

114   *Colonial Law Making*

Citing articles 69–77 of the Criminal Code, which dealt with sedition, but without specifying exactly which articles had been contravened by whom, the judges sentenced Khieu and Toung to hard labour for life. Two others, Pau and Yon, were each sentenced to 15 years' hard labour for having encouraged other inhabitants to take part. The other 11 were sentenced to 10 years for a range of activities, including inciting inhabitants, supplying boats, circulating anonymous letters, robbing village chiefs and having magic tattoos they believed would protect them from physical harm. One man, Chan, was acquitted because he was found to have participated under duress.[66]

The minister of justice appealed the judgement.[67] Less than two months after the original trial, the Cambodian Court of Appeal in Phnom Penh found the Peareang Criminal Court judges had failed on largely procedural grounds. The Criminal Court had not specified which articles of the Penal Code had been breached by each defendant and had imposed inconsistent sentences.[68] Nevertheless, the Court of Appeal confirmed that all 15 men were guilty of serious crimes. It convicted Khieu and Toung of leading and organising an armed gang with seditious intentions, crimes that attracted the death penalty, but commuted these sentences to hard labour for life. The 13 other guilty defendants were found to have led and participated in an armed gang and were each sentenced to 15 years' hard labour. In other words, 11 of the defendants had their sentences increased on appeal.

The judgements of the first instance provincial Criminal Court and that of the Court of Appeal reflected differing interests—of the provincial governors on one hand and the protectorate authorities on the other. For the governor of Peareang and the other presiding officials, the first instance trial was primarily a stage on which they sought to shore up their authority over their constituents and to punish their opponents. They made only a cursory attempt to fit their judgement within the framework of the 1911 codes. In its judgement, the Court of Appeal lent an air of formal legality to the reprisals against the protesters that would suit the colonial record. Unlike the provincial

---

[66] Ibid.

[67] The list of appellants includes the name "Ban", which did not appear in the list of defendants in the Court of First Instance. However, this appears to have been a misspelling of "Chan", who was acquitted in the first judgment and again on appeal; see, Kingdom of Cambodia, Court of Appeal, Judgment no. 179 (2nd chamber), 9 May 1916, NAC RSC 16032.

[68] Ibid.

court, the Court of Appeal ignored the human drama of the incident. Yet it, too, sought to cast a certain light on events, as the judges of the Court of Appeal ignored or glossed over questions regarding the actions of the French-controlled militia and of the local administrators who had shot at the protesters.

In some ways, the protectorate administration benefited from the first instance criminal trials of 1916, which enabled the French to remain at arm's length from the harsh retributions that colonial powers invariably applied when local people threatened their authority. The *résident* of Prey Veng, Charles Bellan, under whose watch the Peareang provincial trial took place, certainly considered their rough justice as all that was needed or desirable when he reported to Baudoin.[69] On the other hand, the fact that the governors conspicuously failed to apply the 1911 codes properly further justified French plans to impose new structures of rural administration and indigenous justice.

The 1916 trials also provided another opportunity for King Sisowath to remind the French of his ongoing links with his subjects. Perhaps emboldened after the French called on him to help pacify the population and allowed him to make a rare tour of his realm, the king also sought to influence the trials. First, he wrote to Baudoin to request leniency for a number of his "clients", including some of the 16 defendants from Peareang.[70] In a second letter, the king advised Baudoin to put an end to the trials, arguing that those who had not been found guilty of violence should be acquitted. Appearing to refer directly to the 12 February shootings in Peareang, Sisowath stated that the deaths and injuries were punishment enough. Sisowath tried to reassure Baudoin that the demonstrations had not targeted French rule, but added a gentle barb, reminding the *résident supérieur* that the people deeply resented *corvée* and other imposts.[71]

Available written records suggest King Sisowath rarely openly intervened with the protectorate, but when he did, his abiding influence was clear. In 1916, he, or his advisers, had a better understanding of the mood of the populace than did the French. Whether or not he was influenced by the king's counsel, Baudoin subsequently instructed Charles Bellan, *résident* of the Prey Veng *circonscription*, to put an end

---

[69] Bellan to Baudoin, 23 June 1916, NAC RSC 16032.
[70] Letter No. 23, Sisowath to Résident Supérieur (trans.), 16 May 1916; Letter No. 26, Sisowath to Résident Supérieur (trans.), 10 June 1916, NAC RSC 16032.
[71] Sisowath to Résident Supérieur (trans.), 10 June 1916, NAC RSC 16032.

116 *Colonial Law Making*

to sedition trials.[72] In the following years, Baudoin and the French authorities used the 1916 Affair to justify their decision to push ahead with reforms to the Cambodian and French jurisdiction.

After the 1916 Affair: Cambodian and French Jurisdictions

For the French administration, the 1916 Affair, the Peareang trial and perhaps others like it, provided fresh evidence to justify their long-held plans for further reforms in the Cambodian jurisdiction, particularly the Cambodian provincial courts. But while the 1916 Affair may have added impetus to plans to separate judicial and administrative roles in the provincial courts, it had the opposite effect in the French jurisdiction, where *Résident Supérieur* Baudoin used the unrest to good effect in his struggle with Prosecutor General Gabriel Michel over the courts of the *résidents*.

When calm had generally been restored, the protectorate authorities removed many of the troublesome provincial Cambodian officials and put some on trial for various offences under the 1911 Criminal Code.[73] The following year, the French opened a new School of Administration to provide more rigorous instruction for Cambodian judges and administrators, presaging Governor General Sarraut's 1919 decree that judicial and administrative functions should be separated in all indigenous jurisdictions across Indochina.[74] The same year, a Royal Ordinance declared that Cambodian officials should be divided into administrative (*krom rathabal*) and judicial (*krom tralakar*) branches.[75] The Cambodian governors would no longer preside over local justice, further weakening the role of these once powerful men.

The final blow for the governors came in 1922, when, as part of an Indochina-wide administrative reform, each of the old provinces, or *khet*, was downgraded or abolished. In their place came 14 new provinces, also called *khet*, which coincided with the *circonscriptions* of the French *résidents*. Fourteen Courts of First Instance (*sala dambaung*), each located

---

[72] Baudoin to the Résident of Prey Veng, 26 June 1916, NAC RSC 16032.

[73] Tully, *Cambodia under the Tricolour*, p. 198.

[74] Sorn Samnang, "L'Evolution de la société cambodgienne entre les deux guerres mondiales (1919–1939)" [The Evolution of Cambodian Society between the Two World Wars (1919–1939)] (PhD dissertation, University Paris VII, 1995), p. 72.

[75] Royal Ordinance of 2 May 1919, cited in Sorn Samnang, "L'Évolution de la société cambodgienne", pp. 66–7.

Rural Jurisdictions and the 1916 Affair

alongside the office of a *résident* and staffed by full-time Cambodian judges, replaced the former provincial courts.[76] The 1922 reforms, including the 14 new Courts of First Instance and the separation of judicial and administrative roles, came into effect in 1923. The Cambodian court hierarchy they established would remain largely unchanged until after 1940.

A 1924 text for students of the new School of Administration, written by one of Baudoin's adjutants, Achille Silvestre, frankly explained the need for these latest reforms of the Cambodian jurisdiction. Silvestre wrote that the former governors had lacked time and competence to run the provincial courts in compliance with the 1911 codes. It had been necessary, he argued, to create courts that could be more easily supervised.[77] These changes indeed held clear advantages for French control: every *résident* then had to supervise only one Cambodian court, conveniently located close to his own office.[78] It was no doubt easier for the French to oversee legal procedure in the new courts and therefore to ensure more consistent outcomes for litigants.

But the reforms also made justice more remote from the people, physically and culturally. Most Cambodians would now have to travel much further, often under difficult conditions, to access their local court. Suspects held in pre-trial detention were further away from their families. Like the new provincial governors, these courts were less familiar to Cambodians, more remote and more directly connected with French power.[79]

The 1916 Affair gave impetus to French reforms in the indigenous jurisdiction, which they justified as being in support of the legal principle that judicial and administrative powers should be separate. Yet in

---

[76] Royal Ordinance No. 118, Judicial Organisation of Cambodia, 14 Sept. 1922, rendered into effect by the Governor General, 3 Oct. 1922, NAC Doc, Box 425. The locations of these courts were specified in Royal Ordinance No. 142, Setting the Jurisdictions of the courts of Cambodia, 23 Dec. 1922, art. 8, NAC Doc, Box 425.

[77] Achille Silvestre, *Le Cambodge Administratif: cours professé a l'École d'Administration Cambodgienne* [The Administration of Cambodia: Course for the Cambodian School of Administration] (Phnom Penh: Imprimerie Nouvelle, Albert l'Ortail, 1924), pp. 160–1.

[78] Report of inspection of political and administrative affairs, Prey Veng, 1915. NAC RSC 21180.

[79] Rapport d'ensemble de la Résidence de Kandal, April 1922–24 [Summary Report from the Residence of Kandal, April 1922–24], quoted in Sorn Samnang, "L'Evolution de la société cambodgienne", p. 40.

118   *Colonial Law Making*

the French jurisdiction, Baudoin used the 1916 "effervescence" to the opposite effect in his campaign to keep the French courts in rural Cambodia under the control of the *résidents* rather than French judges. Just prior to Baudoin's posting to Cambodia in 1914, the prosecutor general of Indochina, Gabriel Michel, had manoeuvred to extend the catchment of the French court of Phnom Penh, thus abolishing four *tribunaux résidentiels*.[80] *Résident Supérieur* Baudoin used the unrest in 1916 as further evidence in his campaign to reverse this change and by April of that year, two of these courts had been reinstated.[81]

Single-judge French courts run by justices of the peace with expanded authority were a colonial innovation.[82] What had started as an interim measure became entrenched in many colonies due to chronic shortages of qualified judicial personnel and a perennial lack of funds.[83] These courts gave inordinate power to the magistrate, as he combined the roles of investigator, prosecutor and judge in all but the most serious criminal cases.[84] Such courts were particularly vulnerable to criticism when, as was the case in Cambodia, they were headed by administrators rather than by career judges.[85]

Several senior judges in Saigon and Hanoi had lobbied to replace the administrator-run courts in Cambodia with "regular" courts presided over by career judges, in compliance with the principle of the separation of powers.[86] Prosecutor General of Indochina Gabriel Michel led the judiciary's attack on these courts. He questioned the legitimacy of the *tribunaux résidentiels* and the legal competence of the *résidents*, and was quick to reprimand them for the slightest mistakes.[87]

---

[80] The area involved what had been the regions of Pursat and Kompong Chhnang in central western Cambodian, and Svey Rieng and Prey Veng in the south-east. Low, "Tribunaux Residentiels", p. 83.

[81] Svay Rieng, Quarterly political report (Mar.–May 1916), CAOM RSC 401.

[82] Bernard Durand, "L'impératif de proximité dans l'Empire colonial français: les justices de paix à compétence étendue" [The Imperative of Proximity in the French Colonial Empire: Justices of the Peace with Expanded Competence], *Histoire de la justice* [History of Justice] 17, 1 (2007): 109–26, 212.

[83] Durand, "L'impératif de proximité", p. 216. Regarding the shortages of judicial personnel, see also Blazy, "L'Organisation judiciaire", pp. 742–59.

[84] Durand, "L'impératif de proximité", p. 212.

[85] Ibid.

[86] The magistracy also criticised the *tribunaux résidentiels* in other parts of Indochina; see, for example, Blazy, "L'Organisation judiciaire", p. 526.

[87] See, for example, the prosecutor general's criticism of the Résident of Kompong Chhnang for his handling of the charges against Nguyen van Khanh, 28 Aug. 1905,

The colonial judiciary had a point, in legal principle, and also in terms of consistency with reforms in the Cambodian jurisdiction. The battle between Baudoin and Michel had become personal, and each man tended to ignore the needs of local litigants while also claiming to protect them.[88] For his part, Baudoin targeted the impracticality and inconvenience caused by Michel's interferences in jurisdictional matters. But his concern for the rights of local litigants was also questionable, and he likely abhorred the prospect of having judges who answered to the prosecutor general in Hanoi, rather than to himself, spread across his domain.

Baudoin would also have been conscious that the *résidents* often dealt with highly sensitive cases that could undermine the protectorate administration if not dealt with adroitly. Their courts provided a forum for the *résidents* to mediate relations among ethnic Chinese and Vietnamese and the majority Khmer population. They could rule in cases that threatened France's standing with the local population, such as those involving their Vietnamese employees.[89] They were able to decide lesser criminal cases involving the "troublesome elements" among ethnic Vietnamese who, rightly or wrongly, were often blamed for inciting the Khmer population to lawlessness and banditry.[90] The *résidents* could, it was argued, also protect those, including ethnic Khmer people, who had become victims of indebtedness or had been cheated of their wages.[91]

One civil dispute between two Chinese merchants in the region of Kompong Thom illustrates some of the political and legal complexities the *résidents* faced. In 1920, Chea Kai, who had close commercial ties

---

NAC RSC 16917; see also the complaint from the *résident* of Battambang about the generally unhelpful and legalistic attitude of the prosecutor general, Résident of Battambang to Résident Superior, 22 Sept. 1931, NAC RSC 23005.

[88] Regarding some of the problems caused by Michel's reforms, see Letter from Marie Louis Bramel, Résident of Kompong Chhnang, to Baudoin, 10 Oct. 1915; Letter from Charles Bellan, Résident of Prey Veng to Baudoin, 25 Sept. 1915, NAC RSC 9914. Regarding Baudoin's arguments against the reforms, see Low, "Les Tribunaux Residentiels", pp. 83–6.

[89] See, for example, Court of Kompong Chhnang, Nguyen Long Thi Vs Hai Bao and others, 20 July 1914, NAC RSC 16192.

[90] See, for example: Political Report, Svay Rieng 1st trimester 1918, CAOM RSC 401; State of detainees sent by Kompong Chhnang and Prey Veng since the suppression of the tribunaux résidentiels (undated, circa 1915), NAC RSC 9914.

[91] See, for example: files from Kompong Thom for 1907, NAC RSC 9147, and from May 1920 to June 1922, NAC RSC 9298; from Kompong Cham for 1914, NAC RSC 6192; and from Stung Treng from Jan. 1918 to June 1919, RSC NAC 26530.

120 *Colonial Law Making*

with the protectorate administration in Kompong Thom, sued Ly Eng for debt.[92] Ly Eng, who had also traded with the French, claimed the amount in dispute was his part of the profits from a business partnership between the two men.[93] Chea Kai denied the partnership had ever existed. Ly Eng later counter-sued for loss of earnings and reputation as a result of having been held in debtors' prison for 14 months and for damage to his possessions that Chea Kai had seized. The Kompong Thom *résident* and his staff had to sift through a mass of records to determine if the two men had formed a business partnership. The matter came to court at least five times during 1921 before *Résident* Emile Desenlis finally made a determination in September 1922. By then Chea Kai had died, leaving his estate to two young children.[94] Desenlis found that the two parties owed each other the same amount—a zero sum result.[95] It could hardly have been a coincidence that the case was not resolved until Chea Kai died. During the almost three years that his case against Ly Eng was before the court, at least some of his commercial transactions with the protectorate administration continued. In particular, he supplied food rations for the local prison.[96]

From the point of view of legal principle, the conflicts of interest involved in this case in the French jurisdiction—and that of the 1916 Peareang case in the Cambodian jurisdiction—provided a potent argument for the separation of judicial and administrative functions. But, whereas the 1916 unrest may have provided momentum to divide

---

[92] Sentence Arbitrale du 14 Septembre 1922, entre Héritiers Chea-Kai et Ly-Cam dit Ly-Eng, Tribunal de Kompong-Thom, NAC RSC 13012; for further discussion of this case, see Low, "Les Tribunaux Residentiels", pp. 86–8.

[93] See receipts dated 25 Sept. 1920, 15 Dec. 1919 and 10 July 1920, NAC RSC 13011.

[94] Court of Kompong Thom: Records from the court dated 14 Feb., 12 Sept. and 23 July 1921, NAC RSC 13012; see also record of accounts, date obscured, in the same file.

[95] Sentence Arbitrale du 14 Septembre 1922, entre Héritiers Chea-Kai et Ly-Cam dit Ly-Eng, Tribunal de Kompong-Thom [Arbitration Award of 14 September 1922, between the Heirs of Chea-Kai and Ly-Cam Known as Ly-Eng, Court of Kompong-Thom], NAC RSC 13012.

[96] Record of supplies provided to the prison of Kompong Thom and the register of prisoners (supplier Chea Kai) [Mémoires des fournitures faites à la prison de Kompong Thom et états nominatifs des prisonniers (fournisseur Chea Kai)], NAC RSC 13011; among these receipts, there are some also made out to other providers, including, on at least four occasions, Ly Eng for supply of wood; see Invoice numbers 470, 392, 390 and 379.

functions in the rural courts of the Cambodian jurisdiction, *Résident Supérieur* Baudoin used the same events to argue for restoring the four *résidents'* courts, and returning the geographic reach of the French court of Phnom Penh to what it had been before Michel had intervened in 1914.

Baudoin's feud with Prosecutor General Michel was particularly bitter, and was shaped by the *résident supérieur's* desire for personal control in the protectorate. However, many of the French judges, including Michel, had done little to enhance the reputation of the judicial corps. In 1917, the governor general of Indochina, the respected politician Albert Sarraut, requested the Minister for Colonies to force Michel to retire.[97] Sarraut accused the prosecutor general, whose career he had previously encouraged, of having allowed a clique of self-serving and possibly corrupt judges and clerks (*greffiers*) to dominate the French courts of Indochina.[98] Sarraut also persuaded the French government to dilute the power of the prosecutor general by creating the position of director of judicial administration. This official answered directly to the governor general and was in charge of judicial placements, transfers and promotions across Indochina—tasks that the prosecutor general had previously overseen.[99]

While the colonial judiciary of Indochina considered this move further violated their independence,[100] they had invited such an intervention through the failings of individual judges, and by trying to circumvent the administration's ability to control judicial appointments. The judges of Cochin China in particular had used the fact that they presided over indigenous justice to make knowledge of a local language a prerequisite for many positions.[101] The restrictions on recruitment were later modified to impose a quota whereby three-quarters of vacancies in all but the most junior positions would be reserved for judges

---

[97] Blazy, "L'Organisation judiciaire", p. 732. Michel's name disappears from the list of judicial personnel in Indochina in 1919, see *Annuaire Générale de l'Indochine* (1919) [General Directory of Indochina 1919] (Hanoi: Imprimèrie d'extrème-orient), p. 122.

[98] Ibid., pp. 659–60; Sarraut to Minister of Colonies, 25 Oct. 1917, CAOM GGI 65618.

[99] Blazy, "L'Organisation judiciaire", pp. 735–6.

[100] Ibid.

[101] Minister of Colonies to President of France, 1 Nov. 1911, CAOM GGI 4580; Barnhart, "Violence and the Civilizing Mission", pp. 477–8; Letter from Minister of Colonies to President of France, 1 Nov. 1911, GGI 4580.

122 *Colonial Law Making*

already serving in the colony.[102] In this way, the judges seriously impeded the French minister for foreign affairs' ability to oversee judicial appointments in Indochina. Within the context of this broader conflict between the two arms of the colonial apparatus, Baudoin had all four previously abolished *résident*-run courts reinstated. This was an important victory for Baudoin, and although the issue continued to be raised during the 1920s and 1930s, successive *résidents supérieurs* held firm. Even after some *résidents* asked for relief because their courts had become so busy, the French court of Phnom Penh remained the only French court in Cambodia to be presided over by French judges.[103] The protectorate administration's suspicion of the colonial judiciary also would have favoured Baudoin in his struggle to keep the Cambodian jurisdiction under his control, and out of the hands of French judges.

The Importance of Jurisdictions

Whatever we may think of the comparative advantages of the Cambodian governors' provincial courts (*sala khet*) and the *sala dambaung* that replaced them, or of the French courts of the *résidents* versus courts in which members of the colonial judiciary presided, these tales reveal some of the ways in which colonial jurisdictions mediated social and political relations in rural areas of the protectorate. The French crafted jurisdictions that facilitated their rule. The French jurisdiction, and its sub-jurisdiction that dealt with ethnic Vietnamese and Chinese inhabitants, imposed and enforced divisions that both assisted and justified colonial rule. The courts of the *résidents* allowed these rural colonial administrators to manage the conflicts arising from the very divisions they enforced. Just as the process of separating judicial and administrative functions would lessen the Cambodian governors' prestige and their formal power, Baudoin's successful campaign against the separation of roles in the French rural courts was meant, at least in part, to bolster the standing of the *résidents*. It also enhanced Baudoin's personal hold on the protectorate, as he could make or break the careers of the *résidents*.

Contests in the Cambodian jurisdiction revealed competing notions of the role of law and courts. The French placed monetary limits

---

[102] J. de Galembert, *Les administrations et les services publics Indochinois* [Indochinese Public Administration and Services] (Hanoi: Imprimerie Mac Dinh Tu, 1924), p. 338.
[103] Low, "Les Tribunaux Résidentiels", pp. 85–6.

on the right to appeal civil cases, wishing to stop the higher courts from being flooded with trivial matters. For the French, such measures were rational and practical, but for non-elite Cambodians they redefined which matters were and were not legally significant. Subsequently, law and the courts became more distant, both geographically and in their relevance to the daily existence of ordinary people. However, non-elite Cambodians influenced the impact of the reforms as they adhered to their normal methods of land ownership and their mistrust of colonial rolls and registers.

In the Cambodian jurisdiction, the paradox of French rule also shaped reforms. On one hand, the French needed to subordinate Cambodian officials within their nascent colonial state apparatus. On the other, they relied on those same officials' authority over, and links with, the population. Colonial rule, and in particular the 1911 codes, demanded an impossible balancing act of the Cambodian governors. They tried to navigate a path between subordination to the protectorate administration and maintaining their standing among and domination over the inhabitants of their provinces. In 1916, the judges of Peareang chose to defend their status rather than strictly comply with the 1911 codes. Other provincial criminal courts also imposed overly harsh judgements against accused miscreants. In the process, they provided the French with a further pretext to move ahead with plans to abolish the Cambodian governors' provincial courts.

For the French, the 1911 codes helped to lay the groundwork for the next round of reforms. By the time the protectorate moved to abolish the 52 provinces and their courts, the reformed Phnom Penh courts, operated by judicial officials, had already been in place for several years. Moreover, the 52 provincial governors had had ample opportunity to prove that it was impossible for them to comply with the codes. The 1916 Affair, which the French administration claimed was directed against corrupt Cambodian officials rather than colonial exactions, and the subsequent trials in the local courts, provided the perfect context for further reform.

Historians differ over the impact of the 1922 administrative and political reforms, including legal reforms. Historian Sorn Samnang argues that, although taxes were at times onerous, French rule provided the population some relief from exploitative Cambodian officials.[104] Forest claims, however, that the new administrative arrangements

---

[104] Sorn, "L'Evolution de la societé cambodgienne", pp. 41–3.

124 *Colonial Law Making*

allowed Cambodian mandarins to continue to exercise their "old" power.[105] Historians Pierre Brocheux and Daniel Hémery posit that colonisation may have exacerbated exploitation as it further disrupted the balance that ideally epitomised patron—client relations.[106] The evidence examined in the following pages indicates that it is possible to find support for all of these propositions in the transformed Cambodian jurisdiction.

---

[105] Forest, *Le Cambodge*, p. 110.
[106] Brocheux and Hémery, *Indochina*, p. 285.

6

The Cambodian Courts
after 1922

Jointly presiding, King Sisowath and François Baudoin, the long-term *résident supérieur* in Cambodia, but who was then acting governor general of Indochina, lent an air of authority to the ceremony to open Cambodia's new *Palais de Justice* on 25 April 1925. The opening provided the occasion for a particularly timely display of colonial theatre. Just one week earlier, enraged villagers had murdered the *résident* of Kompong Chhnang province, Félix Bardez, interpreter Sourn and militiaman Leach in the village of Kraang Laev.[1] Bardez's murder shocked the colonial community, and the ceremony for the *Palais de Justice* would have been a perfect opportunity to counter its effect with declarations of Franco-Cambodian collaboration and Cambodian gratitude for French tutelage.

The two events, Bardez's murder and the opening of the new building, neatly characterise the workings of justice in the protectorate. In one sense, the opening of the *palais* was the culmination of over 20 years of reform in the Cambodian jurisdiction and of French claims to be civilising, but not replacing, indigenous justice. The "Bardez affair" highlighted the limits of colonial justice, giving rise not only to a politically managed trial in the French jurisdiction, but also to

---

[1] For an account of the events, see David Chandler, "The Assassination of Résident Bardez (1925): A premonition of Revolt in Colonial Cambodia", originally in *Journal of Siam Society* (Summer 1982), reproduced in David Chandler, *Facing the Cambodian Past: Selected Essays 1971–1994* (Bangkok: Silkworm Books, 1996), pp. 139–58.

126   *Colonial Law Making*

an administrative form of collective punishment carried out in the name of the king.

The two speakers at the 25 April ceremony, French *Conseiller-juriste* (Legal Adviser) Maurice Habert and Cambodian Judge Penn, personified those features of the Cambodian jurisdiction which made it unique in Indochina. As president of the Cambodian Court of Annulment (*sala vinichhay*), Judge Penn headed a hierarchy of indigenous courts modelled loosely on that of France, but in which no French judge officially presided.[2] Judge Penn attributed this fact to Baudoin, whom he thanked for having ensured that it was "Khmer who judge Khmer".[3] In order to achieve this outcome, Cambodian officials had been divided into separate judicial and administrative corps, leading Habert to claim that Cambodians were "the only subjects . . . to whom the French Government presently devolves [your own] independent judicial power".[4]

Located close to the Royal Palace in Phnom Penh, the *Palais de Justice*, which today forms part of the premises of the Cambodian Ministry of Justice, had been designed to symbolise a merger of Khmer traditions with French legal principles and procedures. At the centre of the building sat the Criminal Court (*sala okret*), where all felony cases would now be heard, replacing the indigenous provincial criminal courts, many of which had performed so unsatisfactorily following the 1916 demonstrations.[5] The Cambodian coat of arms adorned the four corners of the room. According to the account of the opening printed in the newspaper *Echo du Cambodge*, two bronze plaques, one in French and one in Khmer, were to be placed respectively at the back of the

---

[2] In the 1922 restructure of the Cambodian court system, the previous Court of Cassation was renamed in French as the Court of *Annulation* (Annulment), but it retained the same Khmer name (*sala vinichhay*). Its role remained the same, that is, to review issues of law and procedure (but not of fact) decided by the lower courts. The Court of Annulment could order a retrial but could not overturn judgements of the lower courts. Royal Ordinance on Judicial Organisation of Cambodia (Protectorate of Cambodia), 14 Sept. 1922, art. 60; Gouvernement Générale de l'Indochine, "Recueil des Actes du Gouvernement cambodgien" [Government of Indochina, Collection of Acts of the Cambodian Government], 2nd Supplement, 1922–23, NAC Doc, Box 425.

[3] Quoted in "Inauguration du Palais de Justice cambodgien", *Echo du Cambodge*, 25 Apr. 1925, NAC RSC 11850.

[4] Ibid.

[5] Royal Ordinance on Judicial Organisation, 1922, art. 60; Recueil des Actes du Governement, 1922–23, p. 82.

Figure 6.1: Cambodian *Palais de Justice*
Source: Possibly copy of old postcard. Supplied by Darryl Collins.

room facing the judges, and on the front of their bench. A mural behind the judges' bench depicts Yama, the god of death and justice, flanked by two figures who hold texts promising rewards to judges who are impartial and so balance the scales of justice, and punishments for those who fail to be impartial and upset the scales.[6] The mural has survived in what is today part of the Cambodian Ministry of Justice.

The offices of the French judicial adviser and the French delegate to the minister of justice sat directly behind the Criminal Court. Along one side of the building lay the courts of Annulment (formerly Cassation, *sala vinichhay*) and Appeal (*sala outor*). On the other side were the Court of First Instance (*sala lukhun*) and that of the Justice of the Peace (*sala lohuk*) for Phnom Penh and the nearby province of Kandal.[7]

---

[6] Thun Theara (trans.); Hel Chamroeun, មរតកយុត្តិធម៌ខ្មែរ [The Heritage of Khmer Justice] (Phnom Penh: eLibrary of Cambodia, 2009) pp. 534–5. https://www.elibraryofcambodia.org/ebook/morrordok-yutithor-khmer-ebook/ (accessed 12 Sept. 2023).
[7] Ibid.

Figure 6.2: Plaque commemorating the inauguration of the *Palais de Justice* in 1925
Source: Photograph by Darryl Collins, 2006.

The ceremony marked more than the opening of a new building. The architecture of the Cambodian jurisdiction had also been redrawn and would remain basically unchanged until late in the Second World War. Most importantly, the 1922 Royal Ordinance on Judicial Organisation in Cambodia had come into effect. The 14 new Courts of First Instance (*sala dambaung* in the provinces and *sala lukhun* in Phnom Penh) were now operating, and Cambodian administrative and judicial roles had been separated. New state justice institutions had formally replaced the personalised networks of patronage and the semi-religious legal texts that characterised pre-colonial methods of legal administration. Judicial decisions involved findings for or against each party according to written laws and procedure. However, these state structures and the codes they administered still claimed traditional authority through continuity with the past.

The 1911 Penal Code had been substantially revised in 1924 and a *Chambre de mises en accusation*, or *sala kromchot* (roughly translated as an indictment chamber), had been established in 1923, as a further development in criminal procedure. A Civil Code had finally been promulgated in 1920 after a compromise on land titling had been reached.

Over the following years there would be other new legislation, including codes of civil and penal procedure in 1938, which expanded the rudimentary procedures established in previous codes.[8] A 1933 Royal Ordinance established an administrative chamber (*krom viveat*) ostensibly to deal with complaints against Cambodian civil servants, although it appears to have remained largely a dead letter.[9] Nevertheless, according to the official French pronouncements, by the mid-1920s Cambodians had been given the framework of a modernised legal system, albeit one that incorporated aspects of Khmer tradition.[10]

At the opening of the *Palais de Justice*, Judicial Adviser Habert went so far as to claim:

> Henceforth, Cambodian litigants enjoy the same guarantees as French litigants. The separation of powers, judicial powers conferred on career judges . . . freely accessible means of legal appeal, a permanent judicial supervision exercised on all procedures by a French magistrate, constitute the solid armature of . . . the most important reform since the establishment of the Protectorate . . . The presence of a French judge at the hearing is sufficient to ensure that . . . rules of procedure are not departed from and that [the necessary dignity is preserved].[11]

Two narratives emerge from the archives regarding the Cambodian jurisdiction in the 1920s and 1930s. According to the official narrative of the protectorate administration, the inauguration of the *Palais de Justice* marked the beginning of a period of consolidation in which Cambodians would learn to occupy their new structures of justice, under

---

[8] Code de Procédure en Matière Pénale [Code of Procedure in Criminal Matters] and Code de Procédure en Matière Civile, 1938 [Code of Procedure in Civil Matters]. NAC Doc, Box 423.

[9] Nicolas, "L'Organisation de la Justice Cambodgienne", pp. 1, 42; Claude-Gilles Gour, *Institutions Constitutionnelles et Politiques du Cambodge* [Constitutional and Political Institutions of Cambodia] (Paris: Librair2e Dalloz, 1965), pp. 365–6.

[10] For a summary of the various adjustments made to the court structures and legal procedures from 1922 to 1940, see Léger, "L'organisation judiciaire du Cambodge", pp. 47, 59–70.

[11] Maurice Habert, Judicial Adviser, speaking at the inauguration of the Cambodian *Palais de Justice*, quoted in "Inauguration du Palais de Justice cambodgien", *Echo du Cambodge*, 25 Apr. 1925. The draft of the speech and a copy of the newspaper article are filed in NAC RSC 11850. The *Echo du Cambodge* was a semi-official French-language newspaper.

French tutelage.[12] Countering this official picture of steady progress towards enlightened justice, a range of French and Cambodian critics complained the Cambodian jurisdiction was repressive, overreaching and administered by inept and corrupt judges.

The international context of rising nationalist and anti-colonial sentiment began to reverberate in Cambodia, but was absent from the official narrative portrayed in reports and in case numbers from the Cambodian courts. Rather than devolving to Cambodians their own independent judicial power, the French administration had tightened its control over the local courts. Moreover, two criminal trials that took place in the French jurisdiction during the 1920s illustrate the limits on judicial independence that were inherent in colonial rule.

The Context: Protection in or from Turbulent Times?

Royal deaths and coronations punctuated affairs of state in Cambodia during the 1920s and 1930s. King Sisowath died in 1927; his son, King Monivong, reigned until April 1941. Monivong's 18-year-old grandson, Norodom Sihanouk, then took the throne. Like his two predecessors, Sihanouk was hand-picked by the colonial authorities.[13] Economically and socially, Cambodians experienced considerable changes. In the 1920s France embarked on a programme to develop its colonies, and the protectorate authorities put Cambodians to work completing a network of roads and railways and erecting public buildings.[14] They brought electricity and clean water to Phnom Penh and regional urban centres.[15] French *colons* established rubber plantations in the red-earth territories located mainly in the eastern provinces of Kompong Cham, Kompong Thom and Kratie.[16] While many Cambodians benefited from economic growth and expanding rice yields during the 1920s, prices for their agricultural products fell during the global depression of the 1930s, and

---

[12] Léger, "L'organisation judiciaire du Cambodge", pp. 47–71; Nicolas, "Le Cambodge", pp. 113–54; Nicolas, "L'Organisation de la Justice Cambodgienne".

[13] Tully, *France on the Mekong*, pp. 195–8; Milton Osborne, "King-Making in Cambodia: From Sisowath to Sihanouk", *Journal of Southeast Asian Studies* 4, 2 (1973): 169–85. DOI:10.1017/S0022463400016593.

[14] Tully, *France on the Mekong*, pp. 257–61.

[15] Ibid., pp. 260–1.

[16] Slocomb, *Colons and Coolies*; Mitch Aso, "Rubber and Race in Rural Colonial Cambodia (1920s–1954)", *Siksacakr* 12–13 (2010–11): 127–38.

the protectorate's demands for tax revenues increased, leading to considerable hardship.[17]

Meanwhile, political change in countries such as China, Japan, India and Russia helped to inspire agitation closer to home, including in the Vietnamese regions of Indochina.[18] Both the French colonial administration and the Cambodian royalist elites must have been alarmed by the growth of radicalism in Vietnam, but events in Siam/Thailand would also have concerned them.[19] Cambodia's King Monivong in particular would have abhorred the 1932 "revolution" that established a constitutional monarchy in Thailand, eventually leading King Prajadhipok (Rama VII) to abdicate. The Bangkok government replaced him with nine-year-old Ananda Mahidol (Rama VIII), who was then living in Switzerland and would not return to Thailand until 1945.[20] *Résident Supérieur* Baudoin and his successors worked hard to isolate Cambodia from such influences.

Of course, the French could not keep Cambodia entirely cocooned from events occurring next door. As nationalist and communist ideas spread in the Vietnamese territories, they inevitably also reached Cambodia and Laos, despite the authorities' best efforts.[21] Amid considerable economic and social change, differing currents within the

---

[17] Tully, *France on the Mekong*, pp. 266–8; Chandler, *History*, pp. 196–8.

[18] For events in Vietnam during the 1920s and 1930s, see Goscha, *Modern History of Vietnam*, pp. 93–186; Ben Kiernan, *Việt Nam: A History from Earliest Times to the Present* (New York: Oxford University Press, 2017), pp. 343–76; David G. Marr, *Vietnamese Tradition on Trial, 1920–1945* (California: University of California Press, 1981), pp. i–127.

[19] Penny Edwards notes that in 1927 Governor General Pasquier supported Monivong to succeed King Sisowath because "he was a 'real Khmer' who felt no attraction for Siam"; see Edwards, *Cambodge*, p. 195.

[20] For differing interpretations of these events, see Arjun Subrahmanyan, "The Unruly Past: History and Historiography of the 1932 Thai Revolution", *Journal of Contemporary Asia* 50, 1 (2020): 74–98; Eugene Mark, "Time to Truly Understand Thailand's 1932 Revolution", *The Diplomat*, 29 June 2017, https://thediplomat .com/2017/06/time-to-truly-understand-thailands-1932-revolution/ (accessed 11 June 2020); Thongchai Winichakul, "Toppling Democracy", *Journal of Contemporary Asia* 38, 1 (2008): 11–37; Chaiyan Rajchagool, *The Rise and Fall of the Thai Absolute Monarchy: Foundations of the Modern Thai State from Feudalism to Peripheral Capitalism* (Bangkok: While Lotus, 1994).

[21] Stuart-Fox, "French in Laos", pp. 130–4; Brocheux and Hémery, *Indochina*, pp. 283–4. Ethnic Vietnamese and Chinese communists began agitating in the rubber plantations and in certain workplaces in Cambodia from the 1930s, but communist cells, affiliated to the Indochinese Communist Party, remained very

132   *Colonial Law Making*

Cambodian elite became more pronounced. Khmer nationalism began to have an impact on colonial rule during the decade 1935–45.[22] Many elite Cambodians remained firm Francophiles, yet resented certain aspects of colonial rule. The Khmer-language newspaper *Nagaravatta* was founded in 1936 and became a popular forum for discussions of concepts of nationhood and nationality among some members of the Buddhist Sangha, high-school graduates and civil servants.[23] Huy Kanthoul, who briefly served as prime minister after the Second World War, remembered the 1930s as a time when he, like other young educated Cambodians, "became interested in the future of my country".[24]

Although the French often portrayed non-elite Cambodians as docile and passive, this had never been accurate. The 1916 Affair had demonstrated that many resented and mistrusted the authorities, both Cambodian and French, to whom they paid taxes and other imposts. Banditry remained a perennial problem in certain areas, and bandit leaders often espoused anti-authoritarian views.[25] In the late 1920s, the syncretic Cao Dai religious sect threatened social hierarchies in certain parts of the country, dismaying the French administration and the Cambodian monarchy. Cao Dai leaders promoted Vietnamese–Khmer cooperation and championed mythical figures such as Neak Mian Bon, a prince who, according to Khmer folklore, would deliver the people from misery. King Monivong and leaders of the Buddhist clergy united with the French to demand that the sect be suppressed in Cambodia.[26] These myriad events, taken as a whole, set the scene for a contest of ideas about the nature and the practice of the judicial system in Cambodia, pitting the official view of progress against the narratives of French and Cambodian critics.

The Official Narrative of Steady Progress

The 1922 reforms had abolished the 51 provincial courts, which had been headed by Cambodian governors, and put in their place 14 Courts of

---

small and subject to severe repression from the colonial security forces. See Ben Kiernan, *How Pol Pot Came to Power* (London: Verso, 1985), pp. 8–10.

[22] Edwards, *Cambodge*, pp. 210–41.

[23] Ibid., pp. 216–27; Chandler, *History*, pp. 194–201.

[24] Kanthoul, *Mémoires*, p. 71.

[25] Tully, *France on the Mekong*, pp. 166–72.

[26] Kiernan, *How Pol Pot Came to Power*, pp. 4–7, 14–15; Tully, *France on the Mekong*, pp. 200–3.

First Instance (*sala dambaung*), staffed by men placed within the judicial corps. These changes completed the foundations for an indigenous jurisdiction unique in Indochina: a separate judicial corps; no officially presiding French judge; and an almost completely rewritten set of codes. Neither the protectorates of Annam and Tonkin nor the semi-protectorate of Laos combined all three of these characteristics. The indigenous jurisdiction of Annam also excluded French judges, but although its pre-colonial court structures and laws had been modified, they had not been replaced.[27] In Tonkin and to a lesser extent Laos, French judges played an increasingly important role, particularly at appeal level. The codes of Laos had also been rewritten, although they borrowed less extensively from French law. Those of Tonkin also retained more aspects of the pre-colonial Code Gia Long, and had been less rigidly codified in the French style than was the case in Cambodia.[28]

One feature common to all the indigenous jurisdictions of Indochina, however, was that, regardless of form, the colonial authorities exercised close control. As judicial adviser in Cambodia, Habert headed a hierarchy of colonial officials who oversaw the Cambodian courts, for which he controlled judicial appointments and other personnel matters and drafted new legislation.[29] He sat with consultative voice in the Court of Annulment and advised on which cases it should hear.[30] Below Habert, French administrators, not judges, continued to supervise each level of the court hierarchy. A French delegate shadowed the Cambodian minister of justice, supervising his correspondence.[31] The delegate also had a watching brief in the Court of Appeal, paying particular attention to criminal matters.[32] Habert later took over these functions.[33] In the provinces, each *résident* monitored the one Cambodian Court of First Instance in his province, vetted judgements, and reported problems to the delegate or adviser, who would then counsel the Cambodian minister of justice to take remedial action.[34]

---

[27] Bonhomme, "L'Annam", pp. 155–74.

[28] Habert, "Le Tonkin", pp. 175–210.

[29] Arrêté of Résident Supérieur, 19 Sept. 1922, art. 2, in *Recueil des Actes du Gouvernement, 1922*, p. 95.

[30] Ibid., arts. 4–6.

[31] Ibid., arts. 16 and 17.

[32] Ibid., arts. 15–19.

[33] Léger, "L'organisation judiciaire du Cambodge", pp. 47, 65.

[34] Arrêté of Résident Supérieur, 19 Sept. 1922, arts. 9, 11.

134 *Colonial Law Making*

This network of supervision closely resembled those in place in the rural areas of Tonkin and in Laos. The major difference was that active members of the colonial judiciary formally played no role in Cambodia, whereas they did in Tonkin and Laos, particularly at appeal level.[35] Habert was a judge, but he had been seconded to work under the *résident supérieur*. Neither he nor the delegate to the Cambodian minister for justice formally adjudicated, although the senior Cambodian judges doubtless followed their advice.

Judicial Adviser Habert acted as a bridge between the Cambodian courts, the protectorate authorities and the colonial judiciary. He would have had to walk a careful path between the expectations of his judicial colleagues and those of the *résident supérieur*, and he appears to have been eminently well placed to do so. Habert had worked as the prosecutor in the French court of Phnom Penh in 1918–19, so would have been known and presumably acceptable to Baudoin, whose influence over the protectorate continued even during the years he was acting as governor general of all Indochina.[36] To find a judge acceptable to Baudoin was likely not an easy task. In 1925 he enlisted the support of King Sisowath to prevent another judge whom he did not like, Louis Charles Motais de Narbonne, from filling in for Habert while he went on leave.[37] There may also have been some nepotism involved in Habert's appointment as judicial adviser, as he was a close relative of the then director of judicial administration for Indochina, Alfred Habert, who would have signed off on his secondment.[38]

As well as the presence of the judicial adviser, who in French eyes leant an air of legal legitimacy to the Cambodian jurisdiction, a hierarchy of reports and statistics promoted the official narrative. Starting with the records kept by the Cambodian court officials, reports filtered up through the *résidents*, the judicial adviser and the *résident supérieur*,

---

[35] Habert, "Le Tonkin"; Cressent, "Administration mixte: le Laos", pp. 82–112.

[36] Farcy and Fry, *Annuaire rétrospectif.*

[37] See Baudoin to Governor General, 2 Sept. 1925; King Sisowath to Résident Supérieur (trans.), 1 Sept. 1925, CAOM RSC 618/6135. Motais de Narbonne, who presided in the 1925 Bardez trial (see below) and Baudoin were known to dislike each other; see extract from the newspaper *Courrière Saïgonnais*, 12 Dec. 1925, in CAOM RSC 261.

[38] Regarding their relationship, see Letter from Lortat Jacob to French Minister for Colonies, 3 Dec. 1929. Archives de La Contemporaine, site de Nanterre, Fonds LDH [Archives of La Contemporaine, Nanterre Campus, Collection of the League for the Rights of Man] (France), F Delta Res Box 798/85.

to the governor general of Indochina and then to the French minister of colonies.

The narrative was also occasionally reproduced for public consumption in France, for example in a document called *La Justice en Indochine* (Justice in Indochina) prepared for the 1931 International Colonial Exhibition in Paris.[39] Raoul Nicolas, who was acting judicial adviser while Habert was on leave, drafted the chapter on Cambodia. He carefully listed and explained the various reforms initiated by the French. With an eye for legality rather than the facts, he claimed that before King Norodom gave his consent for them to do so in 1884, the French had not become involved in Cambodian justice.[40] He explained the 1911 reforms in some detail and then noted that problems with implementation had arisen because of the ongoing combination of judicial and administrative functions, and because Cambodian officials could not adapt to new ways. Nicolas then claimed that the reforms of 1922 were working well, under the guidance of the judicial adviser, because Cambodian judges were willing to "follow the advice given to them". He also wryly noted that the judicial adviser had the power to recommend promotions and other benefits.[41]

In his annual report for 1927, newly appointed *Résident Supérieur* Le Fol emphasised two indicators that the French administration considered important measures of progress in the Cambodian jurisdiction. Firstly, the *résident supérieur* noted that in the previous year there had been only four official complaints against the Cambodian courts, and three of these had been dismissed.[42] Secondly, he reported that the only defendants held in any kind of pre-trial custody for more than six months were those awaiting the outcome of an appeal to the Court of Annulment.[43]

Based on these measurable outcomes, which are indeed important signs of the health or otherwise of courts of justice, Le Fol considered that "the Cambodian judicial personnel have shown themselves, [to be] up to the mission that has been vested in them".[44] At the same time, Le Fol praised an innovation which, in order to meet the protectorate's

---

[39] Direction de L'Administration de la Justice, *La justice en Indochine*.

[40] Nicolas, *Le Cambodge*, p. 126.

[41] Ibid., p. 139.

[42] Rapport d'ensemble sur la situation du Cambodge, Année 1925–26 [Overview Report on the Situation of Cambodia, Year 1925–1926], CAOM RSC 432.

[43] Ibid.

[44] Ibid.

136   *Colonial Law Making*

perennial concern to balance its budget, may have actually facilitated bribe-taking by court officials. He noted with satisfaction that revenue from court fees had increased markedly (up from 14,589 piastres in 1925 to 24,848 in 1926) thanks to a new regulation that allowed the court clerks to keep a small percentage of each fee they received.

New and revised legislation also contributed to a picture of steady progress, in tune with the sought-after "evolution" of Cambodian society. In 1926, defendants in criminal matters were granted limited access to legal aid, and, two years later, court fees in criminal matters were abolished.[45] It is also true that by 1932 Cambodian litigants had gained some right to legal representation, as discussed in the following chapter. The Penal Code was again revised in 1934, and in 1938 new codes of Civil and Criminal Procedure came into effect. The 1938 Code of Criminal Procedure introduced a prosecution service into the jurisdiction.[46] Before then, criminal investigations and hearings had taken place without the intervention of a prosecutor, and the Cambodian minister for justice had performed many of the functions normally carried out by the prosecutor general under French law. These changes were introduced cautiously and with certain safeguards. For example, Judicial Adviser Léger reported that in order to avoid abuses arising from the "litigious spirit of the oriental", the minister for justice retained final say over which cases should go ahead even after prosecutors received the right to declare if there was a case to answer.[47]

Court statistics formed the basis for much of the official narrative, and case numbers from the new Courts of First Instance in the 1920s and 1930s would have been reassuring. Importantly, there was an almost sevenfold increase in the number of civil matters adjudicated in the Courts of First Instance between 1924 (1,946 cases) and 1939 (13,481 cases), as illustrated in Table 6.1. Because private citizens rather than the colonial state initiated civil cases, these figures provided some evidence that a growing number of Cambodians trusted the courts.[48] The sharpest rise in civil case numbers occurred in 1938 and 1939, and Judicial Adviser Léger hinted that this may have been at least partly due to the

---

[45] Rapport d'ensemble sur la situation du Cambodge, Année 1925–26, CAOM RSC 432.

[46] Léger, "L'organisation judiciaire du Cambodge", pp. 47–90.

[47] Ibid., pp. 59–70.

[48] Overview on the Progress of the Indigenous Judicial service in Cambodia in 1927, NAC Doc, Box 422.

new Civil Procedure Code, which, for the first time, established a role for Cambodian bailiffs (*huissiers*), who had the power to enforce payment of damages and transfers of property ordered by the courts.[49] A further reason, not stated by Léger, may have been the courts' authority to issue certain certificates related to civil status. For example, in 1939, the normally quiet court of Kompong Speu reported a sudden increase in demands for *jugements supplétifs d'actes de naissance*, or retrospective court-registered birth certificates, perhaps indicating that the colonial state, and its requirements for civil registration, were reaching new layers of the population.[50]

The protectorate authorities would likely also have been satisfied by the fact that appeals in civil cases increased at a slower rate than cases at first instance. This would seem to indicate that the protectorate had had some success in discouraging Cambodians from burdening the higher courts with what were, in the views of the French, trivial or hopeless civil-case appeals.[51] Even so, the 1938 Code of Civil Procedure placed a 30-year time limit on individual cases, suggesting that there was still some room for improvement.[52]

Judicial Adviser Léger also claimed progress in the area of criminal law. As well as the reductions in time spent on remand mentioned above, he asserted that the 1938 Code of Criminal Procedure, which he had drafted, had led to an immediate drop in the number of trials of alleged criminal misdemeanors.[53] He asserted this was because, for the first time, the code empowered officials in the Cambodian Courts of First

---

[49] Annual Report of the Judicial Adviser (Léger), 1939–40, CAOM RSC 692; Ministerial Circular No. 11, 2 Feb. 1927, reproduced in *Recueil des Actes du Gouvernement Cambodgienne, 3ème supplément, années 1926, 1927, 1928, 1929 et rapels d'années antérieurs (1929)* [Collection of Acts of the Cambodian Government, 3rd Supplement, Years 1926, 1927, 1929 and Recalls of Previous Years (1929)], NAC Doc, Box 425.

[50] Report from Résident of Kompong Speu, June 1940, CAOM RSC 692. Regarding the need for a court order, see Code Civil et Procédure Civile Cambodgiens [Cambodian Civil Code and Civil Procedure], 1920, Book One, Chapter Two, Section IV, art. 73. NAC Doc, Box 423.

[51] Léger, "Rapport de Présentation", 25 Mar. 1938. Minimum limits had been imposed on the value of cases that could be appealed; in the 1938 code, the limit for most cases was 300 piastres; see Code de Procédure en Matière Civile, 20 Dec. 1938, art. 98, NAC Doc, Box 423.

[52] Léger, "Rapport de Présentation", 25 Mar. 1938.

[53] Misdemeanours (eng.), *délits* (fr.) or *batolmeus* (kh.).

138   *Colonial Law Making*

Table 6.1: Cases processed in Cambodian jurisdiction, 1924–26 and 1936–39[55]

Type of Case	1924	1925	1926	1936	1937	1938	1939
Civil							
First Instance	1,946	2,222	2,147	3,578	4,977	11,164	13,481
Appeal	337	406	465	205	234	348	519
Annulment	259	322	436	469	580	728	898
Misdemeanour							
First Instance	4,288	5,464	4,898	9,209	9,704	9,504	7,709
Appeal	744	753	682	1,027	1,170	1,124	1,351
Annulment*	277	198	146	245	232	263	274
Felony							
Criminal Court	187	190	187	318	232	217	289
Accusation Chamber**	538	450	410	526	636	548	711
Annulment	111	43	79	108	77	75	93
Petty							
First Instance	344	325	490	3,316	3,586	3,748	4,296
Annulment	11	15	23	79	54	42	48

Notes: * *sala vinichhay*
** *sala kromchot*, or chambre de mises en accusation

Instance to declare the accused had no case to answer.[54] If Léger's analysis was correct, then this reform had indeed led to fewer people being tried needlessly.

Table 6.2 gives a breakdown of the number of new cases *registered* in each Court of First Instance in 1932 and 1939, showing regional variations in the rate of misdemeanour cases. There was a sharp increase in Kompong Cham, the centre of the rubber industry, and also significant rises in Kompong Thom and Siem Reap, but numbers declined in Phnom Penh, Svay Rieng and Takeo. The reasons for these regional differences are not apparent from the reports. Kompong Cham experienced an influx of migrant labour and no doubt an increase in criminal activity

---

[54] Annual Report of the Judicial Advisor, 1939, CAOM RSC 692.
[55] Figures for 1924–26 come from Rapport d'ensemble sur la situation du Cambodge, Année 1925–26, CAOM RSC 432 Rapports. For 1936–39, see Rapport Annuel: Justice Cambodgienne [Annual Report: Cambodian Justice], 1940, CAOM RSC 692. During the 1920s, reporting periods corresponded to calendar years; by the 1930s, the reporting period ran from June to May.

The Cambodian Courts after 1922

Table 6.2: Cases registered in Courts of First Instance, 1932 and 1939[56]

Court of First Instance	New Cases registered 1932			New Cases Registered 1939		
	Civil	Misde-meanours	Total	Civil	Misde-meanours	Total
Phnom Penh	308	2,296	**2,604**	2,000	1,186	**3,186**
Battambang	265	868	**1,133**	1,865	908	**2,773**
Kampot	31	531	**562**	627	453	**1,080**
Kompong Cham	178	884	**1,062**	1,952	1,338	**3,290**
Kompong Chhnang	84	318	**402**	177	567	**744**
Kompong Speu	49	412	**461**	449	453	**902**
Kompong Thom	43	344	**387**	254	550	**804**
Kratie	7	135	**142**	183	184	**367**
Prey Veng	35	658	**693**	452	647	**1,099**
Pursat	67	258	**325**	244	248	**492**
Siem Reap	42	245	**287**	1,837	314	**2,151**
Stung Treng	1	93	**94**	19	20	**39**
Svay Rieng	101	780	**881**	1,021	225	**1,246**
Takeo	101	624	**725**	1,306	248	**1,554**
Total	**1,312**	**8,446**		**12,386**	**7,341**	

related to the rubber industry, although matters involving the largely Vietnamese migrant workforce would have been heard in the French jurisdiction.

I have compiled Tables 6.1 and 6.2 from various different reports that were either written by the judicial adviser (Habert or Léger) or that were likely drafted by him. The next chapter discusses claims by at least one critic that the court statistics were, at best, unreliable. The main point of these figures is that they were the foundation for the narrative of steady progress, of an operational court system and of growing confidence in the Cambodian courts. There is likely some truth in them. For example, the growing number of civil matters may indicate that at least some Cambodians found the courts a useful forum in which to settle their claims. In general, French reports painted the courts as institutions in training, guided by their own close supervision and tutelage.

---

[56] Figures for 1932 from General Report on the Functioning of the Cambodian Judicial Services in 1932, NAC RSC 18405. Figures for 1939 from Annual Report of the Judicial Advisor, 1939, CAOM RSC 692.

140   *Colonial Law Making*

Within their framework of steady progress, the judicial advisers acknowledged there were some teething problems, for which they usually blamed backward and corrupt Cambodians. In 1927, four years after the new Courts of First Instance had started operating, Habert reported there was:

> an emerging competitiveness between administrative and judicial personnel . . . [Cambodian functionaries] do not willingly accept being definitively deprived of all juridical power, particularly in penal matters. It is equally probable that the senior dignitaries of the Crown do not appreciate the benefits of a reform that shields justice from their influence, where it was formerly dominant.[57]

That same year, a small group of Cambodian local government officials had called for a Court of First Instance in every district (*srok*), which would essentially have meant a return to the status quo before 1922. The disgruntled officials blamed the new courts for being too lenient, claiming this led to an increase in the rate of petty crime.[58]

It fell to Judge Khoun Nay, president of the Phnom Penh Court of First Instance (*sala lukhun*), to respond to these particular criticisms. A nine-page rebuttal, which appears to have been originally written in French, circulated under his name.[59] In it, Khoun Nay claimed that many critics of the new courts were barely literate and that former provincial governors, many of whom had been demoted as a result of the 1922 reforms, resisted the changes because the old system had allowed them to "condemn accused at will".[60]

The decision to abolish or downgrade the previous provinces and to do away with their courts had been a serious rupture for rural Cambodian elites. When he was still the head of the Cambodian Court of Cassation, Judge Keth had advised a more incremental approach, fearing that the necessary infrastructure did not exist for the new courts, and wanting to avoid widespread redundancies that might result when

---

[57] Overview on the Progress of the Indigenous Judicial service in Cambodia in 1927, NAC Doc, Box 422.

[58] Extracts from an undated meeting of the Indigenous Consultative Assembly, forwarded to Habert on 8 Aug. 1927, NAC RSC 36097.

[59] Khoun Nay to Habert, 27 Oct. 1930, NAC RSC 31174. This document is in French and is not marked as a translation. See also Habert's cover note attached to statistics from the courts, 16 Oct. 1930, NAC RSC 31147.

[60] Ibid.

the 51 provincial courts were abolished.[61] The French ignored the judge's advice because it did not fit their budget or their schedule.[62] Although there may not have been as many redundancies as Judge Keth had feared, he was probably right to counsel a more gradual approach because some courts indeed lacked suitable premises and encountered considerable confusion and resistance regarding their role.[63]

Colonialism, Independent Justice and the Separation of Powers

In this atmosphere, the Cambodian judges depended on the French administration to shield them against their critics. A level of trust, and mutual respect, developed between Judicial Adviser Habert and his successor Léger and the senior Cambodian judges who, for example, organised a ceremony to farewell Habert when he left Phnom Penh in 1935.[64] Another event which indicates that the French were confident in the loyalty of the Cambodian judges was the formation in 1936 of a judicial association, called the *Amicale de la Magistrature*. The colonial administration usually viewed any indigenous organisation with deep suspicion, but in this case one official even went so far as to question if it was necessary to appoint anyone to monitor the first meeting of the *Amicale*, although Léger eventually kept an eye on the event.[65]

The judicial advisers wielded a great amount of power over the indigenous jurisdiction. Even when it came to drafting new laws, they enjoyed a relatively free hand. They no longer had to submit to the cumbersome Franco-Khmer committee structures that had been required

---

[61] Minister of Justice to Résident Supérieur, 14 Feb. 1921, and Note, President of the Court of Cassation, 2 Mar. 1921 (original in French), in NAC RSC 20674.

[62] Note on judicial organisation in Cambodia, 2 Mar. 1921, NAC RSC 20674.

[63] Sorn, "L'Evolution de la société cambodgienne", pp. 58–9. Regarding teething problems in various provinces, see Kompong Thom Political Report, 4th trimester 1923, 9 Jan. 1924, CAOM RSC 374. Kampot Political Report, 15 June 1923, CAOM RSC 358.

[64] Report in *La Dépeche*, 1 Apr. 1935. The journal was published by Henri Chavigny de Lachevrotière, a Saigon-based journalist who also operated a rubber plantation in Cambodia in the region of Kampot. Copies for 1935 and other years are available in the National Archives of Cambodia.

[65] Note to the Résident Supérieur, On the subject of the general assembly of the Amicale de la Magistrature cambodgienne [Association of the Cambodian Judiciary] in 1936, 23 Dec. 1936, NAC RSC 28283.

142   *Colonial Law Making*

to ensure the 1911 codes were acceptable to the king and the Cambodian Council of Ministers. While Habert and Léger still claimed to take account of Cambodian law and custom, Cambodian input appears to have been limited and at the whim of the judicial advisers themselves. For example, Léger noted that when drafting the 1938 Civil Procedure Code, he had, apparently as he saw fit, convened informal meetings with Cambodian judges at which they had the chance to comment on, learn about and on occasion suggest changes to his work.[66]

Even the claim that no French judge served in the Cambodian courts was, in practice, difficult to sustain. As they mentored Cambodian judges, the judicial advisers and the *résidents* also ensured that the Cambodian courts operated in line with the interests of the protectorate administration. For example, Habert closely monitored potentially sensitive cases, such as charges of rape against two members of the Indigenous Guard, or the accidental death of a judge at the hands of a local commune chief.[67] In 1934, a French journal published an article, purportedly written by an anonymous "Cambodian Mandarin", which accused the French of exceeding their mandate, including in the area of justice.[68] The author's main grievance was against the extent of French control over the Cambodian courts, and in particular against the role of the judicial adviser: "He is, in fact, if not in law, the grand chief of Cambodian justice and of Cambodian judicial personnel . . . These new attributions . . . appear fairly difficult to reconcile with the provisions of the Treaty of 1863."[69]

In 1928 *National Geographic* published a photograph entitled "the Cambodian courts".[70] Taken in the main courtroom of the *Palais de Justice*, a clearly European judge sits in the middle of the bench. This

---

[66] Ibid.

[67] Criminal Court, Judgment no. 26, 6 Dec. 1930, NAC RSC 18405. See also various correspondence regarding the death of Judge Lamouth, 25 June to 8 July 1930, NAC RSC 18405. According to Léger, in 1936 all penal cases in which members of the militia were defendants were moved to the French court, see Léger, "L'organisation judiciaire du Cambodge", p. 67.

[68] Anonymous, "La politique indigène de la France au Cambodge, appréciée par un Mandarin Cambodgien" [French Indigenous Policies in Cambodia, as Perceived by a Cambodian Mandarin], *La Revue du Pacifique* [The Pacific Review] 3 (1934): 143–57.

[69] Ibid., p. 155.

[70] Thanks to Dr Darryl Collins for giving me a copy of this picture. Unfortunately I could not attain the licence to reproduce it here. The picture appeared in *National Geographic*, Sept. 1928, XIV.

may well be Habert himself. He is flanked by Cambodian judges. On the wall behind them is the mural warning the judges to be impartial. The image illustrates French claims to have synthesised modern French legal principles and procedures with Cambodian custom.

What, then, of Habert's assertions regarding the separation of powers and independence of the judiciary? The separation of judicial and administrative roles made the Cambodian courts more independent in that it reduced the ability of non-judicial members of the Cambodian elite to interfere. However, Habert's concept of judicial independence did not incorporate any sense of a Cambodian judiciary that acted autonomously from the protectorate administration. Legal historian Laurent Manière posits that in the French colony of West Africa, indigenous jurisdictions became, de facto, an extension of the Indigénat, the extrajudicial code under which administrators could bypass the courts and inflict summary punishments. In other words, the indigenous courts merged with the colonial administrative apparatus.[71] In Cambodia, the situation was more tempered, but the effect was similar. The Indigénat no longer applied, and a French judge, the judicial adviser, leant a veneer of judicial independence to the indigenous courts, even though he ultimately answered to the *résident supérieur*. Nevertheless, while they may have completed the division of administrative and judicial functions in the Cambodian jurisdiction, the 1922 reforms had not separated judicial and administrative powers. Rather, the reforms had completed a transfer of control of the judicial power exercised in the Cambodian jurisdiction from the Cambodian elite to the French administration.

Trials in the French Jurisdiction

As the anonymous Cambodian mandarin had noted in the article in which he denounced the role of the judicial adviser, members of the Cambodian elite were well aware that the protectorate administration adopted directly opposing attitudes to the separation of judicial and administrative functions in the French and Cambodian jurisdictions. Colonial administrators had ensured that only in Phnom Penh did French judges preside over a French court, leaving administrators to act as judges in the provincial French courts. However, two high-profile cases in the French court of Phnom Penh, one in 1924 and the other in

---

[71] Manière, "Deux conceptions de l'action judiciaire".

144   *Colonial Law Making*

1925, demonstrated that even judge-run colonial courts were subject to administrative interference, particularly when French interests or prestige were at stake.

In 1924, French writer André Malraux and an accomplice, Louis Chevasson, appeared in court charged with stealing bas-reliefs from the temple of Banteay Srey in the north-western region of Siem Reap.[72] Charges against Malraux's wife, Clara, were dismissed because it was presumed she had participated out of obedience to her husband. The three had indeed plundered the carvings, but Malraux claimed they had not broken the law because Banteay Srey temple was not then listed as a protected site.[73] The original prosecutor in the matter had been on the point of declaring there was no case to answer, but he was suddenly replaced, and Malraux was tried and found guilty in the French court of Phnom Penh.[74] Malraux became an outspoken critic of the colonial regime in Indochina and argued, plausibly, that his trial had been fixed. His case became a cause célèbre among senior literary figures in France, who called for his acquittal, questioning the legitimacy of the colonial courts.[75]

We can only wonder what members of the Cambodian elite made of this case. Those who spoke or read French would have heard, for example, of André Breton's open letter in defence of Malraux, which was widely circulated in local newspapers. They would have been aware that Malraux was no friend of the French administration of Indochina.[76] Writing many years later, former prime minister Huy Kanthoul supported Malraux's claim that he had been singled out because he was a critic of the French colonial regime. Huy Kanthoul also echoed Malraux in pointing out that many a colonial official had plundered local antiquities with impunity.[77]

The second notable trial would certainly have reverberated among the Cambodian elite as it concerned the murder of *Résident* Félix Bardez

---

[72] Walter G. Langlois, *André Malraux: The Indochina Adventure* (Westport, CT: Praeger, 1966), pp. 25–51; Raoul Marc Jennar, *Comment Malraux est devenu Malraux: de l'indifférence politique à l'engagement* [How Malraux Became Malraux: From Political Indifference to Engagement] (Perpignan: Cap Bear, 2015), p. 43.

[73] Langlois, *André Malraux*, p. 37.

[74] Ibid. See also Jennar, *Comment Malraux*, p. 43.

[75] See André Breton, "Pour Malraux" [For Malraux], *Echo du Cambodge* [Cambodia Echo], 27 Sept. 1924, and "Chronique judiciaire" [Legal Chronicles], *Echo du Cambodge*, 11 and 18 Oct. 1924.

[76] Breton, "Pour Malraux".

[77] Kanthoul, *Mémoires*, p. 55.

The Cambodian Courts after 1922   145

and his two Cambodian assistants, Leach and Sourn, just one week before the opening of the *Palais de Justice*. Because one of the victims of the crime was a French citizen, the matter went before the French Criminal Court of Phnom Penh, presided over by three French judges. As the 18 defendants were Cambodians, two indigenous assessors, chosen from an approved list, advised the French judges.[78] According to one newspaper report, there were two assessors and two reserves or assistants appointed in the Bardez case. The paper named them as: Mr Kim An, governor of Kompong Speu province; Mr Mong Khonn, chief of Kien Svay district; and the two *suppléants* were Mr Mau, assistant to the Cambodian minister of defence, and Mr Yea, governor of Svay Rieng province.[79]

The trial centred on competing interpretations of the murders. The prosecution maintained they had been instigated by bandits intent on theft, and were devoid of any political significance.[80] Countering this, three of the defence lawyers argued that the villagers had acted spontaneously and collectively, provoked by Bardez's arrogance and the villagers' reluctance to pay taxes from which they saw little benefit.[81] Thirteen of the 18 defendants were convicted. One was sentenced to death and 11 to hard labour on the notorious prison island of Poulo Condor in Cochin China for periods ranging from five years to life.[82] One defendant, a minor, was also sentenced to an adult prison, but one that was less harsh than Poulo Condor.[83]

What we know of the events indicates the murders were not premeditated. Rather, they resulted from Bardez's arrogant and inept behaviour. He and his staff had foolhardily arrived in the village of Kraang Laev to collect outstanding taxes during the Khmer Buddhist New Year celebrations, a very important holiday for Cambodians, which

---

[78] Morché, "Organisation Judiciaire de l'Indochine", pp. 9–39, see p. 17.

[79] "Affaire Bardez en cour d'assises" [The Bardez Affair in the Court of Assises], in *Echo Annamite* [Annamite Echo], 8 Dec. 1925.

[80] Ligue des Droits de l'Homme [League for the Rights of Man], *L'Affaire Bardez aux Assises de Phnom Penh* [The Bardez Affair in the Court of Assises of Phnom Penh] (Saigon, 1926).

[81] Closing statement of defence lawyer Gallet, in Ligue des Droits de l'Homme, *L'Affaire Bardez*, pp. 43, 50.

[82] See Cour Criminelle. Assassinat de M Bardez, Résident de France à Kg Chhnang, [Criminal Court. Assassination of Mr Bardez, Resident of France in Kompong Chhnang] CAOM RSC, 261.

[83] Ibid.

occurs during the hottest part of the year. Bardez ordered all the adult male inhabitants to stand in the midday sun until all their debts to the colonial state had been paid. When one woman came forward to pay the taxes owed by her husband, Bardez refused to release the man. The two sides then seem to have panicked and the crowd set upon Bardez and his staff. The prosecution later claimed the villagers' attack had been planned and encouraged by several "outsiders" who wanted to rob Bardez. Conveniently, these outsiders were killed during or immediately after the melee and so were never put on trial. Instead, the 18 villagers were arrested and indicted. Fifty-six years later, Ben Kiernan interviewed one of the defendants, Sok Bith, who had been sentenced to 15 years in prison. Bith's account suggests that he indeed remembered the event as something spontaneous and unplanned.[84]

Two of the defence lawyers, *Maîtres* Robert Lortat-Jacob and Gallet, were members of the local chapter of the *Ligue des droits de l'homme* (League for the Rights of Man), the influential French human rights organisation.[85] Gallet was also the head of the Saigon bar. Lortat-Jacob and Gallet openly questioned the legitimacy of the trial and the investigation that led to the indictment of the 18 defendants. The lawyers severely criticised two French administrators, Paul Bonnet and Maxime Chassaing, the same man who later wrote the introduction to the article by the anonymous Cambodian mandarin.

Résident Supérieur Baudoin was also taking an active interest behind the scenes. Maxime Chassaing sat in the trial in his role as inspector of political and administrative affairs, reporting to the Indochina administration in Hanoi.[86] Baudoin had asked him to monitor the proceedings and to report back to him, particularly if any evidence emerged that would contradict the protectorate's "preliminary conclusions" about the case.[87] Defence lawyer Lortat-Jacob accused Chassaing of directing the

---

[84] David Chandler discusses Bith's interview with Kiernan; see Chandler, "The Assassination of Résident Bardez", pp. 142–57.

[85] See the critical accounts "from our special correspondent" under the heading "Affaire Bardez en cour d'assises", in *Echo Annamite*, 8, 11, 12 Dec. 1925, and subsequent issues. For coverage that was unashamedly in favour of the Protectorate authorities, and of Baudoin in particular, see *Echo du Cambodge*, "Avant le procès de l'affaire" [Before the Trial of the Case], 12 Dec. 1925.

[86] Bardez to the Inspector of Political and Administrative Affairs, 13 Dec. 1925, CAOM RSC 261. See Lortat-Jacob's discussion of Chassaing's role, in Ligue des Droits de l'Homme, *L'Affaire Bardez*, p. 103.

[87] Baudoin to Chassaing, 13 Dec. 1925, CAOM RSC 261.

The other official singled out by the defence lawyers was Paul Bonnet, one of Baudoin's protégés, who had replaced Bardez as *résident* of Kompong Chhnang, the province where the murders took place. As the judge of the local French court in Kompong Chhnang, Bonnet led the initial investigation (*instruction*) into the deaths of Bardez and his two colleagues. The defence team mocked Bonnet's lack of legal qualifications and insinuated he could hardly be trusted to investigate his predecessor's death objectively.[90] After the trial, Lortat-Jacob cited what he said were first-hand accounts claiming that Bonnet's staff had intimidated witnesses and tortured some suspects.[91] For example, a man called Preap Choun had been held in detention for 25 days, regularly beaten, had red ants let loose on his head, and had a revolver fired next to his ear, because he would not admit to having taken part in the killings. Parents of two of the accused claimed the local authorities had threatened to lock them up if they attempted to travel to Phnom Penh to consult lawyers who might defend their sons.[92]

Résident Supérieur Baudoin in particular, and the colonial administration in general, were determined to portray the "Bardez affair" as a common crime rather than an outburst of anger over colonial taxes. Even in 1938, when the French Popular Front government declared an amnesty for political prisoners, the local branch of the *sûreté* refused to release the few defendants from the "Bardez case" who were still in prison. The *sûreté* stated that the case had never been political and so the prisoners should serve their full sentences.[93] Yet, beyond the trial, the protectorate administration demonstrated the lie to their claim that the murders were devoid of political significance when they authorised collective, extrajudicial punishment of the whole village of Kraang Laev. With

---

[88] Ligue des Droits de l'Homme, *L'Affaire Bardez*, p. 103.

[89] Chandler, "The Assassination of Résident Bardez", p. 153.

[90] Ligue des Droits de l'Homme, *L'Affaire Bardez*, p. 46.

[91] Lortat-Jacob, *Sauvons l'Indochine*, p. 92.

[92] Ibid., pp. 92–6.

[93] Extracts from the note of the Sûreté on activities of a political nature in Cambodia, 1–31 Mar. 1938, NAC RSC 14331.

148 *Colonial Law Making*

French approval, King Sisowath decreed that all the inhabitants of the village must perform acts of penitence to atone for the way in which they had affronted royal and French prestige.[94] The village was renamed *Derichan* (meaning bestial), and its inhabitants received special identity cards that marked them as coming from such a shameful place.[95] The villagers may not have been conscious nationalists, but their actions in Kraang Laev exposed their hostility to the relations of extraction and force inherent in colonial domination.

At a time when Judicial Adviser Habert was hailing the separation of judicial and administrative functions in the Cambodian jurisdiction, the Bardez affair demonstrated that even the courts of the French jurisdiction in Indochina served to support colonial rule. This point is hardly surprising to any student of European colonialism, yet it is important when considering the colonial legal legacies. Even though the colonial judiciary went to pains to protect their independence from the administrative arm of the colonial state, that independence was, to say the least, qualified. Moreover, when French prestige or authority was attacked, the colonial authorities resorted once again to the Cambodian king. This time they used him as a convenient vehicle to move beyond state law to impose collective punishment on the villagers of Kraang Laev. In doing so, they once again facilitated the notion that the king was above the law.

Towards an Initial Balance Sheet

According to the official colonial narrative, the inauguration of the *Palais de Justice* in 1925 marked a watershed between a previous period of fundamental reform and a new era of further consolidation. In trying to draw a balance sheet regarding this narrative, there are markers of progress towards a modernised French-style legal system. Even if it did not represent a true separation of judicial and administrative powers, the differentiation of administrative and judicial roles among Cambodian officials may well have lessened the ability of some non-judicial Cambodian officials to influence the courts. The reformed jurisdiction may have provided a more consistent and steadily more effective form of administering law than had existed before the French arrived.

---

[94] Chandler, "The Assassination of Résident Bardez", p. 154; Tully, *France on the Mekong*, p. 300.
[95] Tully, *France on the Mekong*, p. 300.

Moreover, a layer of Cambodians embraced aspects of the modernising project espoused by the colonial administration, including its legal reforms.[96] Even though they had to navigate between the demands of colonial and Cambodian power, men like Judges Keth and Khoun Nay, who occupied senior positions in the new state-centred structures, seem to have appreciated the ideals of an impartial, rule-bound justice. Their interests may not have merged with those of the colonial power, but at times they may have felt more affinity towards their French patrons than towards some other layers of the Cambodian elite for whom the new laws and courts were a serious rupture with tradition, and contrary to their interests.

Nevertheless, apart from the critical narratives discussed in the following chapter, it is necessary still to interrogate concepts such as the separation of powers and judicial independence when applied to the protectorate. As the trials in the French jurisdiction demonstrate, these democratic principles would inevitably be, at best, limited within the decidedly undemocratic context of colonial rule. The Cambodian indigenous jurisdiction was characterised by highly paternalistic colonial oversight coupled with opportunist references and concessions to a certain view of Khmer tradition. In this light, the separation of judicial and administrative functions is better termed a transfer of control of the Cambodian jurisdiction from the Cambodian elite to the French administration, rather than a move towards the separation of powers.

The following discussion of critical narratives regarding the Cambodian jurisdiction during the 1920s and 1930s illustrates that even loyal members of the Cambodian elite who supported many principles of French justice had a lively understanding of the structural barriers that colonial rule placed in the way of achieving them.

---

[96] Edwards, *Cambodge*, pp. 91–4.

7

Lawyers and Other Critics

When Judicial Adviser Maurice Habert told the audience at the 1925 opening of the *Palais de Justice* that henceforth Cambodian litigants enjoyed the same guarantees as French litigants, he omitted the right to legal representation. Until 1932, lawyers were forbidden in the Cambodian jurisdiction. For many years, the colonial administration in Indochina had tried to keep French lawyers on a tight rein and in particular to ban them from indigenous courts.[1] Cambodians, too, were banned from representing their compatriots on a professional basis.

Alongside the official narrative of steady progress, critical narratives contained both French and Cambodian perspectives, encapsulated in the debate over the right to legal representation and in written critiques by two lawyers: colonial *avocat défenseur* Robert Lortat-Jacob, a member of the French League for the Rights of Man and one of the outspoken members of the defence team in the "Bardez case" discussed in the previous chapter; and Cambodian Penh Nouth, a former employee of the French administration turned lawyer who, in 1940, penned a set of complaints and suggestions (*voeux*) regarding indigenous justice. Nouth's written critique provides a frank perspective of a Cambodian who worked within the system, something that is very rare in the colonial archive. Like Lortat-Jacob, Nouth questioned many of the claims that underlay the official narrative of steady progress, but his critiques went beyond those of his French colleague, questioning some fundamental underpinnings of colonial law.

---

[1] Garrigues, "Administration unique", pp. 60–4.

Legal Representation and Lortat-Jacob

Robert Lortat-Jacob was an abrasive man, who often vehemently criticised what he saw as grave injustices in both the French and Cambodian jurisdictions.[2] He had arrived in the colony as a junior magistrate in 1916 but left that position within two years to become an *avocat défenseur* in the French jurisdiction, working mainly in Cambodia.[3] He used his connections in the League for the Rights of Man and Citizen in France to voice his disgust with perceived injustices in the colony, focusing particularly on the ways in which colonial law differed from that of the metropole. According to some of his detractors, Lortat-Jacob was often motivated as much by personal interests and vendettas as by a genuine concern for the rights of France's citizens, subjects and protégés in Indochina.[4] He singled out *Résident Supérieur* Baudoin, accusing him of being corrupt, but also railed against Alexandre Varenne, the first member of the French Socialist Party to be appointed governor general of Indochina (1925–28).[5]

In 1930, Lortat-Jacob wrote an open letter to the French minister of colonies, listing a number of injustices in Indochina.[6] Regarding the French jurisdiction, he echoed some of the major grievances of the French legal fraternity in Indochina: that the role of the director of the administration of justice was an affront to judicial independence; that 1897 reforms to criminal procedure in France had not been applied in Indochina; and that the judicial role exercised by the *résidents* violated the principle of the separation of powers.

Lortat-Jacob also railed against the indigenous jurisdiction in Cambodia. He claimed the protectorate leadership would not circulate the new Cambodian codes because they wanted to conceal the fact that they blatantly transgressed French legal principles.[7] He excoriated the

---

[2] See, for example, *Le populaire d'Indochine* [The People of Indochina], 20, 25 and 27 May 1935. Copy available in the National Archives of Cambodia.

[3] Farcy and Fry, *Annuaire rétrospectif*.

[4] See various correspondence between the Résident Supérieur and the Prosecutor General during 1931, NAC RSC 23001; Résident of Prey Veng to Résident Supérieur, 21 Dec. 1928, NAC RSC 9295.

[5] Lortat-Jacob to Victor Basch, 14 Feb. 1927, Archives de La contemporaine, site de Nanterre, Fonds LDH (France), F Delta Res Box 798/83 (2121–21490); Lortat-Jacob, *Sauvons l'Indochine*.

[6] Lortat-Jacob, Open Letter to the [French] Minister of Justice, 30 Jan. 1930, CAOM GGI 65840; Lortat-Jacob, *Sauvons l'Indochine*.

[7] Lortat-Jacob, Open Letter to the [French] Minister of Justice.

Figure 7.1: Prince Monivong and Governor General Alexandre Varenne, Phnom Penh, 1926. Monivong ascended the throne in 1927 (r. 1927–41).[8]

Cambodian Penal Code of 1924 as an instrument of repression, particularly for its harsh censorship laws but also because Article 13 classified legal representation in exchange for remuneration in the indigenous Cambodian jurisdiction as an act of trafficking in influence, punishable by up to five years in prison.[9] In France, Etienne Antonelli, politician and fellow member of the League for the Rights of Man and Citizen, raised some of Lortat-Jacob's concerns on the floor of the National Assembly. Noting the prohibition on lawyers, and censorship provisions that were then the harshest in all of Indochina, Antonelli reportedly told the French parliament that some parts of the 1924 code were "shocking for our European mentality".[10]

---

[8] Source: Blog Kampot la prospère—années 60: "Sous le protectorat, visite au Cambodge du Gouverneur Général de l'indochine, Alexandre Varenne, 22 Février 1926". http://kampot.over-blog.com/2016/02/sous-le-protectorat-visite-au-cambodge-du-gouverneur-general-de-l-indochine-alexandre-varenne.html (accessed 2 October 2022). Varenne was governor general, 1925–28.

[9] Habert to Résident Supérieur, 29 Aug. 1927, NAC RSC 36097; 1924 Penal Code (Kingdom of Cambodia), art. 311, NAC Doc, Box 423.

[10] Quoted in "Les lois que l'on cache" [The Laws That They Hide], *Les Annales Coloniales* [Colonial Annals], 13 Feb. 1930, reproduced in NAC RSC 23051. Director of Political Affairs, Ministry of Colonies, to the Governor General of Indochina, 20 Jan. 1930, NAC RSC 23051.

It was possibly due to Lortat-Jacob's lobbying that in 1927 the French minister for colonies directed the governor general of Indochina to reconsider the question of legal representation in the Cambodian courts.[11] The minister's request was duly passed to the new *résident supérieur* in Cambodia, Aristide Le Fol, and to Judicial Adviser Habert. The two men were obliged to take some action, but they both opposed the proposition that litigants should have recourse to lawyers in the Cambodian jurisdiction, giving reasons that reflected the paternalistic approach to the Cambodian courts that ran throughout the official narrative. Perhaps justifiably, they feared that Cambodians could be easily led into hopeless and costly litigation by unscrupulous French lawyers touting for business.[12] They also rejected the idea of allowing Cambodian lawyers in the courts, seemingly for similar reasons. For example, Judicial Adviser Habert argued at the time that, by monitoring the courts, he and the *résidents* guaranteed the litigants' rights better than lawyers would.[13] Further, he maintained that to insert a third level between judge and litigant would be contrary to Cambodian custom. He claimed that the Cambodian judges still often mediated civil matters before they went to trial and that lawyers would impede "such a simple and paternal administration of justice".[14]

Faced with the need to respond to the minister's demands that the issue be reconsidered, but not wanting to allow lawyers in the local courts, *Résident Supérieur* Le Fol organised a series of consultations with the members of the various *Conseils de Résidence* (Councils of the Residencies), which were generally tame consultative bodies in each province chaired by the local *résident*. Each *résident* asked the hand-picked members of his council to give their opinions on two options: either to allow French lawyers to appear in the Cambodian jurisdiction; or to allow Cambodian "defenders" to represent clients in the local courts.[15] Chairing the meetings, the relevant *résident* briefed council

---

[11] Habert to Governor General, 16 Mar. 1927; and Aristide Le Fol to Governor General, Sept. 1927, NAC RSC 36097.

[12] Habert to Résident Supérieur, 29 Aug. 1927, NAC RSC 36097; Barnhart, "Violence and the Civilizing Mission", p. 482. Governor General Sarraut made a similar complaint about French lawyers in 1917, see Sarraut to Minister of Colonies, 25 Oct. 1917, CAOM GGI 65618.

[13] Habert to Résident Supérieur, 29 Aug. 1927, NAC RSC 36097.

[14] Ibid.

[15] *Conseils de Résidence* were established in 1903. Their official role was to provide feedback on the local budget. See Brocheux and Hémery, *Indochina*, app. 3, p. 386.

154   *Colonial Law Making*

members on the two options, usually making it clear that the *résident supérieur* strongly opposed both. For example, in Kompong Cham province, councillors heard that: defence lawyers would create an imbalance between the parties to cases as there were as yet no Cambodian prosecutors; lawyers would encourage pointless lengthy litigation; there was a dearth of suitably qualified Cambodians; and French lawyers, who relied on their eloquence, could not generally speak Khmer. Moreover, it would be "difficult if not impossible to subject French lawyers to the authority of a Cambodian judge".[16]

After hearing these views of the *résident supérieur*, the members of the Kompong Cham assembly "unanimously and spontaneously" rejected both propositions, crying "*pas d'avocat*" (no lawyers).[17] The councils in all the other provinces also voted against allowing French lawyers into their jurisdiction, but some defiantly voted in favour of Cambodian lawyers.[18] In Svay Rieng province, the councillors unanimously demanded "the initiation of a corps of [Cambodian] defenders, of a prosecution service and of [assistance] for those who need legal aid".[19] Several other councils were split, with significant minorities voting in favour of admitting Cambodian lawyers.[20] Ignoring these dissenting voices, Habert reported that the consultative bodies had been "unanimously won over"[21] to oppose both forms of representation.

Just five years later, however, Habert, and presumably the *résident supérieur*, had had a change of heart. The judicial adviser wrote that Cambodia's level of "economic and intellectual development"[22] now warranted a role for lawyers in its indigenous jurisdiction. Rather than any radical change in Cambodian society, this about-face was likely due to further pressure from Paris, inspired at least in part by the efforts of lawyer Lortat-Jacob and the League for the Rights of Man. Habert himself drafted what would become the 1932 Royal Ordinance Organising

---

[16] Extracts from meetings of the Indigenous *Conseils de Résidence* forwarded to Habert on 8 Aug. 1927, NAC RSC 36097.

[17] Ibid.

[18] Ibid., reports from Battambang, Pursat and Kampot.

[19] Ibid., report from Svay Rieng.

[20] Ibid., reports from Takeo, Prey Veng and Kandal.

[21] Habert to Résident Supérieur, 29 Aug. 1927, NAC RSC 36097.

[22] Habert, "Representation of litigants before the Cambodian courts", 26 Feb. 1932, NAC RSC 27999.

Lawyers and Other Critics 155

and Regulating Legal Defence Before the Cambodian Courts.[23] The ordinance sanctioned two forms of representation. Litigants could attain special dispensation to be represented by a nominated relative or co-litigator, or they could engage the commercial services of a lawyer of Cambodian nationality.[24] French lawyers were still excluded. Cambodians eligible to become lawyers came to be known as *metheavy*. To be eligible, they had either to have completed some legal training or have worked for at least six years in a senior position in the Cambodian or protectorate administrations.[25]

Like Cambodian judges, the *metheavy* had to wear a special costume that combined the French cravat with more traditional Khmer dress, including a *sampot* (sarong), another example of the way in which the physical trappings of the jurisdiction symbolised the purported fusion of Cambodian tradition and French justice, but that also distinguished Cambodian lawyers from their French counterparts.[26] The 1932 ordinance ensured that the Cambodian lawyers enjoyed neither the status nor the power of French colonial lawyers.

Most importantly, the *metheavy* could be disbarred and prosecuted if they breached any of the stringent libel and censorship laws of the 1924 Penal Code. Among these provisions, Article 304 punished "harmful criticisms" (*critique injurieuse*) of the French or Cambodian administration with up to three years in prison. Such criticisms did not have to cause harm, but could be punished if they were merely deemed to have been "conceived in a spirit of malevolence or hostility".[27] Article 305 punished displays of irreverence or disrespect towards the administration with up to a month in prison, and Article 299 gave the Council of Ministers the power to issue a Royal Ordinance outlawing any activities that were deemed contrary to public order or good morals, or were disrespectful towards the king, the royal family or the national religion. Clearly, no Cambodian lawyer would get away with impugning the protectorate authorities in the way lawyers Lortat-Jacob and Gallet had done in the

---

[23] Royal Ordinance 15 Mar. 1932, Organising and Regulating Legal Defence Before the Cambodian Courts, in *Recueil de législation et jurisprudence coloniales, 1932* [Collection of Colonial Legislation and Jurisprudence, 1932], ed. P. Dareste and G. Appert (Paris: Challamel, 1933), p. 478.

[24] Ibid., arts. 1–10.

[25] Ibid., arts. 12–13.

[26] "Inauguration du Palais de Justice cambodgien", *Echo du Cambodge*, 25 Apr. 1925, NAC RSC 11850.

[27] 1924 Penal Code (Kingdom of Cambodia), art. 304, NAC Doc, Box 423.

156   *Colonial Law Making*

Bardez trial. In the event, honest *metheavy* found it difficult to make a living from their work, particularly because Cambodian litigants could also choose to be represented by relatives or other representatives who, although they were not meant to levy charges, began actively to compete with the recognised lawyers.[28] In September 1940 one local lawyer, Penh Nouth, encapsulated many of these problems, making it clear that over seven years after they were first admitted to practice, Cambodian lawyers still found it difficult to represent their clients effectively.

The Views of Lawyer Penh Nouth

A French translation of Penh Nouth's critique exists in the colonial archives, thanks to the French security police (*sûreté*), whose agents monitored any activity they thought might be suspect.[29] Nouth had sent the document to his friend, *Oknha* Mar Tes, who was a delegate for the eastern province of Kompong Cham to the Chamber of Representatives of the People, which had previously been known as the Indigenous Consultative Assembly of Cambodia. The chamber comprised all members of the provincial *Conseils des Résidences*, the electoral college for which was considerably expanded in June 1940.[30] Penh Nouth seems to have hoped that Mar Tes might table the document at an upcoming meeting of the chamber. His friend likely never received Nouth's letter, as the *sûreté* intercepted it and forwarded it to Maxime Léger, who had replaced Habert as the judicial adviser.

     Penh Nouth may have held a personal grudge against the protectorate administration. He had worked in the office of the *résident* of Kompong Cham province for over 20 years and had resigned with some bitterness in early 1930, disgruntled that, after so many years of service, the French authorities declined to extend a period of leave without pay to allow him to work for the newly established Sino-Cambodian Society of Industry and Commerce.[31] Regardless of his personal feelings, Nouth's years in the service of the *résident* would have allowed him to

---

[28] Penh Nouth, "Exposé des voeux" [Statement of Wishes], 27 Sept. 1940, NAC RSC 23292.

[29] Tully, *France on the Mekong*, p. 289.

[30] Brocheux and Hémery, *Indochina*, app. 3, p. 385; Royal Ordinance on the Administration of the Kingdom, No. 97, Preamble & Titres III and IV, arts. 7–15, in *Bulletin Administratif du Cambodge* [Administrative Bulletin of Cambodia], 5 July 1940, pp. 1747–55.

[31] Personnel file, Penh Nouth, NAC RSC 11949.

develop a good understanding of the way the French administration operated. Judicial Adviser Léger would claim that Nouth's suggestions showed he did not understand the intricacies of Cambodian law, but Nouth implied that the French administration did not know, or ignored, what really happened in Cambodian courts. The lawyer comprehended the double standards of colonial justice, including the very limited rights guaranteed to litigants in the Cambodian jurisdiction. He explained to Mar Tes that he had already relayed his concerns many times to the Cambodian minister of justice and claimed that his views were based on extensive practical experience.

Under three themes—codes, judges and lawyers—Nouth addressed most of the issues the French lawyer Lortat-Jacob had raised over ten years earlier. For example, he echoed Lortat-Jacob's claim that Khmer-language versions of the legal codes were still not freely available. But whereas Lortat-Jacob used metropolitan French law as the benchmark of what law should be, Nouth requested more Cambodian involvement, and asserted that some French-derived laws were not suited to local conditions.

Nouth challenged the very underpinnings of colonial law in the protectorate, jurisdictions that discriminated on the basis of race. Whereas Lortat-Jacob tended to dismiss the indigenous Cambodian jurisdiction because it was run by Cambodians, and joined with the colonial judiciary in arguing for more French judges (and lawyers) to work in the Protectorate, Nouth focused on the fact that ethnic Europeans, Vietnamese and Chinese had been removed from the remit of Cambodian law. He wrote that Cambodia was governed by a sovereign whose laws should apply to all those who lived on its territory. Moreover, the ethnic Khmer majority should not have to bear the "double yoke" of being subject to one set of laws in ethnically mixed cases, which were heard in the French jurisdiction, and to Cambodian laws in the indigenous jurisdiction in cases that involved only Khmers.

Most members of the Cambodian elite outwardly supported French rule, and many became enthusiastic Francophiles, but that did not preclude a certain unease at colonial overreach, in breach of the 1863 Treaty of Protection. In the eyes of men such as Penh Nouth, ethnically based jurisdictions not only breached Cambodian sovereignty but were also highly discriminatory: firstly, because while Vietnamese who travelled to Cambodia from other parts of Indochina were subject to *Annamite* law, administered by the French courts, ethnic Khmer people in the Vietnamese territories were not subject to Cambodian law; secondly, the Cambodian jurisdiction was based on the notion that Cambodian law, and Khmer people, were less "advanced" in European eyes than

158 *Colonial Law Making*

the laws and peoples of, say, Vietnam and China. Judge Khoun Nay, who in 1927 defended the new Courts of First Instance against criticisms that they were too soft on crime, showed that he, too, was acutely aware of how the French viewed Cambodians. After defending the new courts, he wryly commented on the apparent anomaly that peaceful Cambodians were subject to harsher penalties for some crimes than were the more troublesome Vietnamese:

> Would it be that the severity [of certain penalties] . . . is more marked in this country because the evolution of the Khmer people is more lagging? That is the only possible argument, but it is necessary to concede that if western civilisation penetrates more slowly in Cambodia it is moreover the same for communist doctrines that stop at the frontier of the country. The Cambodians guard the ancestral dignity of the Khmer race deep in their hearts and are loyalists with regard to *la France Protectrice*.[32]

One French administrator also found cause to regret that the harsher laws applied to Cambodians could not also be applied to his fellow countrymen. Achille Silvestre, a long-time colonial administrator with a reputation as a particularly strict enforcer, became *résident supérieur* of Cambodia in 1932. When some of the French-language papers published in Saigon started regularly criticising the protectorate administration and its courts, Silvestre asked the prosecutor general if these papers could be banned from entering Cambodia because they were in breach of the censorship laws of the 1924 Cambodian Penal Code.[33] Although he was sympathetic to Silvestre's dilemma, the prosecutor general advised that under no circumstances could legislation of the Cambodian government apply to French-owned publications. No matter how disruptive some French journalists had become, to suggest that they should be subject to the same laws as Cambodians would have unacceptably breached the legal hierarchies of status on which French rule rested. This small incident highlights the racially based discrimination involved in the way the French worked to engineer the laws and courts of the Cambodian jurisdiction, something of which Penh Nouth, Judge Khoun Nay and other members of the local elite were acutely aware.

---

[32] Khoun Nay to Habert, 27 Oct. 1930, NAC RSC 31174.
[33] Silvestre recounted his exchange with the prosecutor general in a letter to the governor general, 26 Sept. 1934, NAC RSC 23060.

Another of Penh Nouth's demands regarding the writing of new laws was bound to raise the ire of Léger, who had drafted at least two codes since taking up the position of judicial adviser.[34] Nouth argued that without input from locals, particularly Cambodian lawyers, many aspects of the codes were and would remain meaningless.[35] By way of a rebuttal to the idea that Cambodians should be consulted on the laws of their country, Léger resorted once again to blaming tradition. He wrote that "unwittingly, I am sure, [Penh Nouth has] touched on the very foundation of Cambodian royalty: he poses a democratic principle within an absolute monarchy".[36]

Leaving aside Léger's cynical dismissal, there is other evidence to support Nouth's claim that some aspects of French-derived laws and procedures were inappropriate or impossible to implement. One recurring problem affecting the separation of judicial and administrative functions was that investigating judges in the Courts of First Instance tended to ask administrative officials in the districts and the communes to interview witnesses or investigate crimes, instead of doing it themselves.[37] This may have been due to ignorance or laziness, but, according to Judge Nginn of the Criminal Court, the court officials may also have delegated their duties because it was simply impractical for them to travel to the scene of the crime, or for witnesses to leave their village to travel to the new courts, which for most people were located much further away than the old provincial courts had been. Farmers would often have had to give up at least a day's work to attend the provincial court, and even more if required to make a deposition to officials of the Criminal Court in Phnom Penh. Judge Nginn's report appears to confirm Penh Nouth's claim that some of the new codes were unrealistic in the Cambodian context.[38]

Rather than these logistical difficulties, Nouth's main grievances concerned the numerous difficulties faced by Cambodian lawyers, which fell into two categories: the tight constraints within which lawyers were

---

[34] Léger was largely responsible for drafting the Civil and Criminal Procedure Codes of 1938; Maxime Léger, "Presentation Report", 25 Mar. 1938, NAC Doc, Box 423.

[35] Penh Nouth, "Exposé des voeux".

[36] Léger to chief of Cabinet of *Résidence Supérieur*, 27 Nov. 1940, NAC RSC 23292.

[37] President Criminal Court to the Minister of Justice, 2 June 1927, NAC RSC 18405.

[38] Report on the Criminal Session of the 4th Semester 1932, President Criminal Court to Minister of Justice, 1 Feb. 1933 (trans.), NAC RSC 18405.

160   *Colonial Law Making*

forced to practise, and their lesser status compared with French lawyers, but also, and perhaps most importantly, corruption among judges and court clerks. Regarding lawyers' status and their formal ability to act for their clients, Nouth had good reason to claim that, in criminal matters, the scales of Cambodian justice were heavily weighted in favour of the prosecution. He wrote that prohibitions against criticising public officials and the Cambodian and French administrations made it impossible for lawyers to represent clients effectively in criminal trials. Limits on the fees lawyers could charge inhibited them from making a decent living. He also resented the lower status of Cambodian lawyers compared with their French counterparts, and even demanded the right to use the French title *avocat*, rather than the Cambodian term *metheavy*. He wrote: "It is not possible to have two weights and two measures in Cambodian justice and French justice: if the French defender is called '*avocat*', the Cambodian defender should also be called '*avocat*'."[39]

As well as the formal limits on Cambodian lawyers, Penh Nouth maintained that a corrupt and incompetent judiciary actively impeded their work. He claimed that judges resented lawyers for preventing them, the judges, from dealing directly with the accused in order to solicit bribes. The judges tended to punish an accused person who engaged a lawyer by placing him or her in pre-trial detention and refusing bail. Such an order could be overturned only through appeal to the *sala krom-chout* (the *Chambre de mises en accusation*), based in the Criminal Court of Phnom Penh. This caused such delays that the accused often spent more time in pre-trial detention than the length of the maximum sentence warranted by his or her alleged offence. Those who were finally acquitted in effect served time for daring to hire a lawyer. On the other hand, if the accused was represented by a member of his or her family or a nominated representative not bound by the same rules as the lawyers, the judge and his clerk could negotiate directly with them, and grant bail in return for a certain consideration.

French lawyer Lortat-Jacob and members of the indigenous councils had made claims about corrupt practices during the 1920s.[40] Nouth's exposé differed from theirs because he detailed at least some of the ways in which corruption occurred, using French-derived legal procedure. Moreover, he claimed that corruption was the norm rather than the exception, writing that it was rare "that a judicial matter does not

---

[39] Penh Nouth, "Exposé des Voeux".
[40] Lortat-Jacob, Open Letter to the [French] Minister of Justice.

occasion an arrangement".[41] In Penh Nouth's opinion, so little had changed as a result of the reforms of the courts enacted in the 1920s that litigants still considered it was accepted practice to offer gifts to court officials, just as they had done in pre-colonial times. Nouth suggested that one way to deal with the problem might be to grant litigants exemption from prosecution if they informed on the court officials who solicited bribes. Léger dismissed the idea as contrary to the law, and it is easy to imagine that such a measure could create new opportunities for bribery. The idea, however, indicates Nouth's perception that only drastic and innovative measures could address judicial corruption.

The official narrative of the protectorate also acknowledged that corruption was a problem, blaming Cambodian judges for their stubborn attachment to "old" ways.[42] Yet the evidence suggests that, beyond changing the laws, the colonial power made minimal progress in moving beyond these "old" ways. Over the years, French officials often referred to the potential formation of a new judicial cadre whose French-inspired legal education would complete the new Cambodian jurisdiction.[43] They appear to have made only meagre investment in any attempt to attain this goal. Although the annual caseload of the Cambodian courts increased from 10,500 in 1925 to 13,142 in 1931, the number of judges declined from 86 to 78.[44] To meet the increased demand for judges, certain categories of administrative officials were authorised to transfer into the judiciary, diluting the notion of career judges recruited through competitive exams that had been envisaged in the 1922 reforms.[45] By 1943, there were still only 79 Cambodian judges.[46]

Legal education also lagged, despite claims to the contrary.[47] In 1943, Raoul Nicolas, who was then a senior judge in the French Court of Appeal in Hanoi, listed the qualifications of 67 of the 79 Cambodian

---

[41] Penh Nouth, "Exposé des voeux".

[42] Habert to Résident Supérieur, 16 June 1932, NAC RSC 14344. See also Report accusing President Hing of the Battambang *sala dambaung* of corruption, 16 June 1933, NAC RSC 35913.

[43] See, for example, Nicolas, "Le Cambodge", p. 126; Political Report, Kampot, 15 June 1923, CAOM RSC 358.

[44] Résident Supérieur to Governor General, 26 June 1932, NAC RSC 14344. It should be remembered that, in most cases, judges sat in panels of three.

[45] Royal Ordinance No. 157, 7 Dec. 1932, NAC RSC 28235.

[46] See, for example, Nicolas, "L'Organisation de la Justice Cambodgienne", p. 41.

[47] Ibid. See also curricula vitae of some senior judges in "Model for establishing details for the *Société d'Édition Anglaise*", The Europa Publications Ltd, 9 Apr. 1935, NAC RSC 37015.

162   *Colonial Law Making*

judges then in service: 1 held a law degree (*licencié*) from France; a further 6 had attended courses (not necessarily in law) at one of the *grandes écoles* in Hanoi or France; 9 had completed the *baccalauréat*; 7 had attained the first stage of the *baccalauréat*; 42 judges had graduated from the two-year course at the Cambodian School of Administration; and 2 had certificates of senior primary studies.[48]

Lack of education was certainly not the only cause of judicial corruption, as evidenced by Judicial Adviser Habert who, towards the end of his tenure, wrote that he still relied heavily on five senior judges whose "dignified private lives, serious Buddhist convictions, as well as their very modest fortunes"[49] attested to their integrity, something that could not, he said, be guaranteed in the more recent, supposedly better educated recruits. Yet, the most common qualification for judges—the two-year course at the School of Administration, where classes were often delivered by French-speaking experts—must have been hardly sufficient, even for those judges who were sincerely committed to the law and adequately fluent in French to fully understand what their teachers were saying.[50]

Internal reports confirmed that some judges indeed lacked the capacity to apply the law. For example, in 1927, Judge Nak, who was president of the Cambodian Criminal Court, found that the work of the judges in the Phnom Penh Court of First Instance was "close to perfect", but in the provinces the record was mixed. He singled out one judge from Kompong Cham who, through "manifest indolence", dismissed an accusation of murder against a "vulgar criminal, the terror of Kossotin (Koh Sautin)". There were also irregularities in Battambang and in Pursat, where the president of the court was "not brilliant".[51]

Nouth's assertion that such irregularities were the norm rather than the exception undermined the French administration's official narrative. Orderly records were an important way of ensuring transparency and compliance, so it is likely that local court officials did not always complete them honestly. The court records sat alongside other reports and official statistics used by the administration to bolster its view of

---

[48] Nicolas, "L'Organisation de la Justice Cambodgienne", p. 41. Regarding Nicolas' career, see Farcy and Fry, *Annuaire rétrospectif*. In late 1943, Nicolas became president of the Court of Appeal in Hanoi; he retired in Dec. 1947.

[49] Habert to Résident Supérieur, 16 June 1932, NAC RSC 14344.

[50] In his Presentation Report of 25 Mar. 1938 on the 1938 Code of Civil Procedure, NAC Doc, Box 423, Léger thanked the president of the French Court of Phnom Penh, who also taught civil law at the School of Administration.

[51] President of the Criminal Court to Minister of Justice, 2 June 1927, NAC RSC 18405.

progress in the Cambodian jurisdiction. Whether these additional sources reliably revealed a pattern of improvement in the activities of the courts is, to say the least, open to further investigation.

Judicial Adviser Léger's written rebuttal of Penh Nouth's claims and demands failed to address most of the substantial issues that had been raised. Instead, he claimed that Penh Nouth did not understand the laws of his own land or that he had transgressed Khmer tradition by suggesting democratic ideas, such as that Cambodians should be consulted before new laws were enacted. Léger caricatured some of Nouth's suggestions, for example for public education regarding basic legal principles. Other issues he simply brushed over, or implied that nothing could be done. He did not, of course, address Nouth's criticisms regarding the discrepancies between the French and Cambodian jurisdictions, and the allocation of legal rights based on ethnicity. Léger forwarded his response to Nouth's demands to the *résident supérieur*, and the two men agreed that all Cambodian *metheavy* should be invited to a meeting at which Léger would explain Nouth's errors.

The Other Side of the Balance Sheet

How, then, to interpret the balance sheet of the justice system under the protectorate in the years leading up to the Second World War? The reformed Cambodian jurisdiction may have delivered more consistent outcomes, and the court statistics indicate that Cambodians made good use of the court system in adjudicating their civil disputes.

However, many of the claims of the official narrative of steady progress were clearly not true, starting with the 1925 opening of the Cambodian *Palais de Justice,* where Habert said that Cambodian litigants enjoyed the same guarantees as French litigants. Even those rights that Habert mentioned—separation of judicial and administrative functions, formation of an independent judiciary, the right to appeal and supervision of courts by a French judge—were, arguably, window dressing that disguised the way in which the protectorate had harnessed the indigenous Cambodian jurisdiction to facilitate French rule.

Then there were the rights that Habert did not mention, in particular the right to legal representation, which, even when finally granted, was highly circumscribed. As a result, in penal matters the defendants' main guarantees rested with the chance that their case might come to the notice of the judicial adviser or the local *résident* who fitted oversight of a Court of First Instance among his many other duties. The harsh censorship laws inhibited the rights of Cambodians to free speech, even

164   *Colonial Law Making*

compared with the other colonised populations of Indochina, not to mention French citizens. To most Cambodians, the new state laws and courts remained mysterious and inaccessible, and, as Penh Nouth claimed, many assumed that practices of tribute- and gift-giving applied there as they always had in their interactions with power.

Leaving aside Habert's hubris, there was another element of fantasy in the legal institutions of the reformed Cambodian jurisdiction, many of which were enacted in legislation but only partially realised in practice. The codes remained unknown and foreign to most of the population, and even some judges and lawyers struggled to understand them. The separate corps of judges was established but not adequately trained. Combined with the tight restrictions placed on lawyers, there was no chance for an autonomous legal profession, or legal complex, to emerge, something that historians of other colonial legal legacies have deemed necessary if colonial rule was to lead to sustainable rule of law.[52] The official narrative of progress might suggest that Cambodian justice institutions simply needed more time to evolve under French guidance before they could become more independent and more than instruments of control. However, the counter-narrative suggests that was never the intention, and that the indigenous courts were effectively a part of the colonial administrative apparatus. This is most apparent in the workings of ethnically based jurisdictions, resented even by seemingly loyal Cambodians such as Khoun Nay, and by Penh Nouth, who appears also to have been in favour of general principles of French justice.

Whether a case of steady progress or of a constrained system of justice in the service of colonial rule, focus on the courts appears to have diminished during the Second World War. Germany's invasion of France in 1940 brought an end to the French Third Republic, whose representatives had governed Indochina, including Cambodia, for over 60 years. The Free French government in exile, led by Charles de Gaulle, opposed the Vichy regime, but the majority of French colonies, including Indochina, formally sided with Vichy. Some officials chose to support de Gaulle and, in Indochina, were confined in concentration camps.[53]

---

[52] Dezalay and Garth, *Asian Legal Revivals*; Halliday and Karpik, "Political Liberalism in the British Post-Colony", pp. 3–55.

[53] Romerio, *Le Métier de magistrat*, pp. 43–4; see also Tully's mention of concentration camps where suspect Cambodians and Vietnamese were interred. *France on the Mekong*, p. 365.

The Vichy regime took control of Indochina in late 1940 and replaced what historian Eric Jennings calls the Third Republic's "pro forma republicanism" with a selective mix of monarchism, ethnic chauvinism and conservative social mobilisation.[54] In Cambodia, however, the Third Republic's versions of the colonial civilising mission and of indirect rule through protectorates had laid the basis for Vichy rule, which promoted the young King Sihanouk and gave him a popular public role that the French had denied to Kings Sisowath and Monivong.

The main legal developments during and immediately following the war concerned the nature and constitution of the Cambodian state. Cambodian nationalism became more public and more important, influenced by a range of ideologies. After the war, the French allied with the Francophile King Norodom Sihanouk against more radical, potentially republican or communist tendencies. They reinforced the notion that Cambodia and Cambodians were irrevocably destined to be ruled by some form of paternalistic, or authoritarian, monarchism. In doing so, they were continuing the theme on which the protectorate had operated and that had been refined under Vichy. The French used royal power to authorise and legitimise legal reforms, and in the process laid the foundations for a state centred on the king. He was the source of law, and also the link between the secular and the religious. The legal institutions, and the ethos of royal power established under the protectorate, would prove a convenient foundation for Sihanouk's own forms of semi-benign personalised rule.

---

[54] Eric T. Jennings, *Vichy in the Tropics: Pétain's National Revolution in Madagascar, Guadeloupe, and Indochina, 1940–1944* (New York: Stanford University Press, 2001), p. 31.

8

Constitutions and Independence

On 19 February 1955, King Norodom Sihanouk summoned members of the Cambodian government, the diplomatic corps, advisers, and members of the international commission overseeing the 1954 Geneva Accords to a three-hour audience in which he outlined his plans to modify Cambodia's 1947 constitution.[1] Sihanouk blamed many of his country's problems on political parties and their representatives, who, once elected, failed to listen to the people or respond to their needs. He proposed more direct ties between the king—himself—and the common people, who, he said, loved him. The National Assembly, or parliament, should be replaced, Sihanouk thought, by a body of locally elected commune chiefs, supplemented by provincial and national popular assemblies.[2] Although in private at least one diplomat suspected Sihanouk's model would suit Cambodia, the audience did not react favourably.[3] Facing opposition, the king eventually abdicated the

---

[1] The 1954 Geneva Accords resulted from a conference held in July of that year to discuss peace arrangements in the Korean peninsula and to try to bring an end to conflict in the French colony of Indochina. The Vietnamese military victory over the French at Dien Bien Phu occurred in May 1954. See Kau Sokhon, "Introduction", in Norodom Sihanouk, "Étude Corrective de la Constitution Accordée par SM le Roi du Cambodge en 1947" [Corrective Study of the Constitution Granted by His Majesty the King of Cambodia in 1947], *France-Asie: revue mensuelle de culture et de synthèse Franco-Asiatique* [France-Asia: Monthly Review of Culture and of Franco-Asiatic Synthesis] 11, 108 (May 1955): 654–63; Michael Vickery, "Looking Back at Cambodia", *Westerly* 4 (1976): 14–28.

[2] Kau, "Introduction", p. 654.

[3] Regarding the British representative's views, see David P. Chandler, *The Tragedy of Cambodian History: Politics, War and Revolution since 1945* (Bangkok: Silkworm

throne in favour of his father and assumed the title of *Samdech Upayuvareach* ("the prince who has been the king"), in order to play an active role in government. With this dramatic gesture, he could intervene in Cambodian politics but retain his royal cachet.[4]

Whereas this story has so far focused on the structural and contingent transactions that made the common codes and courts under the protectorate, this chapter turns towards constitutional law in the years leading up to and immediately following Cambodia's independence from France in 1953–54. National and international politics, and Sihanouk's personal ambitions, rightly dominate histories of this time. The fate of the country's first constitution, adopted by an assembly of democratically elected Cambodians six years before independence, was inextricably linked with domestic political power struggles. The differences over how to interpret, and then to change, the constitution had their roots in the legal and ideological legacies of the protectorate. France's claim that its protection brought civilising influences to Cambodia while also protecting tradition had given rise to an ideology in which religion, the crown, and the state remained entwined. Although the country's legal codes appeared secular, the ideology of the protectorate asserted that the law drew its authority from a semi-divine monarch, the source of law and the symbol of the nation. The dependent judicial system established under the protectorate contributed to a legacy of royal/colonial paternalism and was bound to impede future efforts to enforce a constitutional separation between executive, legislative and judicial powers.

This chapter follows the evolution of colonial policy and of constitutional law, initially under the French Vichy regime, then during the short-lived independent Kingdom of Kampuchea, and finally during the return to French rule after the Second World War. A 1941 law adopted under Vichy rule created an embryonic constitution for Cambodia within the protectorate, promoting a conservative form of royal power. In 1947, a series of political manoeuvres resulted in a constitution that purported to establish a parliamentary democracy, contrary to the wishes of the colonial authorities and conservative royalist elites. From 1947 until independence in 1953, the French and the young King Sihanouk's closest advisers worked to undermine the democratically elected legislature, subverting the fledgling constitution.

Books, 1991), p. 77, quoting British Public Records Office, Foreign Office 371/117124, British Legation, Phnom Penh's 109, 20 Mar. 1955.

[4] See, for example, Chandler, *Tragedy*, pp. 77–80.

168 *Colonial Law Making*

After independence Sihanouk adapted the colonial-era ethos of royal authority to place himself in charge of the constitution, experimenting with forms of popular democracy under his direct control. Although not entirely uncritical, several contemporary eminent French legal scholars wrote theoretical justifications for Sihanouk's actions, lending them some constitutional legitimacy.[5] These scholars accepted and perpetuated the notion that Cambodian tradition and culture suited royal absolutism rather than parliamentary democracy. Sihanouk manipulated and transgressed the constitution to suit his political project. In some respects, his approach resembled France's use of the 1863 Treaty of Protection, which the French used to justify their presence but the terms of which they frequently transgressed. The 1947 constitution played an analogous role for Sihanouk: he subverted and rewrote it, but did not annul the constitution, which remained the founding document of his nation.

The second part of this chapter returns briefly to the evolution of broader legal institutions, tracing their trajectory after independence. Cambodia retained close ties with France in these years, and there was no revolutionary rupture or clean slate on which to create new laws and systems of governance. As a result, the basic structures of laws and courts created for the Cambodian jurisdiction under the protectorate remained in place. Any potential that may have existed under the provisions of the 1947 constitution to support the development of independent legal institutions failed under the weight of both domestic political manoeuvring and the dependent, rudimentary legal institutions left in place by the protectorate.

Constitutional Competitions

Between 1940 and 1955, when King Sihanouk abdicated the throne in order to play an active role in politics, Cambodians lived through four phases of political control, each of which reflected broader regional and global events. The first phase began in July 1940, when Indochina came under control of the pro-fascist Vichy regime. During the second phase, from March to August 1945, Cambodia was nominally independent under Japanese tutelage. Then, from late 1945 until 1953, France's postwar Fourth Republic re-established a form of protectorate in the wake

---

[5] For example, Gour, *Institutions Constitutionnelles*; Imbert, *Histoire des institutions khmères*.

of the Second World War. The final phase started in 1953, when Cambodia became effectively independent.[6] The politics of each of these four periods influenced constitutional law and contributed to an ethos of conservative monarchism that provided the foundations for Sihanouk's own approach to the 1947 constitution.

After signing an armistice with Germany, whose troops had occupied Paris in 1940, France's Marshal Pétain established a pro-fascist puppet regime in the city of Vichy, in unoccupied southern France. The Vichy administration assumed control of Indochina and of many other French colonies until France was liberated from German occupation in 1944. In late July 1940, Pétain appointed Admiral Jean Decoux to the position of governor general of Indochina, replacing General Raoul Catroux. Both deliberately and inadvertently, Vichy's policies in Cambodia nourished an already emerging notion of Cambodian national identity that linked Khmer ethnicity with a romanticised, arguably ahistorical view of Khmer tradition. Penny Edwards describes this ethos of "Khmerness" as a "bricolage of ideas and influences that had crystallized around the monuments of Angkor".[7]

Decoux promoted a scheme for a federation of Indochinese monarchs united under French tutelage. In Cambodia, Decoux intensified previous efforts by the French to base their rule on claims to be protecting Khmer monarchical traditions, and in 1941 he selected the 19-year-old Prince Norodom Sihanouk to succeed King Monivong. The young king became the poster boy for Decoux's efforts to rally local populations to the banner of their respective monarchs. Sihanouk was more glamorous and appeared more compliant than both the older King Sisavang Vong of Luang Prabang, in neighbouring Laos, and Emperor Bao Dai at Hue in Vietnam, who was wary of being seen as a French puppet.[8] Decoux also opened up more low- and middle-level administrative positions for Cambodians and established a patriotic national youth organisation, the

---

[6] The following account draws on general histories of Cambodia and Indochina during this period. On Cambodia: Tully, *France on the Mekong*, pp. 437–99; Chandler, *Tragedy*, pp. 1–121; Milton E. Osborne, *Sihanouk, Prince of Light, Prince of Darkness* (Chiang Mai: Silkworm Books, 1994), pp. 1–122; Michael Vickery, "Looking Back at Cambodia", p. 14; Kiernan, *How Pol Pot Came to Power*, pp. 41–134. On Indochina: Goscha, *Modern History of Vietnam*, pp. 194–268; Kiernan, *Việt Nam*, pp. 376–91; Martin Stuart-Fox, *A History of Laos* (Cambridge: Cambridge University Press, 1997), pp. 59–134.

[7] Edwards, *Cambodge*, p. 242.

[8] Goscha, *Modern History of Vietnam*, pp. 266–7.

170 *Colonial Law Making*

Yuvan, which provided many young people with their first experience of mass organisation.[9]

Decoux had Sihanouk take a more active public role than had been allowed his predecessors under the protectorate. The young king became head of the Yuvan and travelled the country, meeting with adoring crowds. Such an atmosphere of ethnic pride and royalist propaganda must have been a heady coming of political age for the young man fresh out of high-school, whom Decoux hailed as a living symbol of the ancient glories of Angkor.[10] In these conditions, Sihanouk came to understand the potential power of direct contact with his subjects and no doubt imbibed some sense of divine right.[11]

Governor General Decoux's vision of an Indochinese federation included a "modernising" French overlay, which appeared to contradict his efforts to foster ethnic pride and respect for cultural tradition in the separate regions of Indochina. He sparked openly anti-French demonstrations in Cambodia when his administration tried to replace the Khmer script with the roman alphabet and the Khmer Buddhist calendar with the Julian calendar.[12] Decoux had also planned to impose uniform laws across Indochina, but was deposed before they could be implemented.[13] These new codes would have applied to all ethnicities and would likely have replaced the Cambodian codes and jurisdictions. If it had been implemented, this reform may also have met strong opposition in Cambodia as it would have overturned the fiction—convenient to both the colonial power and to the royal and religious elites—that the Cambodian codes had modernised rather than largely replaced the pre-colonial sacred legal texts.

An Indochinese federation held little appeal to any in the Cambodian elite who feared their country was to be subsumed within a larger Vietnamese-dominated polity. Contrary to his intentions, Decoux's policies nurtured already nascent nationalist sentiments and

---

[9] On the significance of the Vichy regime for Cambodia, see Tully, *France on the Mekong*, pp. 363–80; Chandler, *History*, pp. 194–206; Edwards, *Cambodge*, pp. 231–41.

[10] Edwards, *Cambodge*, p. 232.

[11] Osborne, *Sihanouk*, p. 33.

[12] Tully, *France on the Mekong*, pp. 372–7; Kiernan, *How Pol Pot Came to Power*, pp. 42–5; Edwards, *Cambodge*, pp. 233–8.

[13] Admiral Decoux, *À la barre de l'Indochine: Histoire de mon Gouvernement Général 1940–1945* [At the Helm of Indochina: History of My Government-General 1940–1945] (Paris: Soukha, 2013. First published Librairie Plon, 1949), pp. 336–7.

political divisions among the Cambodian elite. On the one hand, a conservative strain of nationalism benefited from Decoux's promotion of the monarchy. At the same time, various less ardently monarchist trends had begun to take political form among often younger, educated layers of society. Different visions of the way the nation should be constituted and governed began to emerge. Over the coming years, political divisions would deepen and lead to conflict, including over the writing of the first national constitution in 1947.

Constitutions

One of the last acts of the French Third Republic in Cambodia had been a new law which was in effect a proto-constitution. It laid the foundations for a monarchical system of government, albeit ultimately under French control. In July 1940, just days before Decoux replaced him, Governor General Catroux together with King Monivong promulgated Kram No. 1 on the Administration of Cambodia. This new law departed in several ways from previous legislation under the protectorate. First, rather than taking the French administration as its starting point, Kram No. 1 outlined a rudimentary Cambodian system of governance, although still under French supervision. The new law defined the respective powers of the king, the Council of Ministers, individual ministers, and provincial chiefs to issue certain laws, regulations and directives, many of which had Khmer titles that are still used today.[14]

French constitutional-law expert Claude-Gilles Gour called Kram No. 1 a constitutional reform.[15] While the governor general of Indochina had previously had the power to enact certain laws for all the countries in the colony, from 1940 his laws would have to be reissued as *kram* before becoming law in Cambodia.[16] Nonetheless, Kram No. 1 still limited the role of the monarch, largely along the lines of the

---

[14] Below *kram* (laws), which were issued by the king, came *kret*, decrees issued directly by the king or by the Council of Ministers with approval of the king. The Council of Ministers could issue lesser regulations, called *samrach*, without the king's signature as long as they had the approval of the French *résident supérieur*. Individual ministers could issue *prakas*, and provincial regulations became known as *deka*. See Kram No. 1 on the Administration of Cambodia, 1940, art. 2.

[15] Gour, *Institutions Constitutionnelles*, p. 35. The *kram* is available in *Bulletin administratif du Cambodge*, 5 Aug. 1940, p. 1609.

[16] Ibid., p. 36.

172   *Colonial Law Making*

dispensation King Norodom had conceded in 1897.[17] Governor General Catroux and King Monivong had envisaged Kram No. 1 as part of a mildly liberalising package of reforms that also included slightly more representative indigenous assemblies.[18] Decoux quickly abandoned these, but retained Kram No. 1, which would have meshed with his policy to promote Indochina as a federation of monarchies under French tutelage. The new *kram*'s real potential as a royalist constitution became apparent in March 1945, when occupying Japanese forces temporarily ousted the French administration.

Japanese troops had been stationed in Indochina since 1940. Japan was allied with Germany in the Second World War, and by extension with the collaborationist French Vichy regime. Hence, instead of replacing the colonial apparatus as it did in British-ruled Malaya and the Dutch East Indies, Japan collaborated, albeit uneasily, with Vichy's representatives in Indochina. This coexistence ended soon after the Vichy regime collapsed in 1944. On 9 March 1945, Japanese troops turned on the French across Indochina and encouraged the monarchs of Laos, Vietnam and Cambodia to declare independence, although the region remained under Japanese control.[19]

King Sihanouk proclaimed the independent Kingdom of Kampuchea. He announced that he had taken over the functions of the *résident supérieur* and reissued Kram No. 1, minus all references to the French.[20] For several months Sihanouk also became prime minister, which meant that, formally, he wielded a great amount of power. However, he appears mainly to have remained a figurehead and in early August he was replaced as prime minister by Son Ngoc Thanh, following a semi-coup mounted by seven young Cambodians.[21] As far as they still operated at this time, the Cambodian courts had their first experience

---

[17] An annex to the *kram* slightly expanded on the 1897 powers. Acting with the agreement of the *résident supérieur*, the monarch could grant reprieve for the death penalty and reduce prison sentences; grant or revoke Cambodian nationality; and nominate members of the Council of Ministers.

[18] Brocheux and Hémery, *Indochina*, app. 3, p. 386.

[19] Emperor Bao Dai proclaimed the independent Empire of Vietnam. In Laos, after King Sisavong and Crown Prince Svangvatthana had remained loyal to France, the Japanese appointed Prince Phetxarat as Prime Minister of Luang Prabang. See Stuart-Fox, *History of Laos*, pp. 56–7.

[20] Gour, *Institutions Constitutionnelles*, pp. 40–1; Philippe Preschez, *Essai sur la Démocratie au Cambodge* [Essay on Democracy in Cambodia] (Paris: FNSP, Centre D'Etude des Relations Internationales, 1961), p. 13.

[21] Osborne, *Sihanouk*, pp. 42–5; Kiernan, *How Pol Pot Came to Power*, pp. 49–51.

of working without oversight from the French *résidents* and judicial adviser. Cambodian judges presided in what had been the French jurisdiction, hearing cases against ethnic Vietnamese and Chinese inhabitants.[22]

The new regime lasted only six months, until Japan surrendered in August 1945 and the French quickly reclaimed their colony. However, the brief interlude of "independence" had allowed latent divisions among the Cambodian elite to come into play. In the weeks before the Japanese surrender, when the pro-Japanese nationalist, Son Ngoc Thanh, seized the prime ministership he pledged his loyalty to the monarchy and to the Buddhist religion, but Sihanouk mistrusted and disliked Thanh who had replaced him as prime minister and who was very popular with ordinary people.[23] In October 1945, the French arrested and exiled Thanh with the help of the British colonel Edward Murray, who had been sent to oversee the Japanese surrender.[24] Thanh's arrest was therefore the beginning of a period of collaboration between the returned French colonial administration and the conservative royalist elites, particularly the king's inner circle of advisers, who worked together to combat pro-independence and potentially republican currents.

France's postwar colonial policy had been determined at the 1944 Brazzaville conference in the then French Congo. With no Indochinese representatives present, Charles de Gaulle's wartime French government in exile determined the colony would indeed become an Indochinese federation, consisting of the previous five regions of Tonkin, Annam, Cochin China, Laos and Cambodia. The federation was to be part of a French Union that included France plus its colonies.[25]

Cambodians did not universally welcome the French return, although the transition was negotiated more quickly and peacefully than in Laos and Vietnam. In Laos, the French had to dislodge the government of the Lao Issara, which had taken control after the Japanese

---

[22] Léger, "L'organisation judiciaire du Cambodge", pp. 47–71, 70.

[23] Tully, *France on the Mekong*, pp. 388–96; Kiernan, *How Pol Pot Came to Power*, pp. 49–50.

[24] David Chandler and Anthony Barnett, *The Uncrowned King of Cambodia: The Life of Colonel E.D. (Moke) Murray, DSO, OBE, 1910–2002* (forthcoming), Ch. 9. Under the Treaty of Potsdam, the Chinese received the Japanese surrender north of the 16th parallel, and the British to the south; see Stuart-Fox, *History of Laos*, p. 59.

[25] Goscha, *Modern History of Vietnam*, p. 213. French Constitution of 1946, arts. 66–72.

174 *Colonial Law Making*

departure. In Vietnam, by the end of 1946, France was at war with the government of the Democratic Republic of Vietnam led by Ho Chi Minh and the Viet Minh, the communist-dominated national front.[26]

In Cambodia Prince Sisowath Monireth, King Sihanouk's maternal uncle, who became prime minister after Son Ngoc Thanh was arrested, cautiously welcomed the French return to Cambodia as a bulwark against the more radical, potentially republican, nationalists. He negotiated an accord which granted Cambodia a degree of internal self-government, but that reinstated French control.[27] Although the French returned to play a role similar in many respects to the pre-war protectorate, events of the Second World War had diminished their standing.[28] Moreover, in some parts of the country, Cambodian nationalists of differing political orientation were already waging uncoordinated guerrilla resistance.[29]

A Franco-Cambodian Accord agreed in January 1946, declared Cambodia to be an associated state within the French Union. The Accord established a structure of colonial control similar in many ways to that outlined in Kram No. 1 of 1940, but it granted Cambodians some aspects of (supervised) self-government, which were to become increasingly important over the coming years.[30] Even so, the 1863 Treaty of Protection was not formally repealed until 1949.

In Phnom Penh, a French *commissaire de la république* (Commissioner of the Republic), representing both France and the new Indochinese federation replaced the *résident supérieur*. The *commissaire* acted as adviser (*conseiller*) to the king (Accord, Part A. para. 1: 1°, 2°). He had the power to demand an audience with the king, and he co-signed all legislation and related regulations (Accord Part A. para. 2: 2°). Six regional *conseillers* replaced the 14 provincial *résidents* of the pre-Second World War protectorate (Accord Part C. para 1.). The accord recognised seven

---

[26] Stuart-Fox, *History of Laos*, pp. 59–66; Goscha, *Modern History of Vietnam*, pp. 231–2.

[27] Tully, *France on the Mekong*, p. 403.

[28] Ibid., p. 425.

[29] See John Tully's analysis of the Khmer Issarak Insurrection in Tully, *France on the Mekong*, pp. 457–71; see also Osborne, *Sihanouk*, pp. 52–3; Kiernan, *How Pol Pot Came to Power*, pp. 65–78.

[30] "Accord setting out the provisional modus vivendi between France and Cambodia", *Bulletin administratif du Cambodge*, 7 Jan. 1946, p. 23.

Cambodian ministries, whereas up until 1940 there had only been five.[31] Moreover, working alongside French advisers, the ministers were actually responsible for important aspects of the national administration, including health, education and the Cambodian police (Accord Part D).

In the area of justice administration, old methods of supervision continued, but the Cambodian courts had a little more autonomy than in 1940. Maxime Léger, who had been the pre-war judicial adviser, took up a similar role as adviser to the Ministry of Justice. Léger claimed his influence was significantly less than it had been under the old protectorate. Instead of supervising the courts, he merely "stated his opinion" on matters that came before the *sala vinichhay* (Court of Annulment).[32] However, it would have been difficult, to say the least, for the minister and the judges to ignore his advice.[33] Outside Phnom Penh, the French regional advisers "counselled" the judges of the *sala dambaung* (Courts of First Instance), forwarding reports and recommendations to the Cambodian minister of justice, the *commissaire*, and, no doubt, to Léger.[34]

The 1947 Constitution

As part of the newly re-negotiated French presence, and in order to satisfy international support for decolonisation, a joint Franco-Cambodian drafting commission began work on a national constitution in November 1945.[35] The French-dominated commission drafted a very conservative constitution that reflected the paternalism of the protectorate and of conservative elements in the Cambodian elite, particularly the king's uncle, Prince Monireth. The commission's draft placed ultimate legislative and executive powers in the hands of the king. There were to be indirect elections, via commune and provincial councils, to a largely

---

[31] The seven ministries were: Interior and National Defence; National Education and Propaganda; Justice; Health, Public Works and Communications; Cults and Fine Arts; National Economy; Finances.

[32] Maxime Léger, "Rapport: Sur l'organisation actuelle de Juridictions nationales du Cambodge" [Report on the Current Organisation of the National Courts of Cambodia], *Journal judiciaire de l'Indochine française* [Judicial Journal of French Indochina] 10 (1947): 69–80, see 78.

[33] Kanthoul, *Mémoires*, p. 105.

[34] Accord setting out the provisional modus vivendi between France and Cambodia, Part C. *Bulletin administratif du Cambodge*, 7 Jan. 1946, p. 23.

[35] Gour, *Institutions Constitutionnelles*, pp. 43–4.

176   *Colonial Law Making*

advisory national assembly. Limited male suffrage was to apply until such time as the "evolution of the country" permitted a more generous franchise.[36] The draft captured the paternalistic authoritarianism and the view of Khmer tradition that had underpinned the protectorate.[37]

The French, Prince Monireth and other members of the royal inner circle no doubt anticipated that King Sihanouk would assent to the draft constitution without demur. However, perhaps more in touch with the political mood of his subjects, Sihanouk demanded revisions to the draft and insisted it should first be freely considered by a provisional national assembly.[38] In doing so, he ignited a flame that quickly burned out of control. Sihanouk initially proclaimed that the provisional assembly should be elected by members of the commune councils.[39] However, he also amended the draft constitution to allow universal male suffrage, and, by some means, the electoral law for the provisional assembly included this right. Universal male suffrage opened the way for a range of other liberalising reforms. Ahead of the elections for the provisional assembly, Sihanouk issued a series of *kram* granting his subjects unprecedented rights, including freedom of assembly, of speech and of organisation, and thus the right to form political parties.[40]

In September 1946, the newly formed Democrat Party, led by the capable politician Prince Yuthevong, won 50 of the 67 seats in the provisional assembly. With such an overwhelming mandate, the Democrats transformed what had been intended as a pro-forma consultative body into a constituent assembly, despite Sihanouk's reported efforts

---

[36] Gour, *Institutions Constitutionnelles*, p. 45.

[37] Ibid., p. 44, quoting from the doctoral thesis of Jean Larché, "L'evolution du statut du Cambodge" [The Evolution of the Status of Cambodia] (University of Paris, 1948), no page reference given.

[38] Ibid., p. 47.

[39] Royal proclamation of 13 April 1946, quoted in Gour, *Institutions Constitutionnelles*, p. 47. Preschez claims that in this proclamation Sihanouk stated his intention to give his people the most democratic rules possible, see Preschez, *Essai sur la Démocratie*, p. 16.

[40] Commentators are unclear as to whether universal male suffrage was first inserted into the draft constitution or into the 31 May law on the election of the provisional assembly. Gour claims the 31 May law was the first mention of universal male suffrage and that the amendment to the constitution flowed from there, see Gour, *Institutions Constitutionnelles*, pp. 46–8. Osborne states that Sihanouk had already insisted, probably with French support, on amending the draft constitution to allow for universal male suffrage; see Osborne, *Sihanouk*, pp. 50–1.

to prevent them.[41] Instead of dutifully endorsing the draft constitution, the deputies wrote a completely new one. French legal scholar Claude-Gilles Gour likened these events to those of the French Revolution when the *États Généraux* (Estates General) of 1789 proclaimed itself a constituent assembly.[42] Chandler characterises the confrontation between the newcomers in the Democrats and the old-time royal elites as "unseemly" rather than revolutionary.[43] He is correct to the extent that Prince Yuthevong and his colleagues stressed their loyalty to the king. They made a show of meeting with Sihanouk to gain his consent to the new constitution, ensuring it would appear as "a freely made grant of the king".[44] Nevertheless, the Democrats had challenged the ideological foundations of French rule and the theory of royal power it had helped to perpetuate.

Over the years leading up to independence, the 1947 constitution became a weapon in the political confrontation between the progressive Cambodian elites on one hand, and the royalist conservatives and the French on the other. The constitution drew extensively on that of France's postwar 1946 Fourth Republic, putting in place a radical form of parliamentarism.[45] In France, this engendered unstable government. In Cambodia, where a fledgling and inexperienced government was still subject to colonial rule, it was doomed to fail.

The way in which the Cambodian constitution distributed legislative and executive powers seemed designed to create conflict between the National Assembly and the king. Members of the assembly had final say over appointing the cabinet, or Council of Ministers (arts. 79–80), which it could dissolve through a vote of no confidence (arts. 84–5). The assembly also had the right to call individual ministers to account for the way they handled their portfolio (art. 83). On the other side, the king could dissolve the National Assembly on the proposal of the Council of Ministers (art. 38). The king also had the power to designate the prime minister, subject to the National Assembly's approval (art. 39). He could delay promulgating legislation enacted by the assembly by demanding that the legislators reconsider draft laws (art. 36).

---

[41] Gour, *Institutions Constitutionnelles*, p. 49; Preschez, *Essai sur la Démocratie*, p. 22.

[42] Gour, *Institutions Constitutionnelles*, p. 49.

[43] Chandler, *Tragedy*, p. 29.

[44] Gour, *Institutions Constitutionnelles*, p. 49.

[45] For a summary of the fall of the Fourth Republic, see Sowerwine, *France since 1870*, pp. 281–91.

The Democrat-controlled assembly had attempted to impose a constitutional monarchy in which the king reigned but did not rule. This form of government requires a fine balance between the throne and the state which can be difficult to maintain even in the most stable and oldest of constitutional monarchies.[46] After independence, when Sihanouk began to chafe at his lack of political power, he argued that because the constitution had been granted by the king, as stated in its preamble, he, the king, therefore also had the right to change it.[47] These tensions came to a head in the events known as the 1952 coup.

From the time the new constitution became law in 1947, the colonial administration began to undermine the National Assembly and the Democrat-led government. Cambodian ministers were still subject to French advisers, many of whom delighted in exploiting their ministers' relative inexperience, for example, by entangling them in petty procedural issues.[48] Moreover, the national economy had been devastated by the Second World War, and large sections of the population were experiencing severe hardship. By 1948 the Cambodian government "faced almost insurmountable problems of inflation, shortage of revenue, growing insurgency, and lawlessness, all exacerbated by foot-dragging from the colonial administration".[49] Sihanouk, too, continued to mistrust the Democrats. In 1949 he took advantage of disunity within the party to dissolve the National Assembly. He installed a new government with his ally, Yem Sambaur, as prime minister. That same year delegates to the French Union Assembly voted for more autonomy for Vietnam and Cambodia. As a result, the French National Assembly repealed the 1863 Treaty of Protection and granted the Cambodian government control of many areas of the administration. Only the economy, finance, police and the justice system remained with the French.[50] The Democrat-led government therefore had considerable power which perhaps made Sihanouk and the French administration more determined to assert their power.

---

[46] See, for example: Stephen Sedley, "Knife, Stone, Paper", *London Review of Books* (1 July 2021): 17–19; Jenny Hocking, *The Palace Letters: The Queen, the Governor-General, and the Plot to Dismiss Gough Whitlam* (Melbourne: Scribe, 2020).

[47] Preschez, *Essai sur la Démocratie*, pp. 48–9.

[48] Kanthoul, *Mémoires*, pp. 105–6.

[49] Chandler, *Tragedy*, p. 39.

[50] Ibid., pp. 42–57.

Despite the best efforts of the king and the French, elections in 1951 again delivered an overwhelming majority to the Democrats. Until then, Sihanouk had more or less abided by the constitution, but he grew increasingly suspicious of certain Democrat leaders, particularly after the return from exile of the very popular Son Ngoc Thanh in 1951. After his short term as prime minister in the last days of the Japanese-dominated Khmer Republic, Thanh had been arrested and exiled by the French in late 1945. In 1951 he returned to Phnom Penh greeted by enthusiastic crowds. Both the French and Sihanouk resented Thanh's popularity and his nationalist rhetoric. The French in particular insisted that Thanh was linked to the Democrats, who had indeed offered him a cabinet position, which Thanh had refused. In March 1952, Thanh and a few supporters left Phnom Penh to try to unite guerrilla forces fighting for independence from the French.[51] Sihanouk and the French used Thanh's departure for the *maquis*, and subsequent student demonstrations around the country, to accuse the Democrats of fomenting "insecurity and treason".[52]

On 15 June 1952, a new contingent of French troops arrived unannounced in Phnom Penh and surrounded the National Assembly building, while French tanks appeared along major thoroughfares of the capital.[53] It cannot have been a coincidence that, on the same day, Sihanouk dismissed the Democrat-led Council of Ministers and announced that he intended to head an interim government himself.[54] Justifying this move, Sihanouk cited his residual powers in the constitution, but he also reportedly told an American diplomat that he was "not only the giver of the constitution, but [also] the giver of elections".[55] Faced with the presence of French troops, and unwilling to directly defy the king, National Assembly President Sonn Sann "respectfully" informed the monarch that, although his actions appeared unconstitutional, the parliament would vote to endorse them because "all powers emanate from the king".[56] Ironically, by assisting the king to dissolve the National

---

[51] This summary is based on David Chandler's detailed account, see Chandler, *Tragedy*, pp. 59–63.

[52] Chandler, *Tragedy*, p. 61, note 34. Chandler is quoting a despatch to the British legation in Saigon on 18 Apr. 1952. The despatch attributes these words to General Louis Dio, commander of the French forces stationed in Cambodia.

[53] Chandler, *Tragedy*, p. 63; Tully, *France on the Mekong*, p. 449.

[54] Preschez, *Essai sur la Démocratie*, p. 49.

[55] Chandler, *Tragedy*, p. 64, quoting James Guillion, US chargé in Saigon.

[56] Preschez, *Essai sur la Démocratie*, p. 49.

180   *Colonial Law Making*

Assembly and to sideline the Democrats, the French paved the way for Sihanouk to champion Cambodian independence from France.

Soon after his 1952 coup, Sihanouk announced that, over the coming three years, he intended to launch a crusade for independence, end the armed insurrections that were disrupting rural life, implement social and economic reforms and clean up corruption.[57] He could claim to have achieved one of those goals when, in 1953, the French agreed to end their colonial rule in both Cambodia and Laos.[58] Ignoring other factors—such as France's preoccupation with their doomed war in Vietnam—Sihanouk triumphantly claimed credit for the French withdrawal and presented himself thereafter as the father of independence. The last French troops withdrew from Cambodia after the 1954 Geneva Conference on the Problem of Restoring Peace in Indo-China. Out of this conference came the Geneva Accords, which committed Cambodia to hold internationally supervised general elections in 1955.[59] Unwilling to risk another electoral victory for the Democrats, Sihanouk set about preparing for an election that he could control. He first called a tightly managed plebiscite in which citizens voted for or against his crusade for independence.

Boosted by the predictably favourable results, the king then summoned Phnom Penh's notables on 19 February to listen to his proposals for constitutional reform. He presented his audience with a vision of "popular democracy" that would "integrate the good sense, the wisdom, the foresight and the spirit of justice of the Khmer People", under his guidance.[60] Sihanouk had adapted notions of the protectorate whereby a benevolent power would wisely steer Cambodia's "little people" towards modernity and development.[61] He blamed members of political parties in the National Assembly for creating national disunity and for failing to properly represent the needs of their constituents. Sihanouk proposed to replace, or supplement, the National Assembly with a less direct form of representation.

---

[57] Chandler, *Tragedy*, pp. 67–72; Tully, *France on the Mekong*, pp. 475–84.
[58] Stuart-Fox, *History of Laos*, p. 59.
[59] Acte final de la conférence de Genève et déclarations annexes (21 juillet 1954) [Final Declaration of the Geneva Conference and Annex Declarations (21 July 1954)]. www.cvce.eu/obj/acte_final_de_la_conference_de_geneve_et_declarations _annexes_21_juillet_1954-fr-9ccd81ff-64d7-4a46-a71e-590f7e50579e.html (accessed 27 July 2023).
[60] Kau, "Introduction", p. 659.
[61] Chandler, *Tragedy*, p. 77.

The *Sangkum Reastre Niyum* and the 1947 Constitution

When the local elites and the diplomatic community reacted unfavourably to his proposed reforms, Sihanouk abdicated the throne in favour of his father, Suramarit. As Prince Sihanouk with the title *Samdech Upayuvareach* (the prince who has been the king), he was free to take an active role in politics while retaining his high royal status. Although many considered him mercurial and unpredictable, Sihanouk appears to have followed a calculated twofold political strategy after independence: consolidating his hold on political power while attempting to maintain a patina of constitutionality.

In the political arena, Sihanouk established the Sangkum Reastre Niyum (roughly translated: People's Socialist Community), the organisation that would lend its name to the new political regime. The Sangkum's statutes espoused an eclectic ideology that incorporated notions of the monarchy and the past glories of Angkor; the trinity of nation–religion–king; and a vision of popular democracy and socialism.[62] In practice, the Sangkum operated on the basis of loyalty to Prince Sihanouk.[63] Civil servants were strongly encouraged to join, and members were forbidden from belonging to a political party. Although officially not a political party, the Sangkum became an effective electoral vehicle. When Sihanouk finally called elections for the National Assembly, as required under the Geneva Accords, the Sangkum fielded candidates in every seat and won almost 83 per cent of the vote.[64] Candidates who stood against the Sangkum did so at considerable risk.

Sihanouk's second strategy was to amend the constitution. In 1956, 1958, 1959 and several times thereafter, Sihanouk initiated important amendments to the constitution, apparently to lend legal legitimacy to his new regime. At times, he used it to sanction political methods that he had tried and found effective. For example, he initiated Khmer National Congresses and national referenda or plebiscites as extra-constitutional processes but had them incorporated into the constitution

---

[62] Statuts du Sangkum Reastr Niyum [Statutes of the Sangkum Reastre Niyum], art. 3. The French version of the statutes is reproduced in Gour, *Institutions Constitutionnelles*, pp. 417–23.

[63] Preschez, *Essai sur la Démocratie*, p. 59.

[64] Ibid., pp. 61–2; regarding the 1955 election campaign, intimidation and manipulation against non-Sangkum candidates, see Chandler, *Tragedy*, pp. 81–4.

182 *Colonial Law Making*

in 1958 (Title VIII, arts. 92–5). The first Khmer National Congress took place soon after the 1956 elections. It was a mass meeting, called by the Sangkum and open to all members of the population. Thousands of people assembled in the open air near the Royal Palace to listen to a public discussion of set agenda items. By a show of hands, "the people" demanded that Sihanouk become the president of the next Council of Ministers.[65] His father, King Suramarit, duly appointed him.[66]

Henceforth, Sihanouk began to call National Congresses when he wanted to win support for his controversial policies. Phillipe Preschez, a one-time adviser to Sihanouk, wrote a lively summary of the Third National Congress in 1956, when left-leaning Democrats and members of the pro-communist *Pracheachon* party attempted to move a motion for a National Union, aimed at undermining the dominance of the Sangkum. The rowdy debate lasted into the night. Sihanouk tirelessly combated those few delegates brave enough to take an independent stand and castigated them for not joining the Sangkum. Several members of the Democrats were set upon and beaten as they left the meeting.[67] Sihanouk's 1958 constitutional amendment then bound members of the National Assembly to consider recommendations from the National Congress. If the parliamentarians could not agree on a congress motion, the matter would go to a referendum.[68]

In the Khmer National Congress and national referenda, Sihanouk had found forms of popular democracy or dialogue between the people and their royal leader that suited him and that he could control, and he used the constitution to legitimise them. At other times, Sihanouk tried to introduce new, untried constitutional reforms, though most failed to achieve his desired goals. For example, the 1956 amendments established provincial assemblies composed of members elected at commune and district level (Titre VII, arts. 84–7, as amended 1956). Partly because of the low levels of education and high levels of corruption among their members, these assemblies proved a disappointment and ceased operating in 1959.[69]

---

[65] Under the 1947 Constitution the government comprised a Cabinet Council headed by a prime minister. In 1956 this was changed to Council of Ministers and president of the Council of Ministers.

[66] In the following years, Sihanouk would resign and then be reappointed several times. Preschez, *Essai sur la Démocratie*, pp. 77–8; Chandler, *Tragedy*, p. 91.

[67] Preschez, *Essai sur la Démocratie*, pp. 80–1; Chandler, *Tragedy*, pp. 93–4.

[68] Constitution as at 1964, art. 95.

[69] Preschez, *Essai sur la Démocratie*, p. 83.

Sihanouk's longer-term control of the political process rested on his position as head of the Sangkum, as *Samdech Upayuvareach* and on having his dependable father on the throne. He faced a dilemma when King Suramarit died in early 1960. No other candidate for the throne would be as reliably compliant as his father had been. Sihanouk could have re-ascended the throne himself and cast aside any pretence that the country remained a constitutional monarchy. Instead, he arranged that the crown remain vacant under the guardianship of a Regency Council headed by his mother, Queen Kossamak, and her brother Prince Monireth. Then, what had originally been planned as a referendum on Sihanouk's policy of neutrality towards the escalating US war in Vietnam instead became an exercise to endorse this new political arrangement.[70] Voters had to choose between a number of ballot papers expressing views for and against his proposal, one of which carried Sihanouk's picture. A large majority of voters selected the ballot that carried his portrait. To do otherwise might have been tantamount to lèse-majesté.[71]

Following the referendum, the tamed National Assembly adopted resolutions demanding that Sihanouk accept the position of head of state for life. They had first had to pass a special constitutional amendment to allow them to do so (Title 20, art. 122, Constitution of 1964).[72] Even as he worked to render the parliament powerless and to make himself the undisputed leader, Sihanouk remained concerned with "the appearance of maintaining constitutional niceties".[73] In a subsequent interview with the semi-official paper *Réalités Cambodgiennes,* Sihanouk stressed that there had been no *coup d'état* in 1952, saying he had simply acceded to the wishes of the people.[74] Sihanouk's flexible approach to constitutional law had parallels with the ways in which the French had used the 1863 Treaty of Protection to legitimise their rule, while also circumventing and transforming it to suit their ends. With theatrical flair, Sihanouk added in ideas taken from socialism and from the luminaries of the Movement of Non-aligned Countries, with whom he mixed.

In earlier years, the French protectorate had nurtured authoritarian monarchism as a current of constitutional thought, eventually

---

[70] Preschez, *Essai sur la Démocratie*, pp. 90–1.

[71] Ibid., p. 94; Chandler, *Tragedy*, p. 117.

[72] Preschez, *Essai sur la Démocratie*, p. 94.

[73] Osborne, *Sihanouk*, p. 120.

[74] Ibid.

Figure 8.1: Prince Norodom Sihanouk and President Charles de Gaulle, Paris 1964. France funded advisors to the Cambodian government until the late 1960s.

Source: AFP via Getty Images.

giving it legal expression in Kram No. 1 of 1940 and their draft constitution that had been re-written in 1947. Sihanouk built on these legacies and made them his own. French influence in the arena of law and constitutional theory continued after independence. Ever a Francophile, Sihanouk drew succour from visiting French legal scholars, most of whom had come to teach in the new Faculty of Law and Economics. The brilliant polymath Jean Imbert, who served as dean of the faculty from 1958 to 1961, reportedly advised Sihanouk on constitutional matters.[75] Imbert's 1961 work on the *History of Khmer Institutions*, like Claude-Gilles Gour's book on Cambodia's political and constitutional institutions, perpetuated the protectorate's vision of a country tied by tradition to royal power.[76] Although Gour acknowledged that some of Sihanouk's actions had been unconstitutional, he argued that Sihanouk had attempted to develop a non-Western form of democracy that was suited to the country's monarchical traditions. Imbert and Gour both framed the prince's political manoeuvres in constitutional theory and historical continuity.

Many older Cambodians remember the Sangkum as a time of relative peace and prosperity. Education, culture and the arts flourished. By the end of the 1960s, however, the US war in Vietnam and a domestic communist insurgency were enveloping the country. In 1970, pro-US military officials staged a successful coup to remove Sihanouk from power. The National Assembly duly ratified the generals' actions and in April 1972, when the country was already operating under martial law, a new, republican constitution was approved by referendum.[77]

Justice Administration after Independence

On 29 August 1953 the Cambodian judges and the minister of justice must have felt proud as they took control of what had been the French jurisdiction. All its cases, buildings and other resources passed into

---

[75] Jean-Louis Harouel, "Un grand savant et administrateur, Jean Imbert (1919–1999)" [A Great Scholar and Administrator, Jean Imbert (1919–1999)], *Bulletin d'histoire de la Sécurité Sociale* [Bulletin of the History of Social Security] 41 (Jan. 2000): 8–22.

[76] Imbert, *Histoire des institutions khmères*, p. 127.

[77] For an English-language translation of the constitution of the Khmer Republic, see Raoul M. Jennar, ed., *The Cambodian Constitutions (1953–1993)* (Bangkok: White Lotus, 1995), p. 57. Regarding martial law, see Charles Meyer, *Derrière le sourire khmer* [Behind the Khmer Smile] (Paris: Plon, 1971), p. 328.

186   *Colonial Law Making*

Cambodian control.[78] The formerly subordinate indigenous laws and courts, applicable only to those considered to be ethnic Khmer, became the laws and courts of criminal and civil justice for all inhabitants. Cambodian judges were no longer considered unfit to preside in cases that involved people of other ethnicities—Europeans, Vietnamese and Chinese.[79] The French, though, had negotiated some transitional protection for themselves, requiring the Cambodian judges to consult a French adviser in any case that involved a French citizen, and French lawyers who had been practising in the colonial jurisdiction were finally admitted to the Cambodian courts to represent their fellow citizens.[80] Nevertheless, the judges must have celebrated the end of the carefully constructed ethnically based jurisdictional divide between coloniser and colonised. Such a situation would have seemed preposterous to the French 13 years earlier, when Penh Nouth sent his mild critique of Cambodian justice to his colleague Mar Tes, only to have it intercepted and repudiated by the colonial administration.

On one hand, independence brought a momentous change in status for the Cambodian jurisdiction and its personnel. Whereas the constitution, laws, ministers and judges had all previously been subject to French control, Cambodians were now free to determine independently how their country's judicial system would operate. French advisers remained, but they did so at the invitation of the Royal

---

[78] Protocole de transfert au Gouvernement Royal du Cambodge des compétences judiciaires exercées par la France sur le territoire du Royaume, 28 août, 1953 [Protocol of Transfer to the Royal Government of Cambodia the Judicial Powers Exercised by the French on the Territory of the Kingdom, 28 Aug 1953] reproduced in J. Morice, "L'organisation judiciaire du Cambodge: La renaissance d'une justice nationale" [Judicial Organisation of Cambodia: The Renaissance of a National Justice System], *Penant: Recueil Général de jurisprudence, de doctrine et de législation colonials* [Penant: General Collection of Colonial Jurisprudence, Doctrine and Legislation] (1962): 7–35, see 12.

[79] Following the signing of an accord between France and China in 1947, Chinese nationals had been classified as honorary Europeans and therefore subject to the mainstream French jurisdiction rather than its indigenous sub-jurisdiction, which continued to deal with ethnic Vietnamese; see "Circular Relative to the Franco-Chinese Accord of 28 February 1947 and civil status of Chinese nationals, 24 October 1947", *Journal Judiciaire de l'Indochine français* 10 (1947): 111.

[80] Convention on the particular status in judicial matters accorded by the Royal Government of Cambodia to French Nationals, 9 Sept. 1953, arts, 1–2 in Ministère de la Justice, *Recueil Judiciaire* [Ministry of Justice, Judicial Collection] 1 (1954) (Phnom Penh: Royaume du Cambodge), pp. 19–20, NAC Doc, Box 249. This requirement was abolished in 1957, see Morice, "Organisation judiciaire", p. 12.

Government of Cambodia. On the other hand, by the time of independence, the potential of the 1947 constitution to usher in real guarantees of judicial independence and integrity had been at least partially extinguished, along with hopes for a functioning parliamentary democracy. Over the coming years, neither the king nor the legislature was inclined to champion the judicial branch of state power. The protectorate had not engendered respect for the country's judiciary and lawyers, and had left them ill equipped to forge a less subordinate role for themselves.

The most immediate legacy of the protectorate, perpetuated in its dying days, was to undermine the already weak guarantees of judicial independence in the 1947 constitution. The constitution had established a governmental system based on three heads of power—legislative, executive and judicial—exercised in the name of the king (arts. 22–4). Following French practice, the judicial power took a subordinate role. Whereas the constitution dealt in some detail with the operation of the legislature and executive, it devoted only two articles to the judiciary (Title 8, arts. 95–6). The first, Article 95, stated that judicial organisation would be ruled by a special law. Article 96 established a High Council of Magistracy that would guarantee the discipline and the independence of the judges. Members of the council comprised: the minister of justice, as chairperson, two members appointed by the king, two elected by the National Assembly, and two elected by the judges themselves. A further special law was to flesh out how the council would operate (art. 96). Neither of the special laws was ever enacted, leaving the judiciary and the council vulnerable to ad hoc measures and political interference.

The Cambodian constitution provided even fewer specific guarantees of judicial independence than did the 1946 French constitution, on which it drew. Unlike the French constitution, there was no guarantee of tenure, or *inamovibilité*, for adjudicating (sitting) judges, which is normally an important guarantee of judicial independence (French Constitution 1946, Titre IX, art. 84, 3rd para).[81] In another glaring weakness, whereas Article 84 of the French constitution specified that the head of state would appoint judges on the recommendation of the Supreme Council of the Magistracy, the Cambodian constitution was silent in this respect, leaving such details to future legislation.

---

[81] Constitution de 1946, IVe République [Constitution of 1946, Fourth Republic], www.conseil-constitutionnel.fr/les-constitutions-dans-l-histoire/constitution-de-1946-ive-republique (accessed 3 June 2021).

Figure 8.2: Norodom Sihanouk meets Cambodian judges
Source: Meyer collection, undated, National Archives of Cambodia 2096-CM736.hfy.

Predictably, a pre-independence 1947 *kram* had allocated the council a purely consultative role, and the king (under the guidance of the French high commissioner) ultimately decided most issues.[82] Even after independence, despite some initial promise, the council never gained the authority it would have needed if it was to be an effective guardian of judicial probity. In 1954, a new *kram* stated that no judicial appointments, promotions or other movements could be made without the council's consent.[83] According to Gour, the Cambodian judicial corps interpreted this to mean that the council, as in France, had ultimate authority over the career of judges and that the role of the king should be to formally endorse its decisions. However, such an interpretation appears to have clashed with other clauses of the same *kram*, which left the actual administration of judicial appointments in the hands of the minister of justice.[84] The 1954 law also split responsibility for disciplining judges between the minister of justice, the council, and

---

[82] Kram 396, NS 31 Dec. 1947, art. 43, discussed in Gour, *Institutions Constitutionnelles*, p. 369.
[83] Kram 857, NS 9 Mar. 1954, cited in Gour, *Institutions Constitutionnelles*, p. 369.
[84] Gour, *Institutions Constitutionnelles*, pp. 369–70.

the king. Under the Sangkum, Sihanouk made the king the nominal head of the council, further weakening its independence.[85] Rather than guaranteeing the separation of powers and the independence of the judiciary, the council had come to signify the subordination of the judiciary to political and executive control.[86]

Nor were judges and lawyers given the authority they needed. The judiciary may have sought more autonomy in 1954, but they were in no position to champion judicial independence. While there had been individual exceptions, judges generally had not been highly respected under the protectorate by other members of the elite or by the general population. The protectorate had stymied lawyers' attempts to establish an independent legal profession, not to mention one composed of qualified lawyers. In 1951, a new *kram* replaced the 1932 Royal Ordinance Organising and Regulating Legal Defence Before the Cambodian Courts, discussed in the previous chapter, and secured lawyers a greater monopoly on legal representation.[87] However, the legal profession that emerged under the protectorate lacked the social standing and the professional power to become a credible, semi-autonomous social field that may have helped to enforce judicial independence.

One of the glaring barriers facing the Cambodian legal profession, both judges and lawyers, was the historic lack of access to formal legal education. Not until 1949 was a diploma in law offered to students in Phnom Penh.[88] Before that, students had to study in Hanoi or France in order to gain the equivalent of a Bachelor of Laws. After independence, professors from the University of Paris helped to establish what became the Faculty of Law and Economics in 1957.[89] The first cohort of approximately 13 students would have completed the four-year bachelor's degree offered by the faculty in 1961.[90] Early editions of the *Annals of the Faculty of Law and Economics*, which contain some of the courses taught by staff of the faculty, presented an overly optimistic view of law

---

[85] Ibid., pp. 369–70.

[86] Ibid., p. 359.

[87] Morice, "Organisation judiciaire", p. 33; Kram No. 648-NS, Défense en Justice [Legal Defense], 30 Mar. 1951.

[88] Morice, "Organisation judiciaire", p. 19.

[89] Jean Imbert, "Introduction", *Annales de la Faculté de droit de Phnom Penh Tome 1* [Annals of the Faculty of Law of Phnom Penh Vol. 1], (1961) pp. 4–6.

[90] Ibid.

190   *Colonial Law Making*

and legal institutions, given the eventual outcomes.[91] These French legal experts, and the faculty itself, offered a veneer of order and progress to law.

Sihanouk appeared to place great faith in education as a panacea for most ills and was possibly swayed by the *Annals*, which belied the fact that the courts were, reportedly, mired in the corruption that pervaded most areas of the Cambodian public sector after independence.[92] In 1940, lawyer Penh Nouth had intimated that most judges were corrupt and often ignorant of the law.[93] Twenty years later, according to Gour, many serving judges still suffered from severe moral and technical deficits.[94] According to Charles Meyer, a disillusioned former adviser to Sihanouk, corruption had become so egregious by the mid-1960s that lawyers would frankly tell their clients that their capacity to pay would determine the outcome of their case.[95] Sihanouk's response to some of the problems of the legal sector, particularly corruption, was to initiate a series of still-born institutional fixes.

In 1959, the National Assembly enacted the first major reform to legal administration since independence. The "Law on the Reorganisation of Justice" seems to have been designed to enforce the accountability of public officials under criminal law, and to decentralise and streamline criminal justice. However, by 1962 the law was still not in force, as subordinate legislation detailing how the reforms would operate had not been enacted.[96]

In line with Sihanouk's concept of popular democracy, the 1959 law introduced juries in civil and criminal matters, both at first instance and on appeal, but abolished appeals in most less serious matters.[97] In place of one criminal court in Phnom Penh, there were to be eight spread

---

[91] Regarding the predominance of French experts in the faculty, see, for example, a review of the first issues of the *Annales* by F. Derrida, Ch. Buniet and R. Bastannetto, "Annales de la faculté de droit de Phnom Penh", *Revue internationale de droit comparé* 13, 4 (1961): 841–8.

[92] Michael Vickery, *Cambodia 1975–1982* (Bangkok: Silkworm, 1984), pp. 24–8; Meyer, *Derriere le sourire*, pp. 170–9; Chandler, *Tragedy*, pp. 90, 118.

[93] Penh Nouth, "Exposé des voeux", NAC RSC 23292.

[94] Gour, *Institutions Constitutionnelles*, pp. 364–5.

[95] Meyer, *Derrière le sourire*, p. 174.

[96] Gour, *Institutions Constitutionnelles*, pp. 377–87; Morice, "Organisation judiciaire", p. 34.

[97] Law on Reform of Judicial Organisation, Kram No. 320/NS, 30 June 1959, Code of Civil Procedure (as amended in 1963), arts. 229–38, art. 415, art. 8. NAC Doc, Box 257.

across regional centres (art. 2). These measures may have been partly designed to lessen opportunities for judicial corruption, but the provisions that most explicitly addressed the issue concerned the *sala kromchot*, or Court of Indictment, or in French the *Chambre de mises en accusation*. Established in the Cambodian jurisdiction in 1923, the *sala kromchot* heard appeals on rulings by prosecutors as to whether there was a case to be heard in criminal law, on whether the offence was a felony, misdemeanour or petty transgression, and on whether to grant bail. It had previously been attached to the Court of Appeal in Phnom Penh, but the 1959 law made the *sala kromchot* a stand-alone court, where judges were to be assisted by four jurors (art. 11). Article 11 spelt out the real target of the reform: "This court rules on appeals against decisions by the king's Prosecutors that there is no case to answer, including a decision not to pursue a case made in favour of a Prince, a state official, a judge or a notable."

This seems to indicate that members of the elite, including the judiciary, had been avoiding prosecution by having charges against them dropped. Given the extent of elite corruption and the frequent paralyses within the government, it is not surprising that the National Assembly and the government were slow to develop the necessary implementing legislation.

The fate of the High Court of Justice is another example of hollow attempts to make elites accountable before the law. Under the 1947 constitution, government ministers were immune from prosecution in the ordinary courts, but they could be arraigned for serious crimes and misdemeanours by a special High Court of Justice convened by members of the National Assembly.[98] Although they never invoked the High Court, law makers expanded its powers in 1956, as a political weapon against the executive. They made secretaries of state, as well as ministers, subject to the court and declared that these senior government officials could be tried not only for crimes and misdemeanours, but also for serious errors committed in their duties and for failing to defend state security adequately.[99] In 1964, Sihanouk initiated a constitutional amendment to replace the High Court of Justice with what he called a Popular

---

[98] Articles 110–12. On the mixing of powers in the French constitution, see Herbert Weinschel, "The Constitutions of the Fourth French Republic and of the Italian Republic: A Comparative Study", *The George Washington Law Review* 20, 2 (1951–52): 127–73, see 147.

[99] Morice, "Organisation judiciaire", pp. 26–7.

Tribunal.[100] This new court introduced a modified form of trial by jury and was to apply the general law. Four assessors, elected from a carefully selected slate of candidates, were to determine guilt or innocence under the guidance of three legal experts.[101] Like the High Court of Justice, the Popular Tribunals had little if any life.

The protectorate had also had a history of creating empty legal institutions, especially when it came to holding government officials to account. Following the French tradition of separate courts for administrative law, the protectorate had established a *krom viveat* (*contentieux administratif cambodgien*) in 1933. Unsurprisingly, few if any litigants used it to bring complaints against Cambodian administrators. After independence, new legislation progressively reorganised the *krom viveat*.[102] However, like its colonial predecessor, it remained largely ineffectual and only partly operational.[103]

A Legal System That Was Doomed to Fail?

It is artificial to consider what was essentially a process of decline and corruption in Cambodia's already weak legal and constitutional institutions without taking account of the international pressures that Cambodia faced as a result of the war in Vietnam, which inevitably spilled into Cambodia with disastrous results.[104]

With this caveat in mind, the evolution of Cambodia's laws and courts following independence appears to support Matthew Lange's thesis that colonial protectorates failed to build effective state bureaucratic institutions or to replace pre-colonial elites with Western-educated personnel capable of keeping such institutions operating after independence. Indeed, from their return to Cambodia at the end of the Second World War until independence in 1953, the French had

---

[100] Gour, *Institutions Constitutionnelles*, pp. 357, 377–8; Constitution 1964, new arts. 110–12.

[101] Gour, *Institutions Constitutionnelles*, pp. 379–80.

[102] Morice, "Organisation judiciaire", p. 30.

[103] Organisation of the Contentieux Administratif Cambodgien [Cambodian Procedure in Administrative Law], Kram 399-NS 9 Jan. 1948 as amended in 1953 and 1954 in Ministère de la Justice, *Recueil Judiciaire* 2 (1954) (Phnom Penh: Royaume du Cambodge), pp. 59–60, NAC Doc, Box 249; Gour, *Institutions Constitutionnelles*, pp. 365–6.

[104] William Shawcross, *Sideshow: Kissinger, Nixon and the Destruction of Cambodia* (London: Hogarth Press, 1991).

reinforced the power of some older elites. The Cambodian protectorate, however, had been a hybrid of direct and indirect rule. At independence, the French left Cambodia with state institutions that were admittedly weak but that signified vast changes in the way the country was governed. Many of the old elites, such as the former provincial governors, had been displaced, or at least demoted. The corps of dedicated judges created in the early 1920s had usurped the judicial powers that had formerly been so important to the governors. Although forms of patronage persisted, they now operated through modern techniques and institutions.[105]

It seems likely that if French judges had taken over the Cambodian courts, as they took over the indigenous courts of Cochin China, they would have been less subservient to the administration. French lawyers would also have played a more active role. Yet this may have left Cambodian lawyers and judges even less prepared to assume their legal responsibilities at independence, especially given the French had invested so little in legal education for Cambodians. As it was, the protectorate left Cambodia with a dependent set of courts that had operated largely as an instrument of administrative control. Following independence, Sihanouk built on the colonial approach to law and courts. Modern laws and efficient courts may have been desirable, but they were not to place too many fetters on authoritarian rule.

Perhaps the main legacy of the protectorate was ideological rather than practical. There is no doubt that, before the French arrived, Cambodians regarded their king as semi-divine and all powerful. What changed under the protectorate was that the authoritarian colonial state wove royal power into the fabric of the embryonic national institutions, laws and constitutions. Preparing for independence, the colonists tended to re-cast royal power in the light of European absolute monarchs, reinforcing their own methods of rule under the protectorate that depended on the king and the Cambodian elite to keep the peace.

---

[105] Chandler, *Tragedy*, p. 65.

9

Making Law in
Colonial Protectorates

Law played an important role in modern European colonial rule. Law constituted and authorised the colonial presence, was part of the colonial civilising mission and was also part of its means of domination. Colonial legal methods reflected the traditions of their respective metropoles and varied according to the economic structure and political form of each colony. Colonised peoples, even when seemingly pacified, affected all of these factors by resisting, subverting, accommodating and synthesising legal principles and practices, so that, within the overarching requirements of domination, colonial law took shape amid myriad contingent interactions and transactions.

This study of law, jurisdictions and the legal constitution of the colonial and post-colonial state during and immediately after the French protectorate of Cambodia has considered how and why law evolved under the protectorate and some of its post-independence legacies. The French used law to constitute and control the protectorate, particularly through jurisdictions. Structural economic and political factors shaped colonial rule and law. Within those frameworks, law took shape as a result of the quotidian exchanges and transactions among and between colonial authorities and Cambodian elites. The early years of independence show colonial rule had created a dependent legal system whose personnel and institutions failed to play an effective role as a third arm of government. However, the myriad transactions that shaped the Cambodian jurisdiction and that had often been carried out in the language of protection did create a hegemonic view of state law that melded both French and Cambodian formulations. While the result was unique to Cambodia, we can see reverberations in those other nations of the region where pre-colonial monarchs survived European intervention.

Colonial Law: Constituting and Controlling

The 1863 Treaty of Protection established and legitimised the French presence in Cambodia, and constituted it at law, even though the French incrementally breached the treaty's terms. To the extent the French could actually exercise direct control after their long contest with King Norodom, particularly after they forced him to sign the 1884 Convention, they did so in the name of the treaty, which purported to guarantee Cambodia's internal sovereignty. The notion of indirect rule, and the semi-fictional legal principle that the French ruled in the name of the Cambodian king, shaped the political dynamics between the Cambodian elite and the French colonial administration.

The 1884 Convention itself illustrates the legitimising role of written legal agreements, even when signed under coercion. The French treated the convention as an adjunct to the Treaty of Protection. Together they legitimised French rule in the eyes of the colonial administration, of other European powers and, to some extent, of the French public. The convention retroactively authorised actions already taken by the protectorate administration, such as establishing a court of the Indochina-wide French jurisdiction in Phnom Penh.

Did colonial law serve a vastly different function from metropolitan law? Most states seek to clothe their actions in legality, regardless of their political bent. So, what was different about colonial law? First, its origins were foreign and imposed from above, rather than achieved through social and political struggle within the colonised countries. Another feature, common in colonial law but not unique to it, was the overtly racialised nature of the social divisions it established and enforced. Like other European powers, the French used law and legal instruments to establish hierarchies based on ethnicity and status. In this respect, colonial law reverted to what legal theorist Henry Sumner Maine called ancient law—based on status, patronage and prestige.[1] Colonial law also categorised indigenous inhabitants as subjects, protégés and, infrequently, citizens. In these ways it denied colonised peoples equality before the law.

Jack Gin Gary Lee posits that following the abolition of slavery, the definition of the British crown colony narrowed to signify those territories

---

[1] Maine, *Ancient Law*, p. 174.

in which a small European settler population ruled over a much larger population of colonised peoples.[2] Colonial settler minorities sought new ways of creating and enforcing race-based hierarchies of civil status, the legacies of which play out today, for example in Malaysia and Myanmar. In Siam/Thailand, European powers incrementally expanded extraterritorial rights. In response, the Chakri dynasty oversaw the implementation of new legal codes which helped to prevent formal colonial annexation, consolidated their rule, and made ethnicity and royal authority defining characteristics of the nation. In Cambodia, too, citizenship has at times been linked with Khmer ethnicity, echoing the way the French used jurisdiction and other means to create divisions of race and status.

In the early decades of the protectorate, the French used jurisdictions to diminish the reach of the Cambodian courts and to undermine King Norodom's judicial status. Under King Sisowath, they slowly transformed the Cambodian jurisdiction to become a useful instrument of control. As Penh Nouth pointed out in 1940, the scales of Cambodian justice in the protectorate always tipped heavily in favour of the colonial state.[3]

By contrast, the British relied less in their colonies on rigidly quarantined, racially based jurisdictions than did the French, but nevertheless used law to manage and to discriminate against racial groups. For example, in the crown colonies of the Straits Settlements (centred on Singapore) the governor and his legal advisers gained the right to suspend the rule of law in order not only to suppress local opposition to their rule but also to deny certain common law rights and to administer policies of racial differencing.[4] Local rulers in the protectorates of the Malay Peninsula, which incrementally came under a centralised administration based in Singapore, became the titular representatives of indigenous Malays and of Islam, in the face of growing populations of Chinese and Indians, many of whom arrived as free or indentured labour to work on plantations, in mines and in other foreign-run enterprises.[5]

---

[2] Lee, "Plural Society and the Colonial State", p. 238.

[3] Penh Nouth, "Exposé des voeux", NAC RSC 23292.

[4] Lee, "Plural Society and the Colonial State", pp. 238–40; Halliday and Karpik, "Political Liberalism in the British Post-Colony", p. 4.

[5] Amarjit Kaur, "Labour Brokers in Migration: Understanding Historical and Contemporary Transnational Migration Regimes in Malaya/Malaysia", *International Review of Social History* 57, 20 (2012): 225–52, see 227–31; Sunil S. Amrith, "Indians

In Cambodia, driven by considerations of what they saw as necessary, politically convenient and affordable, the protectorate authorities regularly transgressed the principles of French law, including the separation of powers, then in force in France. When the murder of *Résident* Bardez challenged French authority and prestige, colonial officials intimidated and threatened witnesses, turning the trial into an archetypical, and at times farcical, piece of colonial theatre. The *Indigénat*, the ultimate colonial law of exception, which was in force in Cambodia until at least 1912, also buttressed colonial rule by treating petty disobedience and disrespect towards officials as a punishable offence. After the *Indigénat* was no longer in force, the 1924 Cambodian Criminal Code continued this trend, punishing criticism of public officials.

Nevertheless, legality was also a moral benchmark by which critics in France, Europe and Indochina judged the colonial administration. Allegations of illegality influenced French administrators. For example, in 1881 Governor Le Myre de Vilers and Étienne Aymonier searched for a legal justification to establish a French court in Phnom Penh. Lawyer Lortat-Jacob and the League for the Rights of Man publicised what they saw as the denial of defendants' rights and forced the protectorate administration to concede some role for Cambodian lawyers. Learned French jurists, such as Arthur Girault, attempted to develop a theoretical basis for colonial law that separated it from mainstream French legal theory and justified a different status.[6]

Law and legal reform were also part of the civilising mission, an ideology that justified colonisation and that doubtless inspired many a well-meaning colonial official: men such as Adhémard Leclère, who translated (and interpreted) Cambodian legal texts, and Étienne Aymonier, who was outraged by what he saw as the oppressiveness of Cambodian courts. It is easy to imagine that a man such as Judicial Adviser Habert also genuinely believed he was contributing to a more just legal system. He must have drawn great satisfaction from collaborating with those Cambodian judges whose Buddhist beliefs and modest lifestyles, he said, attested to their high moral standards.[7] At the same time, Habert would have had to mediate between the demands of the

---

Overseas? Governing Tramil Migration to Malays 1870–1940", *Past and Present* 208 (2010): 231–61.

[6] Girault, *Principes de Colonisation et de Législation Coloniale.*

[7] Habert to Résident Supérieur, 16 June 1932, NAC RSC 14344.

protectorate administration, his colleagues in the colonial judiciary and his legal principles. Assuming he was genuinely committed to legal principles, his position epitomised the perilous course that honest colonial judges interested in advancing their careers had to steer, something which legal historian Bernard Durand likens to the Greek myth of Jason and the Argonauts sailing down a narrow passage while avoiding crashing rocks from either side.[8]

Referring to the nine British protectorates in the Malay Peninsula, Kobkua Suwannathat-Pian also argues that Britain's primary objective was to impose law and order to protect British interest. However, she states that certain "socio-legal improvements", such as the end of slavery and "proper redress provided by the law to common people", were among the few real benefits of colonial rule for the Malay population.[9]

Did Cambodian people also benefit from France's drive to reform the Cambodian courts and to introduce new codes? Was there a liberatory aspect to colonial law, as colonial powers constantly claimed? Colonisation, it is argued, imposed a legal system which purported to provide legal certainty and some forms of redress for legally recognised wrongs, including for less powerful people. Nevertheless, if the admittedly self-interested comments of the lawyers Penh Nouth and Robert Lortat-Jacob are to be believed, the rights of non-elite people remained a low priority for the protectorate's legal system. The scant evidence regarding the reactions of ordinary people to the reformed legal system suggests that they did not find the courts vastly changed. They approached state law with expectations that gift-giving, patronage and personal connections determined outcomes.

The protectorate worked in diverse ways to create a politically dependent legal system that operated as an extension of its administration. Cambodian judges depended on the judicial adviser and on the provincial *résidents* to supervise their work. They also relied on the French administration to defend them against attacks from other sections of the Cambodian elite. Although men like Habert and Baudoin presented the Cambodian jurisdiction as a justice system in training, regardless of individual intentions, their failure to invest in adequate legal education suggests the colonial regime had little interest in guiding it to stand alone. Moreover, as Habert himself pointed out, training alone would

---

[8] Durand, "Prolégomènes", pp. 1–25.
[9] Suwannathat-Pian, *Palace, Political Party and Power*, p. 26.

not necessarily have created a cadre of Cambodian judges capable of and interested in consistently applying the colonial version of "independent" state law. Lawyers such as Penh Nouth might have contributed to developing a less dependent and more transparent form of justice if they had been less fettered, but the protectorate did all it could to prevent that from happening.

Structures and Trends That Framed Colonial Justice

This book has been a study not only of the role of law in colonising Cambodia, but of the factors that affected the way in which law developed and was used. I have paid a lot of attention to some of the interactions, coincidences and exchanges that affected colonial efforts to define jurisdictions and to impose legal codes. These were often contingent, although they played out within a broader structural context and reflected unequal distribution of power between coloniser and colonised.

How does the example of Cambodia measure against the theories of Dezalay and Garth, Upendra Baxi and Matthew Lange, each of whom posit generalisations regarding the importance of what can loosely be called structural aspects of colonial rule? Dezalay and Garth look for trends in the way colonial rule facilitated the creation of legal capital and legal professions in various Asian countries, arguing that strong legal fields emerged when the law and lawyers also absorbed or brokered other forms of political and economic capital. Lange does not focus directly on law, but he argues that indirect colonial rule generally failed to replace pre-colonial elites and to implant the legal bureaucratic apparatus which he sees as having been a prerequisite for capitalist economic development and liberal democracy. Baxi's proposition that colonial law in India created scripts for governance rather than becoming hegemonic is a counter to Lange's assumption that, at its best, colonial state rule laid the foundations for liberal democracy and strong market-based economic development.

All three works are relevant to the French protectorate of Cambodia, where indirect rule gave birth to a dependent form of justice that did not engender a strong legal field and which was, in many respects, merely a script for colonial governance. Taken together, they explain aspects of the legacy of colonial law and justice in Cambodia.

Dezalay and Garth posit that patterns of colonial investments in law were largely affected by colonial trade, which helped to determine the influence of law, lawyers and the legal field in post-colonial societies.[10] Cambodia was not a colony of trade, and law was predominantly although not wholly an instrument of administration. Domestic trade and commerce remained largely in the hands of Chinese merchants, prompting one French commentator in the early 1920s to characterise Cambodia as a "Chinese colony administered by the French".[11] However, compared with Siam/Thailand, Cambodia did not offer the Chinese elite such scope to manoeuvre between jurisdictions and to profit from competition between the monarchy and rival colonial powers.[12]

Nor did the protectorate mirror the model of the Philippines, where a relatively strong legal profession emerged as a direct result of US investment in colonial state building. The French made considerable investments in creating legal structures in Cambodia, but the meagre resources devoted to legal education were directed towards judges, not lawyers, whom Dezalay and Garth, focusing on countries that inherited some form of Anglo common law, see as the core of a powerful legal field. Although some French lawyers, and in later years some Cambodians, sought to influence justice administration, the colonial state worked hard to minimise their impact. Any legal capital generated under the protectorate remained subsumed within the broader political field dominated by the French administration, rather than taking on a life of its own.

The French did, though, also abolish practices they considered uncivilised, and they attempted to use law to stimulate social and economic change, for example by making land a tradeable commodity and defining which civil disputes were and were not important enough to go before the courts. If French colonial entrepreneurs had had more success and become more numerous in Cambodia, they would likely have demanded more judge-run courts and attracted more lawyers to the French jurisdiction to settle commercial disputes, making it ascendant over the indigenous jurisdiction.

Even then, the strict jurisdictional divides imposed by the French might have allowed the protectorate administration to quarantine the Cambodian courts and to prevent the emergence of a strong, independently minded Cambodian legal profession. Nevertheless, if there

---

[10] Dezalay and Garth, *Asian Legal Revivals*, pp. 1–38.

[11] A. Pannetier, *Notes cambodgiennes: au coeur du pays Khmer* [Cambodian Notes: in the Heart of the Country of the Khmers] (Paris: Centre de documentation et de recherche sur la civilisation khmère, 1983 ed., 1921), p. 57.

[12] Wongsurawat, *The Crown and the Capitalists*, pp. 90–8.

had been more French judges and lawyers in the protectorate, they would likely have scrutinised the administration more closely, and perhaps pressured it to invest more in legal education for Cambodians. Because Dezalay and Garth focus on the legal profession as the holders and wielders of legal, social, family and political capital, their analysis applies to Cambodia only in the negative sense, as the legal profession was so tightly controlled by the colonial state and remained relatively powerless. The indigenous jurisdiction created legal or political capital for the protectorate administration, which could claim to be preparing or laying the basis for a French-style justice system while simultaneously protecting Cambodian tradition. Law remained largely an administrative affair, and an indigenous legal field capable of attracting, mediating or wielding significant influence did not take shape.

Lange's finding that indirect colonial rule precluded development of strong legal bureaucratic structures as the basis for post-colonial, liberal-democratic, market-based states appears apposite to Cambodia, regardless of his view that even in directly ruled colonies the French tended not to develop such structures.[13] Lange observes that British protectorates in Asia combined aspects of both direct and indirect rule, and the same is true of the French protectorate of Cambodia. However, Lange seems to assert that direct rule required colonial civil servants to staff at least the upper echelons of the colonial state bureaucracy. By this criterion, even when it was strongest in Cambodia, French rule was never entirely direct.

Leaving aside how we should define direct rule, the French protectorate in Cambodia indubitably relied on local elites and in this sense left considerable space for pre-colonial structures of patronage and notions of law to continue. However, one of the themes to emerge in this book is that French forms of patronage, personal ambitions and corruption also helped to shape colonial state law. While the structure of the indigenous Cambodian jurisdiction developed in ways that made concessions to the Cambodian elite, animosity between the judicial and administrative arms of the French colonial apparatus was just as influential, especially during the more than ten years when *Résident Supérieur* Baudoin dominated the protectorate. Moreover, the French jurisdiction in Indochina was also subject to overt executive interference.

What transpired in the areas of constitutional law and justice administration in Cambodia during the short period from independence

---

[13] Lange, *Lineages of Despotism and Development.*

in 1953 to the end of the 1960s suggests that the structural legacy of indirect rule went beyond the lack of a strong legal profession and an effective bureaucracy to administer state legal structures. Cambodia's prior status as a protectorate, and the contests between the colonial administration and the local elite—which were carried out in the language of protection—encouraged hybridised concepts of law and of the state, laying the basis for disputes over the king's place within or above the 1949 constitution. The 1863 Treaty of Protection had determined the language in which all parties justified their exchanges. Protection talk, mingled with the colonial ideology of the civilising mission, helped to generate formulations of an immutable Khmer tradition and identity. Colonisers and emerging nationalists alike spoke of modernisation hand in hand with a reawakening, referring to a romanticised Angkorean past and to traditions linked with royalty and religion.[14]

Upendra Baxi prompts his readers to question whether the very structure of colonial rule precluded the development of a legal system that was socially and politically embedded in ways that might be called hegemonic.[15] The laws and structures of the indigenous jurisdiction in Cambodia were certainly mainly foreign, but they incorporated notions of tradition, national identity, royal power and religion which did become hegemonic. The rituals and protocols established under the protectorate linked new legal codes to the pre-colonial legal texts, and through them to royal power and Buddhism. We may call this a legal fiction or colonial propaganda, but it became something more than that. These outcomes were the product of the exchanges and transactions that shaped the Cambodian jurisdiction.

The Contests That Made Colonial Law

Colonial administrators, members of the French colonial fraternity and the Cambodian elite all contributed to shaping the Cambodian jurisdiction, albeit from unequal positions of power and influence. Each approached and used law from different perspectives and with varying interests in mind. French administrators used law and jurisdictions to impose and authorise French rule; to incrementally usurp and undermine the power of King Norodom, the Phnom Penh elites and the

---

[14] Edwards, *Cambodge*, p. 242.
[15] Baxi, "The Colonialist Heritage", pp. 46–75.

provincial governors; to collect their taxes; and to maintain order. For the French judges and lawyers working in Cambodia, law was not only a pillar of French power and prestige. It was also the source of their professional standing and outlook. Their career ambitions and interests led them to clash with the administrative arm of the colonial apparatus, appealing to French legal principles, particularly the separation of powers. This rivalry between the two arms of colonial rule helped to shape both the French and the Cambodian jurisdictions, as powerful administrators successfully manoeuvred to limit the influence of the French judges in the protectorate.

Although the French continued incrementally to expand their control over the protectorate, including its laws and courts, the Cambodian elite retained important elements of power. Formally indirect colonial rule, the protectorate, became entrenched after the rebellion of 1885–86 had put paid to any plans the French may have had to gradually incorporate Cambodia within the directly ruled colony of Cochin China. Thereafter, French rule rested on an evolving modus vivendi with the king and other members of the Cambodian elite. The French worked assiduously to promote and reinforce the king as a figurehead with semi-divine status, in whose name they governed the colony. But while they usurped the king's formal temporal powers, his ties of patronage and protection remained partially beyond French reach. Thus, King Sisowath, whom the French regarded as their man, appeared to be better equipped than they were to quell the 1916 demonstrations against French taxes and the Cambodian officials who collected them. Sisowath also delayed Judge Keth's appointment as president of the Court of Cassation, even if he could not prevent it.

Other members of the elite drew power from their role in the hybrid bureaucracy of colonial rule, working either for the French administration, as lawyer Penh Nouth had done for 20 years, or for the Cambodian apparatus, which the French sometimes referred to as the auxiliary of its rule. In both instances, elite Cambodians operated as the gateway to, or the gatekeepers between, the French administration and the Cambodian peasantry. Like the king, they maintained their own networks of patronage and protection, at least partially beyond French control. As Judicial Adviser Habert noted in 1925, he could trust the Cambodian judiciary only if he or another French official sat in the courtroom to supervise proceedings. Sixteen years later, Penh Nouth claimed that the French were still unaware of much that transpired in the Cambodian Courts of First Instance.

The two arms of the colonial apparatus consciously manoeuvred to maximise their respective advantages, as did members of the Cambodian elite. In what Dezalay and Garth refer to as entwined struggles for control of the colonial state, sectional interests coincided and shifted between and among the French and Cambodian elites.

King Norodom and the early French administrators bartered with each other for legal concessions. Norodom sought to protect his power and therefore his law. Yet he engaged with the colonial game of the written word, issuing numerous Royal Ordinances at the behest of his new protectors. He submitted to French pressures to sign away his powers, but ignored his own ordinances for as long as he could. Norodom also sometimes sought to use the game to his advantage, for example when he tried to shore up his jurisdiction over all "Asiatics" in 1873. He, and his successor, King Sisowath, used the official French discourse, such as their claim to respect Cambodian law, for their own ends.

The Cambodian/indigenous jurisdiction survived this contest and became the main colonial legal legacy, largely as a result of shifting coincidences of interest. French administrators and the Cambodian elite each had their own reasons to prevent the Cambodian courts being handed over to French judges, as had occurred in Cochin China. *Résident Supérieur* Baudoin made the crusade against the French colonial judiciary a leitmotif of his time in Cambodia, and he found ready allies among Cambodians who did not wish to have French judges preside in their courts. Baudoin courted King Sisowath and used the king's formal cachet to impose his own will, for example in choosing a substitute for Habert as legal adviser.

In justice as in other areas of the colonial state in Cambodia, French control rested on collaboration and compromise with members of the Cambodian elite. Justice administration made concessions to Cambodian elite interests but also tolerated, and even encouraged, hybrid notions and practices of law. Although such transactions appear calculated, and on one level certainly were, they also emerged from very different views of law and legal procedure. Beyond conscious jostling for power, therefore, interactions between and among these groups reflected often divergent understandings of law and legal legitimacy. There was often mutual incomprehension; but views of law and the role of the courts and judges also partially overlapped at times, and melded or hybridised at others.

Protectorates, Monarchies and the Constitution of the Nation

In the legal sphere, the outcome of hybrid understandings of law and of competing and coinciding interests produced the Cambodian jurisdiction and ensured it would become the sole jurisdiction after independence. Judicial Adviser Habert glibly claimed in 1925 that the new codes perfectly synthesised Cambodian tradition with French procedure, but the actual synthesis was more complex. The codes were clearly French inspired in form and substance, as well as procedure, although they made concessions to Cambodian tradition and practice, for example in the treatment of the bodies of executed felons, in land ownership and in some aspects of family law. The real synthesis took place in the hybrid notion of state law, which blurred the lines between the secular and the divine, creating a platform for Norodom Sihanouk (as king and as political leader of independent Cambodia) later to subvert the notion that a constitutional monarch was subject to law, rather than vice versa.

In her study of Malaysian kingship, Kobkua Suwannathat-Pian is doubtlessly correct to argue that Western colonial powers consistently underestimated and misunderstood the role royal ceremony and ritual played in Southeast Asian polities, as well as the fluid nature of royal power.[16] The history of the Cambodian protectorate is littered with examples of French transgressions and misunderstandings, from the special court of 1872 that presumed to judge the king's debts, to the 1884 Convention, to their misreading of the role of royal marriages.[17] Yet the protectorate administration also made a great show of participating in and supporting royal ceremonies and rituals, seeking to associate their presence and their power with that of the kings.

This emphasis on royal prestige was most exaggerated in the 1940s, when the young King Sihanouk underwent his political apprenticeship during the years of Vichy rule. Vichy's representative in Indochina, Decoux, attempted to raise the profile of local monarchs in the hope of winning support for French rule, uniting the peoples of Indochina behind their kings under French rule. His ideas built on similar efforts under the Third Republic, which had been most successful in Cambodia,

---

[16] Suwannathat-Pian, *Palace, Political Party and Power*, pp. 16–17.

[17] Jacobsen, "Divergent Perspectives".

206   *Colonial Law Making*

and less so in Vietnam, where the French had an often-troubled relationship with a succession of Nguyen emperors.[18]

By linking their rule with the Cambodian kings, the French ensured the monarchy survived and helped to give it a level of political and symbolic cachet that, in the early years of independence, it was difficult, if not dangerous, to challenge. French-encouraged notions of royal absolutism and unchanging Khmer culture floated among the bricolage of ideas that informed emerging Cambodian nationalism. Colonial state laws claimed continuity with pre-colonial legal texts, including their semi-divine, royally mediated legitimacy. This meant that the process of separating the new state law from pre-colonial religiously inspired law remained incomplete, and to a certain extent the king sat as the nexus between the two.[19]

Whereas direct colonial rule overthrew reigning indigenous monarchs, as in Myanmar and Sri Lanka, Southeast Asian potentates survived various forms of indirect colonisation.[20] The Malay traditional rulers and the Thai monarchy are two cases in point. Like Cambodia, both Malaysia and Thailand emerged from foreign colonial control or influence as constitutional monarchies, and both remain constitutional monarchies today (though since 1932 Thailand has had at least 20 separate constitutional arrangements, punctuated by recurring military coups). Cambodia reinstated a constitutional monarchy in 1993 after a 23-year break, during which it experienced three different regimes, one republican and two ostensibly socialist or communist.[21]

Britain governed its nine protectorates on the Malay Peninsula differently from the ways France ruled Cambodia, including the extent to which it maintained and respected the protocols of indirect rule. Although there were variations between the Federated (FMS) and Unfederated (UMS) Malay States, and among individual states, the British were generally less inclined than the French to promote the Malay rulers' ceremonial role, except in the religious sphere. The British went further towards separating religion and state law than did the French in Cambodia. They created a more centralised, British-run

---

[18] Goscha, *Modern History of Vietnam*, pp. 116, 123, 152–3.

[19] Benton, *Law and Colonial Cultures*, pp. 127–8.

[20] Aldrich, *Banished Potentates*.

[21] The Khmer Republic (1970–75), Democratic Kampuchea (1975–79), Peoples Republic of Kampuchea/State of Cambodia (1979–93).

legal administration that incrementally encroached on indigenous justice, even in the Unfederated Malay States.[22]

Unlike the Cambodian king, who enjoyed a brief period of nominal autonomy under Japanese rule in 1945, the Malay rulers were weakened further by the Second World War and Japanese occupation. When the British resumed control following the end of the war, they seem initially to have planned to merge all the nine states, both FMS and UMS, into one directly ruled crown colony.[23] At that time, it seemed that the cleavage between state law and traditional religious (Islamic) law had been largely achieved under colonial rule.[24] The subsequent negotiations for independence were then led by the legally trained, secular-minded Tunku Abdul Rahman and the coalition headed by the United Malays National Organisation. But all nine Malay rulers nevertheless survived, were consulted in drafting the new constitution and took their seats on the stage to celebrate the formation of the Federation of Malaya in 1957.[25]

Suwannathat-Pian asserts that the independence ceremony of 1957 marked the passing of political power from the British colonial regime, "not to the Rulers, but to the representatives of the people",[26] personified by the democratically elected prime minister, Tunku Abdul Rahman. The newly independent state took the form of a constitutional monarchy and initiated a process that continues today, whereby the rulers of what are now nine states within a national federation elect one among themselves to serve a five-year term as the sultan, or *Yang di-Pertuan Agong*.[27]

However, since independence, some rulers have clashed with the secular state apparatus, attempting to protect and expand their privileged status, but also more recently as a potentially moderating force against

---

[22] Tan Sri James Foong, *The Malaysian Judiciary: A Record* (Selangor Darul Ehsan, Malaysia: LexisNexis, 2017, 3rd ed.), pp. 17–29, 67–70; Gullick, *Rulers and Residents*, pp. 55–6, 338–43; Emily Sadka, "The Residential System in the Protected Malay States, 1874–1895" (PhD dissertation, Australian National University, 1960), pp. 133–5, 250–73.

[23] Suwannathat-Pian, *Palace, Political Party and Power*, p. 128.

[24] Ang and Whiting, "Federalism and Legal Unification", p. 296.

[25] Suwannathat-Pian, *Palace, Political Party and Power*, pp. 330–1. The Federation of Malaya included the nine Peninsular states plus Penang and Malacca; in 1963 it became Malaysia and incorporated Singapore, Sarawak and North Borneo. Singapore left the federation in 1965.

[26] Suwannathat-Pian, *Palace, Political Party and Power*, p. 331.

[27] Constitution of Malaysia, art. 32.

executive overreach.[28] Islam is the official state religion of Malaysia, and each ruler is the head of the religion of Islam in his respective state.[29] Although their role in politics has not been as direct or as substantial as that played by Norodom Sihanouk in Cambodia, individual rulers have, at various times, questioned their position in relation to law, and even challenged or sought to modify certain executive actions.[30] Islamic law has also been resurgent, making inroads into the previously secular civil courts, which may further affect the standing of the rulers as the formal heads of Islam in their state and nationally.[31]

Although the trajectories of each of the Malay Peninsula states, particularly those of individual Unfederated Malay States, varied, British then Japanese rule went further towards eclipsing regal power in Malaysia than did the French in Cambodia. By contrast, the royal family of Siam/Thailand managed, in some ways, to protect itself from colonial domination. While Siam/Thailand formally avoided colonial rule, it became in the views of some contemporary historians a form of semi-colony.[32] This is a problematic and contested idea. On the one hand, Thailand's rulers proudly proclaim theirs as the only state in

---

[28] Andrew Harding, "'Nazrinian' Monarchy in Malaysia: The Resilience and Revival of a Traditional Institution", in *Law and Society in Malaysia*, ed. Andrew Harding and Dian A.H. Shah (London: Routledge, 2017), pp. 72–95; Suwannathat-Pian, *Palace, Political Party and Power*, pp. 342–9; H.P. Lee, *Constitutional Conflicts in Contemporary Malaysia* (Kuala Lumpur: Oxford University Press, 1995), pp. 78–102.

[29] Constitution of Malaysia, art. 3.

[30] Lee, *Constitutional Conflicts*, pp. 78–102.

[31] Regarding the spreading influence of Islamic law, see Amanda Whiting, "Desecularising Malaysian Law?", in *Examining Practice, Interrogating Theory: Comparative Legal Studies in Aisa*, ed. Penelope Nicholson and Sarah Biddulph (Leiden: Martinus Nijhoff, 2008), pp. 223–66; Amanda Whiting, "Secularism, the Islamic State and the Malaysian Legal Profession", *Asian Journal of Comparative Law* 5 (2010): 1–34.

[32] Loos, *Subject Siam*, p. 17; Hong Lysa, "'Stranger within the Gates': Knowing Semi-Colonial Siam as Extraterritorials", *Modern Asian Studies* 38, 2 (2004): pp. 327–54; Benedict Anderson, "Studies of the Thai State: The State of Thai Studies", in *The Study of Thailand: Analyses of Knowledge, Approaches, and Prospects in Anthropology, Art History, Economics, History, and Political Science*, ed. Eliezer B. Ayal (Athens: Ohio University Center for International Studies, 1978), pp. 193–247, see pp. 210–13; Thongchai Winichakul also discussed the status of Siam/Thailand as possibly a semi-colony in a presentation titled "Absolute Monarchy and the Legal State in Thailand", sponsored by the Coral Bell School of Asia Pacific Affairs, Australian National University, 30 Nov. 2021.

Southeast Asia never to have been colonised. On the other hand, the term semi-colony overlooks the fact that while the Chakri dynasty modernised Thai laws and the state apparatus in response to colonial pressure, it simultaneously undertook its own colonial project, cementing the state's hold over peoples and regions that had not previously been wholly subject to its rule.[33]

There are some obvious similarities between the legal reforms in Siam in the late 19th and early 20th centuries and those in Cambodia under the protectorate. In Siam, foreign advisers from a number of countries, including France, wrote new civil and criminal codes and helped the Siamese monarchs to establish new court structures and legal procedures.[34] The key difference with Cambodia was, of course, that the Siamese royal family kept control of this process and used it to cement their own hold on power.[35] The democratic revolution of 1932 challenged but did not permanently curb royal power, and the Thai monarchy continues to influence and to intervene in national politics. Although new, seemingly secular codes replaced the Three Seals Laws, Theravada Buddhism was entrenched as the official religion and became conflated with state power.[36] While there have been many intervening political, economic and social influences over Thai politics, the legal reforms carried out at the turn of the 20th century laid the constitutional basis for the subsequent power of the Thai monarchy.

In Siam, King Chulalongkorn purported to reject tradition in favour of modernity, but it was a non-secular form of modernity that reinforced and retained certain practices that may be considered traditional. The colonial legal legacy in Cambodia in the years immediately after independence resonates somewhat with that of Siam/Thailand, albeit refracted through different forms and degrees of colonial intervention. Although legal reform in the protectorate was largely controlled by and in the interests of French rule, its indigenous jurisdiction, which formed the foundations of the post-independence justice system, also helped to lay the constitutional and ideological basis for a resurgent royal power. Colonial law encoded the link between royal power, religion and

---

[33] Loos, *Subject Siam*, pp. 15–20, 45. Winichakul, *Siam Mapped*, pp. 95–112.

[34] Tamara Loos, "Gender Adjudicated: Translating Modern Legal Subjects in Siam" (PhD dissertation, Cornell University, 1999), pp. 48–90.

[35] Winichakul, "Absolute Monarchy and the Legal State in Thailand"; Anderson, "Studies of the Thai State", p. 207.

[36] Loos, *Subject Siam*, p. 23.

tradition. This was reflected in the 1947 constitution and is still encapsulated today in the official motto of "nation, religion, king" as enshrined in Article 4 of the 1993 constitution.[37]

Over 40 years after Benedict Anderson wrote his analysis of Thai studies, comparisons, for example between Thailand and Myanmar, appear to contradict his hypothesis that more rather than less colonisation would have benefited Thailand (both as a basis for democracy and for economic development). Anderson's insightful and deliberately provocative analysis appears to rest on too rigid an application of an ultimately Western-centric notion of modernity and the nation state.[38] Today, the analysis also appears more questionable as early 20th century colonial legacies may have faded, mediated by post-independence international and domestic events and by different modes of neo-colonial intervention, including "dollar diplomacy".[39]

Beyond Southeast Asia, France's "model" protectorate in Tunisia had been, like Siam, a centre for economic and diplomatic competition between European powers. However, the French gradually established a monopoly on extraterritorial jurisdiction, which was fundamental to their control. They also later established a local Court of Appeal, enforcing the protectorate's separate status from the neighbouring colony of Algeria. Tunisia became a republic soon after independence, reflecting nationalist Habib ibn Ali Bourguiba's political outlook and dominance. Bourguiba had studied law and political science at the Sorbonne, and constitutionalism and modernity were the leitmotif of his anti-colonial struggle. However, he eventually became president for life, and in this respect failed to make a clean break from the legacies of the traditional rulers, the beys, through whom the French had ruled. After independence, the secular state judicial system absorbed the Islamic courts, which had operated as a separate, albeit supervised, jurisdiction under the French. However, Islam and traditionally interpreted sharia law retained a strong hold over sections of the population and are resurgent today.[40]

---

[37] Constitution of the Kingdom of Cambodia, 21 Sept. 1993.
[38] See, for example, Silak Sivaraksa's comment on Anderson, in *The Study of Thailand*, ed. Eliezer B. Ayal, pp. 248–51; also Loos' discussion of modernity, *Subject Siam*, pp. 19–22.
[39] Dezalay and Garth, *Asian Legal Revivals*, p. 59.
[40] Kenneth Perkins, *A Modern History of Tunisia* (New York: Cambridge University Press, 2013, 2nd ed.), pp. 140–1; Annie Deperchin, "Dimensions internationals de l'installation de la justice française en Tunisie: La négociation de l'abandon des

Comparisons and patterns are interesting and often useful, but every experience of colonial rule was unique and is worthy of study. Structural factors, including the exigencies of domination, framed colonial law in Cambodia, but a myriad of more contingent events and coincidences of interest shaped the colonial legacy in each instance. Cambodia's status as a protectorate, and the many meanings of protection played a formative role in colonial law making. Protection talk provided the language for colonial and Cambodian elites to contest and transact over law. In the name of protecting tradition, these contests entrenched an ethos of authoritarianism and of royal rule, limiting any liberating potential that may have emerged from legal reform.

---

justices consulaires" [International Dimensions of the Installation of French Justice in Tunisia: The Negotiation of the Abandonment of Consular Justice], in *La Justice française et le droit pendant le protectorate en Tunisie*, [French Justice and the Law during the Protectorate in Tunisia] ed. Nada Auzary-Schmaltz (Rabat: Institute de recherche sur le Maghreb contemporain, Maisonneuve & Larose, 2007), pp. 29–41.

Bibliography

Archival Collections

National Archives of Cambodia, Phnom Penh (NAC)
  Collection of the Résident Superieur du Cambodge (RSC)
  Documentation Collection (Doc)
Centre des Archives d'Outre-Mer, Aix en Provence, France (CAOM)
  Fonds du Gouvernement Générale de l'Indochine (GGI)
  Fonds du Résident Supérieur du Cambodge (RSC)
  Fonds Ministériels, Nouveau Fonds (FM NF)
  Fonds Ministériels, Ancien Fonds (FM AF)
Archives de La contemporaine, site de Nanterre, Fonds LDH, France

Official Publications of French Government and French Administration of Indochina

Annuaire Administratif de l'Indochine [Administrative Yearbook of Indochina]. Hanoi: Imprimerie d'Extrême-Orient, 1937.

Annuaire de L'Indo-Chine française: Cochinchine et Cambodge [Yearbook of French Indo-China: Cochin China and Cambodia]. Imprimerie coloniale, 1890, 1897.

Annuaire Général de l'Indochine [General Directory of Indochina]. Hanoi: Imprimerie d'Extrême-Orient, 1900, 1914, 1915, 1919, 1920, 1926.

Annuaire Générale de L'Indo-Chine française [« Puis » De L'indochine] [Yearbook of French Indo-China (then Indochina)]. Hanoi: Imprimerie d'Extrême-Orient, 1922, 1929.

Bonhomme, A. "L'Annam", in *La Justice en Indochine* [Justice in French Indochina], Direction de l'Administration de la Justice [Justice in Indochina, Department for the Administration of Justice] (Paris 1931: Indochine Française). Hanoi: Imprimerie d'Extrême-Orient, 1931, pp. 155–74.

Cochinchine française: Les Codes Cambodgiens [Traduits par M. Cordier] [French Cochin China: The Cambodian Codes (Translated by Mr Cordier)], Henri Cordier, trans., Paris: Imprimerie Nationale, 1881.

214   *Bibliography*

Cressent, M.P.E., "à Administration mixte: Le Laos", in [Justice in Indochina, Department for the Administration of Justice] (Paris 1931: Indochine Française). Hanoi: Imprimerie d'Extrême-Orient, 1931, pp. 82–112.

Doumer, Paul. "Situation de l'Indochine française de 1897 à 1901 (Rapport par Paul Doumer, Gouverneur Général)" [The Situation of French Indochina from 1897 to 1901 (Report by Paul Doumer, Governor General)]. Hanoi: F.H. Schneider, 1902.

Galembert, J. de. *Les administrations et les services publics Indochinois* [Indochinese Public Administration and Services]. Hanoi: Imprimerie Mac Dinh Tu, 1924.

Garrigues, E.A.F. " à Administration unique: la Cochinchine", in *La justice en Indochine*, Direction de l'Administration de la Justice [Justice in Indochina, Department for the Administration of Justice] (Paris 1931: Indochine Française). Hanoi: Imprimerie d'Extrême-Orient, 1931, pp. 41–81.

Habert, L.A. "Le Tonkin" [Tonkin], in *La justice en Indochine,* Direction de l'Administration de la Justice [Justice in Indochina, Department for the Administration of Justice] (Paris 1931: Indochine Française). Hanoi: Imprimerie d'Extrême-Orient, 1931, pp. 175–210.

Journal Judiciaire Cambodgien: Publication de législation, jurisprudence et documentation judiciaire Cambodgiennes: années 1927 à 1930 [Cambodian Judicial Journal: Publication of Cambodian Legislation, Jurisprudence and Judicial Documentation: Years 1927 to 1930]. Hanoi: Imprimerie du Gouvernement Générale, 1930.

Journal Officiel du Cambodge [Official Journal of Cambodia]. Phnom Penh: Royaume du Cambodge, 1919–40.

Morché, H. "Organisation Judiciaire de l'Indochine" [The Legal Organisation in French Indochina], in *La justice en Indochine*, Direction de l'Administration de la Justice [Justice in Indochina, Department for the Administration of Justice] (for the Exposition Coloniale Internationale, Paris 1931: Indochine Française). Hanoi: Imprimerie d'Extrême-Orient, 1931, pp. 9–38.

Nicolas, L.P. "Le Cambodge" (Cambodia], in *La justice en Indochine.* Direction de l'Administration de la Justice [Justice in Indochina, Department for the Administration of Justice] (Paris 1931: Indochine Française). Hanoi: Imprimerie d'Extrême-Orient, 1931, pp. 113–154.

Régime Législatif, Administratif et Judiciaire de L'indochine [Legislative, Administrative and Judicial Regime of Indochina]. Paris: Agence économique des colonies françaises, 1944.

Silvestre, A. *Le Cambodge Administratif: cours professé à l'École d'Administration Cambodgienne.* [The Administration of Cambodia: Course for the Cambodian School of Administration] Phnom Penh: Imprimerie Nouvelle, Albert l'Ortail, 1924.

Frequently Quoted Compilations of Colonial Legislation

Dareste, P. and G. Appert, ed. *Recueil de législation & jurisprudence coloniales* [Collection of Colonial Legislation and Jurisprudence] (Paris: Challamel 1898–1935) (*Recueil Dareste*) [Dareste Collection].

Michel, Gabriel. *Code Judiciaire de l'Indo-Chine: lois, décrets et arrêtés concernant le service judiciaire et applicables par Les cours et les tribunaux de l'Indo-Chine 1904–1913* [Judicial Code of Indo-China: Laws, Decrees and *arrêtés* Concerning the Judicial Service and Applicable by the Courts and Tribunals of Indo-China 1904–1913] (Imprimèrie d'extrême-orient, Hanoi 1914) (Michel, *Code Judiciaire*).

Gouvernement Générale de l'Indochine. *Recueil des actes du Gouvernement cambodgien* [Government of Indochina, Collection of Acts of the Cambodian Government], 2nd Supplement, 1922–23 (*Recueil des Actes 1922–3*) [Collection of Acts 1922–3] NAC Doc, Box 425.

Gouvernement Générale de l'Indochine. *Recueil des Actes du Gouvernement Cambodgienne* [Government of Indochina, Collection of Acts of the Cambodian Government], *3ème supplément, années 1926, 1927, 1928, 1929 et rappels d'années antérieurs*, Collection of Acts of the Cambodian Government, 3rd Supplement, Years 1926, 1927, 1928, 1929, and Recalls from Previous Years, 1929], NAC Doc, Box 425.

Treaties and Conventions

Treaty of Amity, Commerce and Protection between France and Cambodia, 11 August 1863, 128 Consolidated Treaty Series, 143.

Declaration between France and Cambodia relative to the Trial of Causes between Europeans, 17 November 1880, 157 Consolidated Treaty Series, 189.

Convention of 18 December 1881: Moving to the Conseil Privé of Cochinchina, the responsibility to judge litigious matters between the Cambodian government and litigants who fall under the French court. In *Annuaire de l'Indo-Chine Française: Cochinchine et Cambodge* [Yearbook of French Indo-China: Cochin China and Cambodia] (1890), 582.

Convention between France and Cambodia for the Regulation of their respective Relations (1884 Convention), signed at Phnom Penh, 17 June 1884, 164 Consolidated Treaty Series, 99.

Accord setting out the provisional modus vivendi between France and Cambodia, *Bulletin administratif du Cambodge* [Administrative Bulletin of Cambodia], 7 January 1946, p. 23.

Cambodian Codes

Civil Code (Kingdom of Cambodia, 1911) NAC RSC 30549.

Code of Criminal Investigation and Judicial Organisation (Kingdom of Cambodia, 1911) NAC Box 423.

Penal Code (Kingdom of Cambodia, 1911) NAC Doc, Box 423.

Civil Code and Cambodian Civil Procedure (Protectorate of Cambodia, 1920) NAC Doc, Box 423.

Penal Code (Kingdom of Cambodia, 1924) NAC Doc, Box 423.

Code of Procedure in Penal Matters (Cambodia, 1938) NAC RSC 4569.

Code of Procedure in Civil Matters (Cambodia, 1938) NAC Doc, Box 423.

Code of Civil Procedure (as amended in 1963) NAC Doc, Box 257.

Cambodian Royal Ordinances and Kram

Royal Ordinance 1 April 1873, *Regarding the legal attributions with regard to Europeans admitted to reside in Cambodia*, CAOM FM AF, 250-0-01 (10) Carton 250.

Royal Ordinance 15 January 1877, *Concerning the reforms introduced in the government and administration of Cambodia*, CAOM GGI 12033.

Royal Ordinance 4 March 1897 (Untitled, regarding diverse aspects of judicial procedure) NAC RSC 32941.

Royal Ordinance 11 July 1897 (Untitled, abolishing slavery and establishing government's right to appropriate unoccupied land), Michel, *Code Judiciaire*, 840.

Royal Ordinance 13 August 1897, *Cambodia: suppression of the Commission of Appeal and of the Mixed Tribunal*, Michel, *Code Judiciaire*, 844.

Royal Ordinance 11 August 1901 (Untitled, establishing committees to revise Cambodian codes) NAC RSC 30549.

Royal Ordinance No. 21, 7 February 1902 (Untitled, regarding civil procedure and composition of courts) NAC RSC 33034.

Royal Ordinance 24 January 1908, *Organising real property in Cambodian and establishing land registers*, NAC RSC 26315.

Royal Ordinance No. 19, 5 May 1905 (Untitled, regarding composition of committees to re-codify Cambodian law) NAC RSC 30546.

Royal Ordinance 14 August 1908 (regarding the case of Nhem and the descendants of Sot) NAC RSC 20644.

Royal Ordinance 13 October 1912 (draft) NAC RSC 36976.

Royal Ordinance No. 118, 14 September 1922, *Judicial Organisation of Cambodia* (*Recueil des Actes 1922–3*) [Collection of Acts 1922–3], 82, also NAC Doc, Box 245.

Bibliography

Royal Ordinance No. 119, 15 September 1922, *On the status of administrative and judicial personnel of Cambodia* (*Recueil des Actes 1922–3*) [Collection of Acts 1922–3], 99.

Royal Ordinance No. 142, 23 December 1922, *Setting the jurisdictions of the courts of Cambodia* (*Recueil des Actes 1922–3*) [Collection of Acts 1922–3], 138.

Royal Ordinance 11 August 1923, *Modifying article 70 of the Code of Criminal Investigation and the creation of an indictment chamber in the appeal court* (*Recueil des Actes 1922–3*) [Collection of Acts 1922–3], 168.

Royal Ordinance 15 March 1932, *Organising and regulating legal defence before the Cambodian courts* (*Recueil Dareste 1933*) [Dareste Collection 1933], 478.

Royal Ordinance No. 157, 7 December 1932 (Untitled, allowing some members of the Cambodian administrative corps to join the judicial corps) NAC RSC 28235.

Royal Ordinance No. 231, 16 December 1938 (Untitled, regarding distribution of the 1938 Civil Procedure Code) NAC Doc, Box 423.

Royal Ordinance No. 97, *On the administration of the Kingdom*, in *Bulletin Administratif du Cambodge* [Administrative Bulletin of Cambodia], 5 July 1940, pp. 1747–55.

Kram No. 1 *On the administration of Cambodia*, 1940, art. 2. In *Bulletin administratif du Cambodge* [Administrative Bulletin of Cambodia], 5 August 1940, p. 1609.

Kram No. 320/NS, 30 June 1959, *Law on reform of judicial organisation*, NAC Doc, Box 257.

French Codes, Decrees and arrêtés

Penal Code (France) 1810 (transcribed by Tom Holmberg, *The Napoleon Series*, https://www.napoleon-series.org/research/government/france/penalcode/c_penalcode3b.html [accessed 16 June 2023]).

Code Pénal (France) 1810, Legifrance: www.legifrance.gouv.fr/affichCode .do;jsessionid=4D177A053C751C9381C678A844DFEE71.tpdila10v_1 ?cidTexte=LEGITEXT000006071029&dateTexte=19940228 (accessed 29 November 2016).

Decree of 6 May 1898 (President of France), *Regarding the reorganisation of justice services in Cambodia* (*Recueil Dareste 1898*) [Dareste Collection 1898], 131–2.

Arrêté of Governor General of Indochina, 13 August 1897, *Regarding suppression of the Commission of Appeal and the mixed courts, attribution of the competence to the court of first instance of matters previously submitted to the mixed jurisdiction* (*Recueil Dareste 1898*) [Dareste Collection 1898], 12.

218   Bibliography

Arrêté of Governor General of Indochina, 18 May 1905 (untitled, regarding
    legislation to apply in territories ceded to France/Cambodia by Saim)
    CAOM GGI 65576.
Arrêté of Résident Supérieur of Cambodia, 19 September 1922 (untitled, re-
    garding the role of the Judicial Advisor) (*Recueil des Actes 1922–3*)
    [Collection of Acts 1922–3], 95.

Secondary Sources

Achour, Sana Ben. "Juges et magistrats tunisiens dans l'ordre colonial", in *La
    Justice française et le droit pendant le protectorate en Tunisie* [French
    Justice and the Law during the Tunisian Protectorate], ed. Nada
    Auzary-Schmaltz. Rabat: Institut de recherché sur le Maghreb contem-
    porain, 2007, pp. 153–73.
Aldrich, Robert. *Greater France: A History of French Overseas Expansion.*
    Basingstoke: Macmillan, 1996.
————. *Banished Potentates: Dethroning and Exiling Indigenous Monarchs
    under British and French Colonial Rule, 1815–1955.* Manchester:
    Manchester University Press, 2018.
Alexandrowicz, Charles Henry. "The Afro-Asian World and the Law of Nations:
    Historical Aspects", *Collected Courses of the Hague Academy of International
    Law*, vol. 123. Leiden: Martinus Nijhoff, 1968.
Amrith, Sunil S. "Indians Overseas? Governing Tamil Migration to Malaya
    1870–1941", *Past and Present* 208 (2010): 231–61.
Anderson, Benedict. "Studies of the Thai State: The State of Thai Studies", in
    *The Study of Thailand: Analyses of Knowledge, Approaches, and Prospects
    in Anthropology, Art History, Economics, History, and Political Science*,
    ed. Eliezer B. Ayal. Athens: Ohio University Center for International
    Studies, 1978, pp. 193–247.
————. *Imagined Communities: Reflections on the Origin and Spread of
    Nationalism.* London: Verso, 1991.
————. *Exploration and Irony in Studies of Siam over Forty Years.* Ithaca:
    Southeast Asia Program, Cornell University, 2014.
Ang, Hean Leng and Amanda Whiting. "Federalism and Legal Unification in
    Malaysia", in *Federalism and Legal Unification, Federalism and Legal
    Unification: A Comparative Empirical Investigation of Twenty Systems*, ed.
    Daniel Halberstam and Mathias Reimann. Dordrecht: Springer, 2014,
    pp. 295–336.
Anghi, Antony. *Imperialism, Sovereignty, and the Making of International Law.*
    Cambridge: Cambridge University Press, 2005.
Anonymous. "La politique indigène de la France au Cambodge, appréciée par
    un Mandarin Cambodgien" [French Indigenous Policies in Cambodia,

as Perceived by a Cambodian Mandarin], *La Revue du Pacifique* [The Pacific Review] 3 (1934): 143–57.

Aso, Mitch. "Rubber and Race in Rural Colonial Cambodia (1920s–1954)", *Siksacakr* 12–3 (2010–11): 127–38.

Au, Chhieng, *Fondement du deuxième traité de Protectorat français sur le Cambodge*, Introduced & edited by Grégory Mikaelian (forthcoming) (Paris, Association Péninsule, Cahiers de Péninsule Vol. 14, August 2023, 356).

Au, Sokhieng. *Mixed Medicines: Health and Culture in French Colonial Cambodia*. Chicago: University of Chicago Press, 2011.

Aun, Wu Min. *The Malaysian Legal System*. Malaysia: Longman, 1990.

Aung-Thwin, Maitrii. *The Return of the Gallon King: History, Law and Rebellion in Colonial Burma*. Ohio: Ohio University Press, 2011.

Aymonier, Étienne. *Le Cambodge: Le royaume actuel* [Cambodia, the Current Kingdom]. Paris: Ernest Leroux, 1900.

Baker, Chris and Pasuk Phongpaichit, trans. and ed. *The Palace Law of Ayutthaya and the Thammasat: Law and Kinship in Siam*. Ithaca, NY: Cornell University, 2016.

Barnhart, James. "Violence and the Civilizing Mission: Native Justice in French Colonial Vietnam, 1858–1914". PhD dissertation, University of Chicago, 1999.

Baxi, Upendra. "Postcolonial Legality", in *A Companion to Postcolonial Studies*, ed. Henry Schwartz and Sangeeta Ray. Oxford: Blackwell, 2000, pp. 540–55.

———. "The Colonialist Heritage", in *Comparative Legal Studies: Traditions and Transitions*, ed. Pierre Legrand and Roderick Munday. Cambridge: Cambridge University Press, 2003, pp. 46–75.

Beard, Jennifer. *The Political Economy of Desire: International Law, Development and the Nation State*. New York: Routledge, 2006.

Bell, John, Sophie Boyron and Simon Whittaker. *Principles of French Law*. Oxford: Oxford University Press, 1998.

Benton, Lauren. *Law and Colonial Cultures: Legal Regimes in World History, 1400–1900*. Cambridge: Cambridge University Press, 2002.

Benton, Lauren and Adam Clulow. "Introduction: The Long Strange History of Protection", in *Protection and Empire: A Global History*, ed. Lauren Benton, Adam Clulow and Bain Attwood. Cambridge: Cambridge University Press, 2018, pp. 1–9.

Betts, Raymond F. *Assimilation and Association in French Colonial Theory, 1890–1914*. New York: Columbia University Press, 1961.

Bhatti, Muhammad Shafique. "Empire, Law and History: The British Origin of Modern Historiography of South Asia", *Pakistan Journal of Social Sciences (PJSS)* 30, 2 (Dec. 2010): 389–400.

220   *Bibliography*

Bignami, Francesca. "Comparative Administrative Law", in *The Cambridge Companion to Comparative Law*, ed. Mauro Bussani and Ugo Mettei. Cambridge: Cambridge University Press, 2012, pp. 145–70.

Blazy, Adrien. "L'Organisation judiciaire en Indochine française (1858–1945)" [The Legal Organisation in French Indochina (1858–1945)]. PhD dissertation, Université de Toulouse, 2012.

Boudillon, A. *La question foncière et l'organsiation du livre foncier en Afrique Occidentale française* [The Question of Real Property and the Organisation of Land Registers in French West Africa]. Paris: Challamel, 1911.

———. *Le régime de la propriété foncière en Indochine* [The System of Real Property in Indochina]. Paris: Émile Larose, 1915.

Bourdieu, Pierre. "La Force du Droit [Eléments Pour une Sociologie du Champ Juridique]", *Actes de la recherche en sciences sociales* [The Force of Law: Towards a Sociology of the Juridical Field, Proceedings of Research in the Social Sciences] 64 (Sept. 1986): 3–19.

———. "The Force of Law: Towards a Sociology of the Juridical Field", trans. and introduction, Richard Terdiman, *Hastings Law Journal* 38 (1987): 805–53.

———. *The Sociologist and the Historian / Pierre Bourdieu and Roger Chartier*, trans. David Fernbach. Cambridge, Malden: Polity Press, 2015.

Bourdieu, Pierre and Loïc J. D. Wacquant. *An Invitation to Reflexive Sociology*. Chicago: Chicago University Press, 1992.

Boyron, Sophie. "Constitutional Law", in *Principles of French Law*, ed. John Bell, Sophie Boyron and Simon Whittaker. Oxford: Oxford University Press, 1998, pp. 147–56.

———. *The Constitution of France: A Contextual Analysis*. Oxford: Hart Publishing, 2013.

Broadhurst, Roderick, Thierry Bouhours and Brigitte Bouhours. *Violence and the Civilising Process in Cambodia*. Cambridge: Cambridge University Press, 2015.

Brocheux, Pierre and Daniel Hémery. *Indochina: An Ambiguous Colonisation, 1858–1954*. 2nd ed., trans. Ly Lan Dill-Klein. Berkeley: University of California Press, 2009.

Brunschwig, Henri. *French Colonialism 1871–1914: Myths and Realities*. London: Pall Mall Press, 1966.

Burns, Peter. "The Netherlands East Indies: Colonial Legal Policy and the Definitions of Law", in *Laws of South-East Asia*, vol. 2, ed. M. B. Hooker. Singapore: Butterworth, 1986–88, pp. 147–298.

Chandler, David. "Cambodian Palace Chronicles (Rajabansavatar) 1927–1949: Kingship and Historiography at the End of the Colonial Era", in *Perceptions of the Past in Southeast Asia*, ed. Anthony Reid and David Marr. Singapore, Kuala Lumpur and Hong Kong: Heinemann, 1979, pp. 189–210.

————. "The Assassination of Résident Bardez (1925): A Premonition of Revolt in Colonial Cambodia", originally in *Journal of Siam Society* (Summer 1982), reproduced in David Chandler, *Facing the Cambodian Past: Selected Essays 1971–1994*. Bangkok: Silkworm Books, 1996, pp. 139–58.

————. "The Tragedy of Cambodian History", in David Chandler, *Facing the Cambodian Past: Selected Essays 1971–1994*. Bangkok: Silkworm Books, 1996, pp. 295–313.

Chandler, David P. *The Tragedy of Cambodian History: Politics, War and Revolution since 1945*. Bangkok: Silkworm Books, 1991.

————. *A History of Cambodia*. 4th ed. Boulder, CO: Westview Press, 2008.

Chandler, David Porter. "Cambodia before the French: Politics in a Tributary Kingdom, 1794–1848". PhD dissertation, Cornell University, 1973.

Chandler, David and Anthony Barnett, *The Uncrowned King of Cambodia: The Life of Colonel E.D. (Moke) Murray, DSO, OBE, 1910–2002* (forthcoming).

Chatterjee, Partha. *The Nation and Its Fragments: Colonial and Postcolonial Histories*. Princeton: Princeton University Press, 1993.

Cheesman, Nick. *Opposing the Rule of Law: How Myanmar's Courts Make Law and Order*, Cambridge Studies in Law and Society. Cambridge: Cambridge University Press, 2015.

————. "Rule-of-Law Lineages in Colonial and Early Post-Colonial Burma", *Modern Asian Studies* 50, 2 (2016): 564–601.

Collard, Paul. *Cambodge et Cambodgiens: métamorphose du Royaume Khmèr par une méthode française de protectorat* [Cambodia and the Cambodians: The Metamorphosis of the Khmer Kingdom by the Method of the French Protectorate]. Paris: Société d'éditions géographiques, maritimes et coloniales, 1925.

Conklin, Alice L. *A Mission to Civilize: The Republican Idea of Empire in France and West Africa, 1895–1930*. Stanford, CA: Stanford University Press, 1997.

Curthoys, Anne and John Docker. *Is History Fiction?* Sydney: University of New South Wales Press, 2006.

David, René and Henry P. de Vries. *The French Legal System: An Introduction to Civil Law Systems*. New York: Oceana, 1958.

Decoux, Jean. *À la barre de l'Indochine: Histoire de mon Gouvernement Général 1940–1945* [At the Helm of Indochina: History of My Government-General 1940–1945]. Paris: Soukha, 2013. First published Librairie Plon, 1949.

Deperchin, Annie. "Dimensions internationals de l'installation de la justice française en Tunisie: La négociation de l'abandon des justices consulaires" [International Dimensions of the Installation of French Justice in Tunisia: The Negotiation of the Abandonment of Consular Justice], in *La Justice française et le droit pendant le protectorate en Tunisie* [French Justice and the Law during the Protectorate in Tunisia], ed. Nada Auzary-Schmaltz. Rabat: Institute de recherche sur le Maghreb contemporain, Maisonneuve & Larose, 2007, pp. 29–41.

Derrida, F., Ch. Buniet and R. Bastannetto. "Annales de la faculté de droit de Phnom Penh" [Annals of the Faculty of Law of Phnom Penh 1961], *Revue internationale de droit comparé* [International Review of Comparative Law] 13, 4 (1961): 841–8.

Derrida, Jacques and Eric Premowitz. "Archive Fever: A Freudian Impression", *Diacritics* 25, 4 (1995): 9–63.

Dezalay, Yves and Bryant Garth. *Asian Legal Revivals: Lawyers in the Shadow of Empire*. Chicago: University of Chicago Press, 2010.

Duguit, Léon. *Traité de droit constitutionnel. 1927–1930* [Treatise on Constitutional Law 1927–1930]. Paris: Ancienne Libraire Fontemoing, 1927.

Durand, Bernard. "Prolégomènes: originalités et conformités de la justice coloniale sous la Troisième République" Prolegomena: Originalities and Conformities of Colonial Justice under the Third Republic], in *Le Juge et l'Outre- mer: Les roches bleues de l'empire colonial* [The Judge and Overseas Territory: The Blue Rocks of the Colonial Empire], vol. 2, ed. Bernard Durand and Martine Fabre. Lille: Centre d'histoire judiciaire éditeur, 2004, pp. 7–42.

———. "L'impératif de proximité dans l'Empire colonial français: les justices de paix à compétence étendue" [The Imperative of Proximity in the French Colonial Empire: Justices of the Peace with Expanded Competence], *Histoire de la justice* [History of Justice] 17, 1 (2007): 209–26.

———. "Les Magistrats coloniaux entre absence et errance" [Colonial Judges: Between Absence and Wandering], in *Le juge et l'Outre-mer, Histoire du droit des colonies: les roches bleues de l'empire colonial* [The Judge and Overseas Territory: The Blue Rocks of the Colonial Empire], ed. Bernard Durand and Martine Fabre. Lille: Centre d'histoire judiciaire, 2009, pp. 47–70.

Duras, Marguerite. *L'Amant* [The Lover]. Paris: Les éditions de Minuit, 1900.

———. *Un Barrage contre la pacifique* [A Wall against the Pacific]. Paris: Gallimard, 1958.

Edwards, Penny. "Womanizing Indochina: Fiction, Nation, and Cohabitation in Colonial Cambodia, 1890–1930", in *Domesticating the Empire: Race, Gender and Family Life in French and Dutch Colonialism*, ed. Julia Clancy-Smith and Frances Gouda. Charlottesville: University of Virginia Press, 1998, pp. 108–30.

———. "On Home Ground: Settling Land and Domesticating Difference in the 'Non-Settler' Colonies of Burma and Cambodia", *Journal of Colonialism and Colonial History* 4, no. 3 (2003). DOI:10.1353/cch.2004.0002.

Bibliography

———. *Cambodge: The Cultivation of a Nation, 1860–1945*. Bangkok: Silkworm Books, 2008.

Ehrentraut, Stefan. "Perpetually Temporary: Citizenship and Ethnic Vietnamese in Cambodia", *Ethnic and Racial Studies* 34 (May 2011): 779–99.

Engel, David M. "Litigation across Space and Time: Courts, Conflict, and Social Change", *Law and Society Review* 24, 2 (1990): 333–44.

Esmein, Adhémar and Henry Nézard. *Éléments de Droit Constitutionnel Français et Comparé*. [Elements of French Constitutional Law and Comparisons, Vol. 1] 7th ed. Paris: Larose, 1921.

Fabre, Martine. "Le magistrat d'outre-mer: L'aventure de la justice" [The Overseas Judge: The Justice Adventure], in *Le juge et l'outre-mer: Les roches bleues de l'empire colonial* [The Judge and Overseas Territory: The Blue Rocks of the Colonial Empire], vol. 2, ed. Bernard Durand and Martine Fabre. Lille: Centre d'histoire judiciaire éditeur, 2004, pp. 71–93.

Foong, Mr Justice Dato James. *The Malaysian Judiciary: A Record from 1786 to 1993*. Kuala Lumpur: Malayan Law Journal, 1994.

Foong, Tan Sri James. *The Malaysian Judiciary: A Record*. 3rd ed. Selangor Darul Ehsan, Malaysia: LexisNexis, 2017.

Forest, Alain. *Le Cambodge et la colonisation française: histoire d'une colonisation sans heurts (1897–1920)* [Cambodia and French Colonisation: History of a Smooth Colonisation (1897–1920)]. Paris: Harmattan, 1980.

Furnivall, J. S. *Colonial Policy and Practice: A Comparative Study of Burma and Netherlands India*. New York: New York University Press, 1956. First published Cambridge University Press, 1948.

Garros, Georges. *Forceries Humaines: L'Indochine litigieuse. Esquisse d'une entente franco-annamite.* [Human Hothouses: Litigious Indochina. Towards Franco-Annamite Understanding] Paris: Delpeuch, 1926.

Girault, Arthur. *Principes de Colonsation et de Législation Coloniale* [Principles of Colonisation and of Colonial Legislation]. Paris: Libraire de la société du recueil général des lois et des arrêts, 1894 and 1904 editions.

Goscha, Christopher. *The Penguin Modern History of Vietnam*. London: Penguin, 2017. First published Allen Lane, 2016.

Gour, Claude-Gilles. *Institutions Constitutionnelles et Politiques du Cambodge* [Constitutional and Political Institutions of Cambodia]. Paris: Libraire Dalloz, 1965.

Guerin, Adam. "Racial Myth, Colonial Reform and the Invention of Customary Law in Morocco, 1912–13", *The Journal of North African Studies* 16, 3 (2011): 361–80.

Guérin, Mathieu. *Paysans de la Forêt à l'Epoque Coloniale* [Peasants of the Forest in the Colonial Era]. Paris: Presses universitaires de Rennes, 2008.

Gullick, J. M. *Rulers and Residents: Influence and Power in the Malay States: 1870–1920*. Oxford: Oxford University Press, 1992.

Halliday, Terence C. and Lucien Karpik. "Political Liberalism in the British Post-Colony", in *Fates of Political Liberalism in the British Post-Colony: The Politics of the Legal Complex*, ed. Terence C. Halliday, Lucien Karpik and Malcolm M. Feeley. Cambridge: Cambridge University Press, 2012, pp. 3–55.

Hansen, Anne Ruth. *How to Behave: Buddhism and Modernity in Colonial Cambodia, 1860–1930*. Honolulu: University of Hawai'i Press, 2007.

Harding, Andrew, *The Constitution of Malaysia: A Contextual Analysis*. Portland, OR: Hart, 2012.

———. "'Nazrinian' Monarchy in Malaysia: The Resilience and Revival of a Traditional Institution", in *Law and Society in Malaysia*, ed. Andrew Harding and Dian A. H. Shah. London: Routledge, 2017, pp. 72–95.

Harding, Andrew and Amanda Whiting. "Custodians of Civil Liberties and Justice in Malaysia: The Malaysian Bar and the Moderate State", in *Fates of Political Liberalism in the British Post-Colony*, ed. Terence C. Halliday. Cambridge: Cambridge University Press, 2012, pp. 247–304.

Harouel, Jean-Louis. "Un grand savant et administrateur, Jean Imbert (1919–1999) [A Great Scholar and Administrator, Jean Imbert (1919–1999)]", *Bulletin d'histoire de la Sécurité Sociale* [Bulletin of the History of Social Security] 41 (Jan. 2000): 8–22.

Hawksley, Charles Michael. "Administrative Colonialism: District Administration and Colonial 'Middle Management' in Kelantan 1909–1919 and the Eastern Highlands of Papua New Guinea 1947–1957". PhD dissertation, University of Wollongong, 2001.

———. មរតកយុត្តិធម៌ខ្មែរ [The Heritage of Khmer Justice]. Phom Penh: eLibrary of Cambodia, 2009.

Hel, Chamroeun, "Introduction to the Land Law of Cambodia" in *Introduction to Cambodian Law*, ed. Hor Peng, Kong Phallack, Jörg Menzel. Phnom Penh: Konrad Adenauer Foundation, 2012, pp. 313–34.

Hobsbawm, Eric. "Introduction: Inventing Traditions", in *The Invention of Tradition*, ed. Eric Hobsbawm and Terence Ranger. Cambridge: Cambridge University Press, 1983, pp. 1–14.

Hocking, Jenny. *The Palace Letters: The Queen, the Governor-General, and the Plot to Dismiss Gough Whitlam*. Melbourne: Scribe, 2020.

Hoeffel, Ernest. "De la condition juridique des étrangers au Cambodge" [On the Legal Status of Foreigners in Cambodia]. PhD dissertation, Charles Hiller University, Strasbourg, 1932.

Hoffman, Katherine E. "Berber Law by French Means: Customary Courts in the Moroccan Hinterlands, 1930–1956", *Comparative Studies in Society and History* 52, 4 (2010): 851–80.

Hong, Lysa. "'Stranger within the Gates': Knowing Semi-Colonial Siam as Extraterritorials", *Modern Asian Studies* 38, 2 (2004): 327–54.

———. "Extraterritoriality in Bangkok in the Reign of King Chulalongkorn, 1868–1910: The Cacophonies of Semi-Colonial Cosmopolitanism", *Itinerario: Journal of Imperial and Global Interactions* 27, 2 (2013): 125–46. DOI:10.1017/S0165115300020568.

Hooker, M.B. *Legal Pluralism: An Introduction to Colonial and Neo-Colonial Laws*. Oxford: Clarendon Press, 1975.

———. *A Concise Legal History of South-East Asia*. Oxford: Clarendon Press; New York: Oxford University Press, 1978.

———. "English Law in Sumatra, Java, the Straits Settlements, Malay States, Sarawak, North Borneo and Brunei", in *Laws of South-East Asia*, vol. 2, ed. M.B. Hooker. Singapore: Butterworth, 1986–88, pp. 299–446.

Hutchcroft, Paul D. "Colonial Masters, National Politics, and Provincial Lords: Central Authority and Local Autonomy in the American Philippines, 1900–1913", *Journal of Asian Studies* 59, 2 (2000): 277–306.

Huxley, Andrew. "Is Burmese Law Burmese? John Jardine, Em Forchhammer and Legal Orientalism", *Australian Journal of Asian Law* 10 (2008): 184–201.

Imam, Vannary. *When Elephants Fight: A Memoir*. Melbourne: Allen and Unwin, 2000.

Imbert, Jean. *Histoire des institutions khmères* [History of Khmer Institutions]. Phnom Penh: Entreprise Khmère de Librairie, Annales de la faculté de droit de Phnom Penh [Annals of the Faculty of Law of Phnom Penh], 1961.

Jacobsen, Trude. "Divergent Perspectives on the Cambodian 'Harem' in the Reigns of Norodom (1863–1904) and Sisowath (1904–1927)", *Working Paper* 133. Melbourne: Melbourne University Press, 2010.

Jacobsen, Trudy. *Lost Goddesses: The Denial of Female Power in Cambodian History*. Copenhagen: NIAS Press, 2008.

James, Eldon R. "Jurisdiction over Foreigners in Siam", *The American Journal of International Law* 16, 4 (1922): 585–603.

Jennar, Raoul Marc. *Comment Malraux est devenu Malraux de l'indifférence à l'engagement* [How Malraux Became Malraux: From Indifference to Engagement]. Perpignan: Cap Bear, 2015.

Jennar, Raoul M., ed. and trans. *The Cambodian Constitutions (1953–1993)*. Bangkok: White Lotus, 1995.

Jennings, Eric T. *Vichy in the Tropics: Pétain's National Revolution in Madagascar, Guadeloupe, and Indochina, 1940–1944*. Stanford, CA: Stanford University Press, 2001.

Joleaud-Barral, J., *La Colonisation française en Annam et au Tonkin* [The French Colonisation of Annam and Tonkin]. Paris: Librairie Plon, 1899.

Kau, Sokhon. "Introduction", in Norodom Sihanouk, "Étude Corrective de la Constitution Accordée par SM le Roi du Cambodge en 1947" [Corrective Study of the Constitution Granted by His Majesty the King of Cambodia in 1947], *France-Asie: revue mensuelle de culture et de synthèse Franco-Asiatique* [France-Asia: Monthly Review of Culture and of Franco-Asiatic Synthesis] 11, 108 (May 1955): 654–63.

Kaur, Amarjit. "Labour Brokers in Migration: Understanding Historical and Contemporary Transnational Migration Regimes in Malaya/Malaysia", *International Review of Social History* 57, 20 (2012): 225–52.

Kiernan, Ben. *How Pol Pot Came to Power*. London: Verso, 1985.

———. *Việt Nam: A History from Earliest Times to the Present*. New York: Oxford University Press, 2017.

Kleinpeter, Roger. *Le problème foncier au Cambodge* [The Land Problem in Cambodia]. Paris: Editions Domat-Montchrestien, 1935.

Kolsky, Elizabeth. "Codification and the Rule of Colonial Difference: Criminal Procedure in British India", *Law and History Review* 23, 3 (2005): 631–85. DOI:10.1017/S0738248000000596.

———. *Colonial Justice in British India: White Violence and the Rule of Law*. Cambridge: Cambridge Studies in Indian History and Society, 2011.

L.F. Untitled review of "Le livre de Vésandar, le roi charitable (Sâlra Maha Chéadok, ou Livre du Grand Jâkata)" [The Book of Vésandar, the Charitable King (Sâlra Maha Chéadok, or the Grand Jâkata)] by Adhémard Leclére, *Bulletin de l'École Française d'Extrême-Orient* [Bulletin of the French School of the Far-East] 3, 1 (1903): 328–34.

Lamant, Pierre L. "Histoire Moderne du Cambodge" [Modern History of Cambodia], *École pratique des hautes études. 4e section, Sciences historiques et philologiques* [Practical School of Advanced Studies. 4th Section, Historical and Philological Sciences] 110, 1 (1978): 1123–8.

Lange, Matthew. *Lineages of Despotism and Development: British Colonialism and State Power*. Chicago Scholarship Online, 2009, DOI:10.7208/chicago /9780226470702.001.0001.

Langlois, Walter G. *André Malraux: The Indochina Adventure*. New York; Washington; London: Praeger, 1966.

Laquièze, Alain. "État de Droit and National Sovereignty in France", in *The Rule of Law: History, Theory and Criticism*, ed. Pietro Costa and Danilo Zolo. Dordecht: Springer, 2007, pp. 261–91.

Leclère, Adhémard. *Recherches sur la législation Cambodgienne (droit privé)*. [Research on Cambodian Legislation (Private Law)] Paris: Challamel, 1890.

———. *Droit Cambodgien* [Cambodian Law]. Paris: Larose, 1894.

———. *Recherches sur la législation criminelle et la procédure des Cambodgiens* [Research on the Criminal Legislation and Procedure of the Cambodians]. Paris: Challamel, 1894.

———. *Recherches sur le droit public des Cambodgiens* [Research on the Cambodians' Public Law]. Paris: Librairie Coloniale, 1894.

————. trans. *Les Codes Cambodgiens* [The Cambodian Codes], vols. 1 and 2. Paris: Ernest Leroux, 1898.

Lee, H.P. *Constitutional Conflicts in Contemporary Malaysia*. Kuala Lumpur: Oxford University Press, 1995.

Lee, Jack Jin Gary. "Plural Society and the Colonial State: English Law and the Making of the Crown Colony Government in the Straits Settlements", *Asian Journal of Law and Society* 2 (2015): 229–49.

Léger, Maxime. "Rapport: Sur l'organisation actuelle de Juridictions nationales du Cambodge" [Report on the Current Organisation of the National Courts of Cambodia], *Journal judiciaire de l'Indochine française* [Judicial Journal of French Indochina] 10 (1947): 69–80.

————. "L'organisation judiciaire du Cambodge et son évolution depuis le traité du Protectorat (1863) jusqu'à la promulgation de la nouvelle Constitution du Royaume Khmer (6 mai 1947)" [The Legal and Judicial Organisation of Cambodia and its Evolution Since the Treaty of the Protectorate (1863) up to the Promulgation of the New Cambodian Royal Constitution (6 May, 1947)], in *Recueil général de jurisprudence, de doctrine et de législation coloniales et maritimes* [General Collection of Colonial and Maritime Jurisprudence, Doctrine and Legislation], ed. D. Penant (Mar. 1950): 47–90.

Lekéal, Farid. "La Place de la justice française dans la distribution des pouvoirs au sein du protectrat tunisien: deux décennies d'ajustement (1883–1903)" [The Place of French Justice in the Distribution of Powers in the Tunisian Protectorate: Two Decades of Adjustment (1883–1903)], in *La Justice française et le droit pendant le protectorate en Tunisie* [French Justice and the Law during the Tunisian Protectorate], ed. Nada Auzary-Schmaltz. Rabat: Institut de recherche sur le Maghreb contemporain, 2007, pp. 43–63.

Lekéal, Farid and Annie Deperchin. "Le protectorat, alternative à la colonisation? Pistes de recherche pour l'histoire du droit" [The Protectorate, an Alternative to Colonisation? Paths of Research for the History of Law], *Clio@Thiemis* [Online], 4, 2011.

Lev, Daniel. "Colonial Law and the Genesis of the Indonesian State", in *Legal Evolution and Political Authority in Indonesia: Selected Essays*. Leiden: Kluwer, 2000, pp. 13–32.

Lilja, Mona. "Discourses of Hybrid Democracy: The Case of Cambodia", *Asian Journal of Political Science* 18, 3 (2010): 289–309.

Loos, Tamara. "Gender Adjudicated: Translating Modern Legal Subjects in Siam". PhD dissertation, Cornell University, 1999.

————. *Subject Siam: Family, Law, and Colonial Morality in Thailand*. Ithaca, NY: Cornell University Press, 2006.

Lortat-Jacob, R.A. *Sauvons l'Indochine* [Save Indochina]. Paris: Éditions de "la Griffe", 1927.

Low, Sally. "Les Tribunaux Residentiels: Disputed Jurisdictions in the Protectorate of Cambodia", *French Colonial History* 16 (2016): 73–102.

Madsen, Mikael Rask and Yves Dezalay. "Pierre Bourdieu's Sociology of Law: From the Genesis of the State to the Globalisation of Law", in *Law and Social Theory*, ed. Reza Banakar and Max Travers. 2nd ed. Oxford: Hart, 2013, pp. 111–27.

Maine, Henry Sumner. *Ancient Law: Its Connection with the Early History of Society and Its Relation to Modern Ideas.* 4th ed. London: John Murray, 1920.

Mak, Phoeun. *Histoire du Cambodge de la fin du XVIe au début du XVIIIe siècle* [History of Cambodia from the End of the Sixteenth Century to the Beginning of the Eighteenth Century]. Paris: École Française d'Extrême-Orient, 1995.

Mamdani, Mahmood. *Citizen and Subject: Contemporary Africa and the Legacy of Late Colonialism.* Princeton, NJ: Princeton University Press, 1996.

Manière, Laurent. "Deux conceptions de l'action judiciaire aux colonies: Magistrats et administrateurs en Afrique Occidentale française (1887–1912)" [Two Conceptions of Judicial Action in the Colonies. Judges and Administrators in French West Africa (1887–1912)], *Clio@Thémis: révue électronique d'histoire du droit* 4 (2011). www.cliothemis.com/Clio-Themis-numero-4 (accessed 31 March 2014).

Manoff, Marlene. "Theories of the Archive from across the Disciplines", *Libraries and the Academy* 4, 1 (2004): 9–25.

Mariol, G. and H. François. *Législation Coloniale* [Colonial Legislation]. Paris: Les Manuels Coloniaux, Librairie La Rose, 1929.

Mark, Eugene. "Time to Truly Understand Thailand's 1932 Revolution", *The Diplomat*, 29 June 2017. https://thediplomat.com/2017/06/time-to-truly-understand-thailands-1932-revolution/ (accessed 11 June 2020).

Marr, David G. *Vietnamese Tradition on Trial, 1920–1945.* Berkeley, CA: University of California Press, 1981.

Martin, Benjamin F. *Crime and Criminal Justice under the Third Republic: The Shame of Marianne.* Baton Rouge: Louisiana State University Press, 1990.

McGeachy, Hilary. "The Invention of Burmese Buddhist Law: A Study in Orientalism", *Asian Law* 4 (2002): 30–52.

Merry, Sally Engle. "Law and Colonialism: A Review Essay", *Law and Society Review* 25, 4 (1991): 889–922.

———. *Colonizing Hawai'i: The Cultural Power of Law.* Princeton, NJ: Princeton University Press, 2000.

———. "From Law and Colonialism to Law and Globalization", *Law and Social Inquiry* 28 (2003): 569–90.

Messaoudi, Layachi. "Grandeur et limites du droit musulman au Maroc" [The Scale and the Limits of Muslim Law in Morocco], *Revue internationale de droit comparé* [International Review of Comparative Law] 47, 1 (1995): 146–55.

Meyer, Charles. *Derrière le sourire khmer*. Paris: Plon, 1971.

Mikaelian, Grégory. "Recherches sur l'histoire du fonctionnement politique des royautés post-angkoriennes (c.1600–c.1720). Appuyées sur l'analyse d'un corpus de décrets royaux khmers du XVIIème siècle" [Research on the History of the Political Functioning of Post-Angkorian Royalty (c.1600–c.1720). Supported by an Analysis of a Body of Khmer Royal Decrees of the 17th Century]. PhD dissertation, University of the Sorbonne, 2006.

————. *Un partageux au Cambodge: Biographie d'Adhémard Leclère. Suivie de l'inventaire du fonds Adhémard Leclère* [A Distributionist in Cambodia: Biography of Adhemard Leclere. Followed by an Inventory of the Adhemard Collection], Paris: Les Cahiers de Péninsule, Association Péninsule, Vol. 12, 2011.

————. "Khmera Lex . . . Sed Lex, Notes sur les possibles fondements juridiques de la violence Khmèr Rouge", [Notes on the Legal Foundations of the Violence of the Khmer Rouge] *Péninsule*, 84 (2022): 73–108.

Morice, J. "L'organisation judiciaire du Cambodge: La renaissance d'une justice nationale" [Judicial Organisation of Cambodia: The Renaissance of a National Justice System], *Penant: Recueil Général de jurisprudence, de doctrine et de législation coloniales* [Penant: General Collection of Colonial Jurisprudence, Doctrine and Legislation] (1962): 7–35.

Moura, J. *Le Royaume du Cambodge* [The Kingdom of Cambodia]. Paris: Ernest Leroux, 1883.

Muller, Gregor. *Colonial Cambodia's "Bad Frenchmen": The Rise of French Rule and the Life of Thomas Caraman, 1840–87*. London: Routledge, 2006.

Mus, Paul. *Le destin de l'Union Française: de l'Indochine à l'Afrique* [The Destiny of the French Union: From Indochina to Africa]. Paris: Editions du Seuil, 1954.

Mutaqin, Zezen Zaenal. "Indonesian Customary Law and European Colonialism: A Comparative Analysis on Adat Law", *Journal of East Asian and International Law* 4, 2 (2011): 351–78.

Nicholson, Pip and Simon Butt. "Official Discourses and Court Oriented Legal Reform in Vietnam", in *Law and Development and the Global Discourses of Legal Transfers*, ed. John Gillespie and Pip Nicholson. Cambridge: Cambridge University Press, 2012, pp. 202–36.

Nicolas, L.P. "L'Organisation de la Justice Cambodgienne" [The Organisation of Cambodian Justice], *La Révue indochinoise juridique et économique* [Indochinese Legal and Economic Review] 21 (1943): 1–68.

Osborne, Milton E. "The Debate on a Legal Code for Colonial Cochin China", *Journal of South-east Asian History* 10, 2 (1969): 224–35.

—————. "King-Making in Cambodia: From Sisowath to Sihanouk", *Journal of Southeast Asian Studies* 4, 2 (1973): 169–85. DOI:10.1017/S0022463400016593.

—————. *Before Kampuchea: Preludes to Tragedy*. First published Allen and Unwin, 1979. Second edition Trinity, Newfoundland: Orchid Press, 2004.

—————. *The French Presence in Cochinchina and Cambodia: Rule and Response (1859–1905)*. Bangkok: White Lotus, 1997. First published Cornell University Press, 1969.

—————. "Peasant Politics in Cambodia: the 1916 Affair", *Modern Asian Studies* 12, 2 (1978): 217–43.

—————. *Sihanouk, Prince of Light, Prince of Darkness*. Chiang Mai: Silkworm Books, 1994.

Pannetier, A. *Notes cambodgiennes: au coeur du pays Khmer* [Cambodian Notes: in the Heart of the Country of the Khmers]. Paris: Centre de documentation et de recherche sur la civilisation khmère, 1983 ed., 1921.

Parry, Clive, ed. *Consolidated Treaty Series: 1648–1919*. Oxford: Oxford University Press, 1969.

Pearson, Trais. *Sovereign Necropolis: The Politics of Death in Semi-Colonial Siam*. Ithaca, NY: Cornell University Press, 2020.

Perkins, Kenneth. *A Modern History of Tunisia*. 2nd ed. New York: Cambridge University Press, 2013.

Persell, Stuart Michael. *The French Colonial Lobby, 1889–1938*. Stanford, CA: Hoover Institution Press, 1983.

Pommier, René. "Le régime de l'indigénat en Indo-Chine" [The Regime of the Indigenant in Indo-China]. PhD dissertation, University of Paris, Faculté de droit, 1907.

Pou, Saveros. "La Littérature Didactique Khmère [Texte Imprimé]: Les Cpap" [Khmer Didactic Literature (Printed Text)], *Société Asiatique* [Asiatic Society] 269 (1981): 454–66.

Preschez, Philippe. *Essai sur la Démocratie au Cambodge* [Essay on Democracy in Cambodia]. Paris: FNSP, Centre D'Etude des Relations Internationales, 1961.

Rajchagool, Chaiyan. *The Rise and Fall of the Thai Absolute Monarchy: Foundations of the Modern Thai State from Feudalism to Peripheral Capitalism*. Bangkok: While Lotus, 1994.

Ranger, Terence. "The Inventions of Tradition in Colonial Africa", in *The Invention of Tradition*, ed. Eric Hobsbawm and Terence Ranger. Cambridge: Cambridge University Press, 1983, pp. 211–62.

Rogoff, Martin A. *French Constitutional Law: Cases and Materials*. Durham, NC: Carolina Academic Press, 2011.

Romerio, François. *Le Métier de magistrat, entretiens avec Robert Hervet* [The Judicial Profession, Interview with Robert Hervet]. Paris: Editions France-Empire, 1977.

Saada, Emmanuelle. "The Empire of Law: Dignity, Prestige, and Domination in the 'Colonial Situation'", *French Politics, Culture & Society* 20, 2 (2002): 98–120.

Sadka, Emily. "The Residential System in the Protected Malay States, 1874–1895". PhD dissertation, Australian National University, 1960.

Sager, Paul. "A Nation of Functionaries, a Colony of Functionaries: The Antibureaucratic Consensus in France and Indochina, 1848–1912", *French Historical Studies* 39, 1 (2016): 145–82.

Samphan, Khieu, "Underdevelopment in Cambodia", extract of translation by Laura Summer, *Indochina Chronicle* (Sept.–Nov. 1976): 2–25.

Sarraut, Albert. *La mise en valeur des colonies françaises* [The Development of the French Colonies]. Paris: Payout, 1923.

Scott, David. *Refashioning Futures: Criticism after Postcoloniality*, Princeton Studies in Culture/Power/History. Princeton, NJ: Princeton University Press, 1999.

Shawcross, William. *Sideshow: Kissinger, Nixon and the Destruction of Cambodia*. London: Hogarth Press, 1991.

Sihanouk, Prince Norodom, with Bernard Krisher. *Sihanouk Reminisces: World Leaders I Have Known*. Bangkok: Editions Duang Kamol, 1990.

Slocomb, Margaret. *Colons and Coolies: The Development of Cambodia's Rubber Plantations*. Bangkok: White Lotus, 2007.

————. *An Economic History of Cambodia in the Twentieth Century*. Singapore: NUS Press, 2010.

Sok, Khin. *Le Cambodge entre le Siam et le Viêtnam* [Cambodia between Siam and Vietnam]. Paris: École Française d'Extrême-Orient, 1991.

Sorn, Samnang. "L'Evolution de la société cambodgienne entre les deux guerres mondiales (1919–1939) [The Evolution of Cambodian Society between the Two World Wars (1919–1939)]". PhD dissertation, University Paris VII, 1995.

Sukhani, Piya, "The Evolving Role of Malaysia's Royalty", *RSIS Commentary* 107–21 (12 July 2021). https://hdl.handle.net/10356/152639 (accessed 13 January 2022).

Sowerwine, Charles. *France Since 1870: Culture, Society and the Making of the Republic*. 2nd ed. Basingstoke: Palgrave Macmillan, 2009.

Spivak, Gayatri Chakravorty. "The Rani of Sirmur: An Essay in Reading the Archives", *History and Theory* 24, 3 (1985): 247–72.

Steedman, Carolyn. "Something She Called a Fever: Michelet, Derrida, and Dust", *The American Historical Review* 106, 4 (2001): 1159–80.

Stuart-Fox, Martin. "The French in Laos, 1887–1945", *Modern Asian Studies* 29, 1 (1995): 113–39.

————. *A History of Laos*. Cambridge: Cambridge University Press, 1997.

Subrahmanyan, Arjun. "Buddhism, Democracy and Power in the 1932 Thai Revolution", *Asian Studies Review* 41, 1 (2017): 40–57.

————. "The Unruly Past: History and Historiography of the 1932 Thai Revolution", *Journal of Contemporary Asia* 50, 1 (2020): 74–98.

Suwannathat-Pian, Kobkua. *Palace, Political Party and Power: A Story of the Socio-Political Development of Malay Kingship*. Singapore: NUS Press, 2011.

Taboulet, Georges. *La geste française en Indochine: Histoire par les textes de la France en Indochine des Origines à 1914* [The French Gesture in Indochina: A History by Texts of France in Indochina from its Origins to 1914]. Paris: Adrien-Maisonneuve, 1956.

Thénault, Sylvie. *Une drôle de Justice: Les magistrats dans la guerre d'Algérie* [A Strange Justice: Judges in the Algerian War]. Paris: Découverte, 2001.

Thompson, Virginia. *French Indo-China*. First published Michigan University Press, 1937. Reprinted London: Octagon Books, 1968.

Thun, Theara and Duong Keo, "Ethnocentrism of Victimhood: Tracing the Discourses of Khmer Ethnicity in Precolonial and Colonial Cambodia", *Asian Studies Review* (forthcoming).

Tully, John. *Cambodia under the Tricolour: King Sisowath and the "Mission Civilisatrice", 1904–1927*. Clayton: Monash Asia Institute, 1996.

————. *France on the Mekong: A History of the Protectorate in Cambodia, 1863–1953*. New York: University Press of America, 2002.

Twomey, Christina and Katherine Ellinghaus. "Protection: Global Genealogies, Local Practices", *Pacific Historical Review* 87, 1 (2018): 2–9.

Tyndale, O.S. "The Organization and Administration of Justice in France, with an Outline of French Procedure with Respect to the Production of Evidence", *Canadian Bar Review* (Nov. 1935): 567–83.

Vickery, Michael. "Looking Back at Cambodia", *Westerly* 4 (1976): 14–28.

————. "The Composition and Transmission of the Ayudhya and Cambodian Chronicles", in *Perceptions of the Past in Southeast Asia*, ed. Anthony Reid and David Marr. London: Heinemann, 1979, pp. 152–79.

————. *Cambodia 1975–1982*. Bangkok: Silkworm, 1984.

Weinschel, Herbert. "The Constitutions of the Fourth French Republic and of the Italian Republic: A Comparative Study", *The George Washington Law Review* 20, 2 (1951–52): 127–73.

Whiting, Amanda. "Desecularising Malaysian Law?", in *Examining Practice, Interrogating Theory: Comparative Legal Studies in Asia*, ed. Penelope Nicholson and Sarah Biddulph. Leiden: Martinus Nijhoff, 2008, pp. 223–66.

————. "Secularism, the Islamic State and the Malaysian Legal Profession", *Asian Journal of Comparative Law* 5 (2010): 1–34.

Winichakul, Thongchai. *Siam Mapped: A History of the Geo-Body of a Nation*. Honolulu: University of Hawai'i Press, 1994.

————. "Writing at the Interstices: Southeast Asian Historians and Postnational Histories in Southeast Asia", in *New Terrains in Southeast*

Asian History, ed. Abu Talib Ahmad and Tan Liok Ee. Singapore: Singapore University Press, 2003, pp. 3–20.

———. "Toppling Democracy", *Journal of Contemporary Asia* 38, 1 (2008): 11–37.

Wongsurawat, Wasana. *The Crown and the Capitalists: The Ethnic Chinese and the Founding of the Thai Nation*. Seattle: University of Washington Press, 2019.

Databases, Presentations, Films, Unpublished Manuscripts

Farcy, Jean-Claude and Rosine Fry. *Annuaire rétrospectif de la magistrature XIXᵉ–XXᵉ siècles* [Retrospective Directory of the Judiciary 19th–20th Centuries] (12 June 2010). Centre Georges Chevrier—Université de Bourgogne/CNRS. http://tristan.u-bourgogne.fr/AM.html.

Kanthoul, Huy. *Mémoires*. Chandler Papers, Monash University, 1988 (accessed 10 March 2016).

Kong, Phirun and Jean-Marie Crouzatier. "Les Études Sur Le Droit Cambodgien". [Studies of Cambodian Law] Paper presented at the Bilan et Perspectives des Études Khmères (Langue et Culture), Phnom Penh, 1995.

Ligue des Droits de l'Homme. *L'Affaire Bardez aux Assises de Phnom Penh* [The Bardez Affair in the Court of Assises of Phnom Penh]. Saigon, 1926.

Panh, Rithy. *La France est notre patrie* [France Is Our Mother Country]. Film. Cambodia; France: Bophana Productions and Catherine Dussart Productions, 2015.

Winichakul, Thongchai. "Absolute Monarchy and the Legal State in Thailand", presentation sponsored by the Coral Bell School of Asia Pacific Affairs, Australian National University, 30 Nov. 2021.

Newspaper and Magazine Articles

"Affaire Bardez en cour d'assises" [The Bardez Affair in the Court of Assises], *Echo Annamite* [Annamite Echo], 8, 11, 12 Dec. 1925.

Breton, André. "Pour Malraux" [For Malraux], *Echo du Cambodge* [Cambodia Echo], 27 Sept. 1924.

"Chronique judiciaire", *Echo du Cambodge*, 11, 18 Oct. 1924.

"Inauguration du Palais de Justice cambodgien" [Inauguration of the Palace of Justice], *Echo du Cambodge* [Cambodia Echo], 25 Apr. 1925.

Kye, Phelim. "Au revoir to T3: merci beaucoup pour les mémoires", *Phnom Penh Post*, 4 Feb. 2000.

"Les lois que l'on cache" [The Laws that They Hide], *Les Annales Coloniales* [Colonial Annals], 13 Feb. 1930.

"Les Résidents ne sont pas meilleurs que les Gouverneurs cambodgiens" [The Residents Are No Better than the Cambodian Governors], *L'Aurore*, 27 Apr. 1935.

Sedley, Stephen. "Knife, Stone, Paper", *London Review of Books*, 1 July 2021, pp. 17–19.

"Un bon administrateur n'est pas forcément un bon magistrat" [A Good Administrator Is Not Necessarily a Good Judge], *Le Populaire de l'Indochine* [The People of Indochina], 22 May 1935.

"Une bonne cause gâté par une défense maladroit" [A Good Cause Spoiled by a Clumsy Defense], *Le Populaire de l'Indochine* [The People of Indochina], 29 May 1935.

Vachon, Michelle. "Judging French Colonialism", *The Cambodia Daily* (Phnom Penh), 6 Oct. 2006, p. 3.

Index

1885–86 rebellion, 64, 66–7, 68–9, 78, 102, 203
1911 codes, 78–80, 87–100, 105–6, 107–13, 115–16, 123–4, 128–9, 135, 142
1915–22 provincial courts' reforms, 100, 103–24, 132–3
1916 anti-tax protests, 98, 101–7, 111–21, 123, 126, 132, 203
1920 codes, 94, 128–9, 216
1922 reforms, 1–2, 12, 15, 25, 78, 116–23, 125–50, 155, 163–5, 191–2, 196
1924 codes, 15, 128–9, 152, 155, 158, 197, 205
1932 "revolution" in Thailand, 131, 209
1938 codes, 129, 136–8, 216

administrative chamber (*krom viveat*) 1933, 129, 192
administrative powers, xxii, 2–3, 17, 25–6, 38–49, 53–100, 102–5, 112–15, 116–49, 151–65, 175–93, 194–211
adultery, 110–11
advisers (*conseillers*), 174–5, 209
    see also judicial/legal advisers
Africa, 11, 13, 36, 38, 39, 64, 72–3, 75, 143, 210
agriculture and rural life, 5, 10, 30–2, 33, 93–5, 101–2, 103–4, 110, 123

Algeria, 38, 64, 72–3, 143, 210
Amicale de la Magistrature (judicial association), 141–2
Ananda Mahidol, King of Siam (Rama VIII), 131
Anderson, Benedict, 8, 42, 208–10
Ang Duong, King, 29, 59, 60, 79
Angkor, 23, 169–70, 181
Annam, xiii, 13, 14, 28–9, 39, 50–3, 62–3, 64, 73, 97, 99, 133, 157, 173
Antonelli, Etienne, 152
archival documents, xv, xxi, xxv, 2–4, 19, 24, 80, 82–4, 156, 162–3, 210, 213–18
Assaud, Prosecutor General Edgard, 86
assimilation/association concepts, French Indochina, 38–9, 141
Au, Chhieng, 66
Au, Sokhieng, 21–2
Augier, François, 55–7
avocats défenseurs, 47–8, 160
Aymonier, Etienne, 33, 57–60, 62–3, 67, 75, 104, 197

bail restrictions, 160
bailiffs (*huissiers*), 137
banditry, 106–7, 119, 132
Bangkok, 52, 54–5, 102
Banteay Srey temple, 144
Bao Dai, Emperor of Vietnam, 169, 172

236 *Index*

Baphnom, 106–7
Baray, 105, 108–9
barbarism allegations, 1, 11–12, 15,
    18, 23, 32–3, 49, 57–61, 75–6
Bardez, *Résident* Félix, xvii, 125–6,
    145–50, 156, 197
Battambang, 29, 37, 79, 105, 119,
    139, 154, 161, 162
Baudoin, François (*Résident
    Supérieur*), 1–2, 21, 44, 47,
    78–80, 97–113, 115–23, 125–8,
    129–30, 131, 132, 134–5,
    146–8, 151, 198–201, 203, 204
Baxi, Upendra, 4, 19, 199, 202
Bellan, *Résident* Charles, 108, 115–16
Bentham, Jeremy, 15
Benton, Lauren, 6, 7, 206
Blazy, Adrien, xxi, 9, 14, 45, 61–4,
    67–9, 71, 87–8, 89, 93, 118, 121
Bonnet, *Résident* Paul, 146–7
Boudillon, A., 93–4, 96
Bourdieu, Pierre, 4
Bourguiba, Habib ibn Ali, 210
Brazzaville conference in 1944, 173
Breton, André, 144
bribery allegations, 27, 32–3, 113,
    160–1, 164, 190–1
Britain, 4, 5–8, 12–16, 24, 37–8,
    40, 51, 54–5, 66, 74–5, 172–3,
    195–201, 206–10
Brocheux, Pierre, 5, 10, 37, 43–4, 53,
    64, 73, 124, 131, 154, 156, 172
Buddhism, 16, 28, 30–1, 36, 45, 49,
    89–90, 100–2, 132, 146, 162,
    170, 173, 202, 209
budget constraints, 43, 136, 141
Burma (Myanmar), Britain, 16, 37,
    51, 66, 196, 210

Cambodia
    pre-colonial Cambodia, xviii,
        5–7, 14, 18, 20, 22, 27–36, 73

pre-colonial court hierarchy,
    32–6
    see also individual topics
Cambodian judges, 2, 14–15, 57,
    63–4, 90–2, 98–9, 103, 116–17,
    126, 134–5, 141–3, 153–5, 161,
    173, 185–8, 197–9
    see also judges
Cambodian lawyers, 153–60,
    193–4, 197
    see also lawyers
Cao Dail religious sect, 132
Caraman, Thomas, 43, 55–6, 57
caste-like strata, 29–31
Catroux, Governor General Raoul,
    169, 171–2
censorship laws, 152, 155, 158,
    163–4
Centre des Archives d'Outre Mer
    (CAOM), xv, xxv, 213
Chakri dynasty, Siam/Thailand,
    7–8, 37, 196, 209
Cham, 31
Champassak, 39
Chandler, David P., xxi, xxv, 10, 17,
    28–31, 35–6, 50–1, 64, 101,
    125, 131–2, 146–8, 166–7,
    169–70, 173, 177–83, 190, 193
Chassaing, Maxime, 146–7
Chea Kai, 119–20
Chevasson, Louis, 144–5
Chhum, Neai Oknha, 86
Chhun, Judge Alexis Louis, 87
China, 51–2, 131, 157–8, 186
Chinese inhabitants, 9, 15, 20, 31–2,
    50, 54–5, 69–73, 87, 95–8, 107,
    119, 122, 131, 139, 157–8, 173,
    186, 196, 200, 204
Chulalongkorn, King of Siam
    (Rama V), 16, 37, 52–3, 88, 209
Civil Codes, 15, 77–80, 92, 93–6,
    110–11, 123–4, 128–9, 136,
    142, 216

civil law, 13–14, 41–2, 66–8, 77–80, 92–6, 110–11, 119–23, 128–9, 136–41, 152–5, 161, 163, 186, 200–1

Civil Procedure Code of 1938, 129, 136–7, 216

civil servants, 5–6, 40, 42–9, 57–8, 104–5, 129, 181–2, 192–3, 201

civilisation-mission colonial narrative, 1, 11–15, 35, 38–9, 43, 49–50, 57–61, 66–7, 75–6, 121, 125–6, 153, 165, 167–8, 194–8, 200–2, 210

Clulow, Adam, 6

Cochin China, 9–10, 13–14, 37–9, 44–8, 51–3, 56, 59, 62–7, 71, 94, 121–2, 173, 193, 203–4

Code of Criminal Investigation and Judicial Organisation of 1911, 77–80, 90–3, 107, 108–9, 112

Code Gia Long, 59, 67–8, 71, 87–8, 133

codes, 10–16, 35–6, 58–61, 66–8, 71–80, 87–100, 105–16, 117, 123–9, 133–8, 142, 152–6, 157–8, 164, 171–6, 185, 188–9, 190–1, 196–7, 205–17

Cold War politics, 7

Collins, Darryl, 127–8, 142

Colonial Exhibition in Paris in 1931, 96, 135

colonisations, 1–29, 35–9, 42–76, 86–8, 121, 125–6, 130–2, 136, 141–3, 153, 165–8, 175–8, 185, 194–211

commerce, 5–6, 10–14, 31, 54, 63, 100, 110–11, 119–20, 155–6, 200

Commissioner of the Republic (*commissaire de la république*), 174–5

common law systems, 12, 13–14, 15, 24, 40, 42, 74–5, 196, 200

commune administrative division from 1908, 104–5, 109, 176

communism, 131–2, 165, 174, 182, 206

complaints' procedures, 90–1, 108, 129, 135, 150–1, 192

concentration camps, French Indochina, 164

Conseil d'état (Council of State), 42

Conseil Privé in Saigon, 56

constitutional monarchies, 8, 18, 26, 131, 178, 183, 195, 205–7

constitutions, 3, 12–13, 18, 25–6, 39–40, 166–93, 201–2, 205–10

consular jurisdictions, 54–5, 61–70

Convention of 1884 (1884 Convention), 63–4, 66–7, 69, 78, 135, 195, 215

corruption allegations, 1, 27–36, 44–9, 57–61, 67, 75–6, 83–7, 111–13, 121–4, 130, 140, 151, 160–4, 180–2, 190–3

corvée, 101, 103–4, 115

Council of Ministers, 70, 82–8, 91, 96–102, 105, 109–10, 142, 155–6, 171–2, 177–9, 182

Councils of the Residencies (*Conseils de Résidence*), 153–4

court administration, xxii, 2–3, 17, 25–6, 38–49, 53–100, 102–5, 112–15, 116–49, 151–65, 175–93, 194–211

Court of Annulment (formerly Cassation, *Sala Vinichhay*), 2, 14, 126–7, 133, 138, 140–1, 175, 203

Court of Cassation, 79, 82, 91–2, 96–100, 110, 126–7, 140–1, 203

court clerks (*greffiers*), xix, 107, 121, 136, 160

court records, deliberately incomplete court records, 162–3

courts, xviii, xix, 1–2, 12, 15, 25–7,
32–6, 39–41, 54–9, 61–80,
87–124, 125–49, 150, 151–65,
168, 172–5, 185–93, 196,
200–11
Courts of Appeal, 9, 14–15, 44,
59–60, 62, 68–9, 71–2, 85–6,
91, 103, 110–12, 114–15, 122–9,
133, 137–41, 160–3, 191, 210
Courts of First Instance (*Sala
dambaung/Sala lukhun*), 78, 91,
103, 114–17, 127–8, 132–3,
136–41, 158–64, 175, 203
Criminal Codes, 15, 77–80, 87–93,
100, 109, 112–16, 123–9, 136–8,
152, 155, 158, 197, 205, 216
Criminal Courts (*Sala Okret*), xviii,
103, 112–14, 123–7, 138, 142,
145, 159–64, 186, 190–1
criminal law, 13–15, 32–6, 42, 48,
58–9, 66, 72–80, 86–93, 100–9,
112–16, 123–9, 133, 136–45,
152, 155, 160–4, 186, 190–1, 197
Criminal Procedure Code of 1938,
129, 136, 137, 216
cultural issues, 8–9, 10–18, 21–3,
28–32, 58–63, 66, 76, 84–5, 88,
98–9, 106–7, 121–7, 142–3, 149,
157, 167–70, 185–6, 194, 201–11

Dartiguenave, Henri, 91, 96
David, René, 40
death penalties, 58–9, 72, 89, 112,
114, 145–6, 172
debt bondage, 84–5, 119
debtors' custody, 84–5, 120
decolonisation support, constitution
of 1947, 175–8
Decoux, Governor General Jean,
169–71, 205–6
delegates, 32–3, 68, 99, 107, 127,
133–4, 156, 159, 178, 182

Democratic Party, 176–80, 182
Desenlis, *Résident* Emile, 120
despotism/barbarism allegations, 1,
11–12, 15, 18, 23, 32–3, 49,
57–61, 75–6
Dezalay, Yves, 4, 10, 17, 18, 164,
199–201, 204, 210
Dien Bien Phu, 166
direct/indirect colonial rule, 4–11,
13–14, 20–1, 37–9, 43–4, 52,
79–80, 165, 193, 195–6,
199–201, 203–9
discrimination, 8, 9, 12–13, 15,
19–20, 157–8, 164–5, 169, 186,
195–6
divorces, 96
"dollar diplomacy", 210
Dong Khanh, Emperor, 52
Doumer, Governor General Paul, 53
Dreyfuss, Alfred, 48
dual-sovereignty concepts, 55–7, 71,
79, 100, 157
Ducos (*Résident Supérieur*), 87
Durand, Bernard, 41, 118, 198
Duras, Marguerite, 45
Dutch East Indies (Indonesia), 14,
16, 38, 172

Echo du Cambodge, 126–7, 129,
146, 155
economic growth from the 1920s, 10,
32, 130–1, 138–9, 154–5, 200
economic/political influences, 2,
4–5, 10–12, 27–8, 79–80,
122–6, 130–1, 154–5, 178,
194–200, 210
education, 4–5, 17, 20, 36, 44–6,
88, 91–2, 108–9, 116–17, 140,
155, 161–3, 175, 182–6, 189–93,
198–201
Edwards, Penny, 21, 22–3, 30, 36,
45, 88, 131–2, 149, 169–70, 202

elections, 18, 176, 179, 180, 181–3
electricity, 130–1
elitist interests, xxii, 2–6, 10–36, 44, 49, 51–80, 82–100, 105–17, 123–4, 128–32, 135, 140–5, 149, 156–9, 167–95, 201–11
employment constraints, gender issues, 45
Entente Cordial between Britain and France in 1904, 38
envoys, 32–3
ethics perspective, colonisation viewing "modes", 19–20, 194–6
ethnic antipathies and colonial encouragement of, 8–9, 13–15, 19–31, 42–5, 49, 55, 62–3, 69–75, 95–8, 119, 157–8, 164–9, 186, 195–6
executive powers, 17, 25, 39–41, 57–61, 177–8, 187–8, 201–11
extraterritoriality issues, 53–7, 196, 210

Faculty of Law and Economics, 185, 189–90
Federated Malay States (FMS), 51, 74, 206–7
Filipino Tagals, 62
fines, 59–60, 73, 109, 110
First World War, 1, 38, 39, 45, 78–9, 103, 104, 116
fishing industry, 103–4
fonctionnaires, 42–9
"foreign Asiatics", 69–70, 71, 95–6, 119, 204
Forest, Alain, 10, 31–2, 44, 51–3, 78, 84–6, 92, 101–9, 111, 112–13, 123–4
Fourès, Julien (*Résident Supérieur*), 63, 68
Fourth Republic, France, 23–4, 168–9, 177

France and French colonial policy, 1, 7, 11–16, 23–5, 31, 36–42, 44–5, 51–79, 89–90, 103–4, 116, 143, 164–75, 177, 183–5, 192, 196–200, 205–11, 217–18
Franco-Cambodian Accord in January 1946, 174–5, 187
French Congo, 173
French Indochina, xiii, xiv, 1–18, 36–76, 78–9, 93, 94–5, 100–24, 132–3, 141, 157, 164, 166–93, 194–211
    definition, 36–8, 51, 195–8
    maps, xiii, xiv, 1, 94–5
French judges, 39–42, 46–7, 55–7, 67–71, 84, 87, 91–2, 97–103, 121–2, 129–30, 133–4, 142–4, 157–9, 193, 200–5
    see also judges
French lawyers, 47–8, 160, 186–7, 193, 200–1, 203
    see also lawyers
French League of the Rights of Man and Citizen, 24, 48, 146–7, 150–4, 163, 197–8
French settlers, 43–7, 53–5, 71, 157
French troops arrival in 1952, 179–80

Gallet, defence lawyer, 145–6, 156
Garth, Bryant, 4, 10, 17, 18, 164, 199–201, 204, 210
gateway/gatekeeper perspectives, elitist interests, 21, 106–7
Gaulle, Charles de, 164, 173, 184
gender issues, 20, 30, 44–5, 57–8, 86–7, 96, 110–11, 142, 176–7, 209
Geneva Accords of 1954, 166, 180, 181
Germany, Vichy rule, 23, 25, 164–5, 167–70, 172–5, 205–6

240 *Index*

Gillet, defence lawyer, 145–7
Girault, Arthur, 197
Goscha, Christopher, 37, 51–3, 131, 169, 173–4, 206
Gour, Claude-Gilles, xxii, 129, 168, 171–2, 175–7, 181, 185, 188, 190–2
governors, 25, 30–6, 44–8, 53, 59–64, 67–8, 78–83, 98, 103–18, 122–6, 128–9, 132–5, 140, 151, 196, 203
    résidents (colonial administrators), 25, 103, 105–9, 112–13, 115, 116–18, 122
Guangzhouwan, 53

Habert, Albert, 134
Habert, Judicial Adviser Maurice, 2, 12, 15, 126, 129–30, 133–5, 139–43, 148, 150–5, 158, 162–4, 197–9, 203–5
Haiphong, 13, 39
Halliday, Terence, 4
Ham Nghi, Emperor, 51–2, 64
Hanoi, 9, 13, 14, 37, 39, 43–4, 118–19, 122, 146, 161–2, 189
"harmful criticisms" (*critique injurieuse*), 155–6, 160, 197
Harouel, Jean-Louis, 185
health services, 21–2
Hémery, Daniel, 5, 10, 37, 43–4, 53, 64, 73, 124, 131, 154, 156, 172
Hertrich, *Résident*, 34–5
High Council of Magistracy, 187–8
High Court of Justice, 191–2
Hindu laws, 16, 35–6
historical-affair perspective, colonisations, 19–20
Ho Chi Minh, 174
Hoeffel, Ernest, xxi, 31, 61–2, 66, 69, 75
Hue royal court, 9, 169

Huy Kanthoul, 45–6, 104–5, 132, 144–5, 175, 178

Imbert, Jean, xxii, 185, 189
imposts, 5, 10, 44, 50–1, 53, 63, 94, 103–4, 115, 131–2, 145–8, 203
independence in 1953–54, xxii–xxiii, 2, 4–5, 7–8, 14–15, 17–18, 24–6, 104, 128, 166–94, 201–2, 209–11
independent judiciary, 39–41, 78–9, 121–2, 126–30, 133, 140–9, 151–65, 172–5, 185–93, 200–11
India, 4, 12, 13–14, 15, 36, 53, 62, 69, 131, 196, 199
indictment chamber (*Sala kromchot*) from 1923, 128, 160, 191
Indigénat code of summary justice, 72–3
indirect/direct colonial rule, 4–11, 13–14, 20–1, 37–9, 43–4, 52, 79–80, 165, 193, 195–6, 199–201, 203–9
interpreters, 35, 68, 88, 121–2, 157
Islamic law (Shariah), 13–14, 16, 31, 74–5, 196, 207–8, 210

Japan, 26, 51, 131, 168–9, 172–4, 179, 207–8
Jason-and-the-argonauts analogy, judges, 41, 198
Jeannerat, Monsieur G. (*Résident*), 82–3
Jennar, Raoul M., 42, 144, 185
Jennings, Eric, 165
judges, 2, 14–15, 27, 32–3, 39–47, 55–7, 63–4, 67–71, 78–9, 84, 87, 90–103, 108–13, 116–22, 126–35, 140–9, 150–68, 172–5, 185–93, 197–9, 200–11

Cambodian judges, 2, 14–15, 57, 63–4, 90–2, 98–9, 103, 116–17, 126, 134–5, 141–3, 153–5, 161, 173, 185–8, 197–9

French judges, 39–42, 46–7, 55–7, 67–71, 84, 87, 91–2, 97–103, 121–2, 129–30, 133–4, 142–4, 157–9, 193, 200–5

judicial/legal advisers (*conseilleurs juristes*), 99, 126–30, 133–43, 150–3, 156–9, 161–3, 175, 178, 184, 186, 197–9, 203–5, 209

judicial powers, xxii, 2–3, 17, 25–6, 38–44, 48–9, 53–100, 102–5, 112–15, 116–49, 151–65, 172–93, 194–211

judicial reviews, 40

jurisdictions and jurisdictional powers, 1–3, 25, 26, 38, 49–76, 87–100, 101–24, 130, 135, 143–8, 170–93, 194–211

justice concepts, xxii, 1–3, 9, 13–18, 32–6, 51–76, 77–100, 101–24, 125–49, 150–65, 194–211

Justice in Indochina 1931 document, 135

justices-of-the-peace powers, 72–3, 97–8, 107, 118, 127

Justice of the Peace (*Sala lohuk*), 127

justifications, colonisations, 11–13, 36–9, 50–1, 53–61, 66–7, 194–5, 198–202, 209–11

Kampot, 61, 64–8, 72, 105, 139, 141, 152, 161

Kandal, 82–3, 117, 127, 154

Karpelès, Suzanne, 45

Karpik, Lucien, 4

Kau Sokhon, 166, 180

Keo, Duong, 28–9

Keth, Judge, 88, 91, 98–100, 140–1, 149, 203

Khan Char, Princess, 84, 99–100

khet (provinces) 1922 reforms, 116–17, 122

Khieu, 113–14

Khmer language versions, codes, 157, 164

Khmer National Congresses, 181–2

Khmer royal law, 35–6, 88–90, 96–100, 155–6, 165, 167–70, 190–3, 202–3, 205

Khoun Nay, Judge, 140–1, 149, 158, 164

Khoun Thonn, 107

Khun Than, Queen (wife of King Norodom), 84–5

Khut, 83

Kiernan, Ben, 131–2, 146, 169–74

Kingdom of Kampuchea, 167, 172–3, 206

Kleinpeter, Roger, 31, 93–5

Kompong Cham, 95, 119, 130, 138–9, 154, 156, 162

Kompong Chhnang, 72, 105, 109, 118–19, 125, 139, 147

Kompong Som court, 61

Kompong Speu, 72, 105, 137, 139

Kompong Thom, 105, 119–20, 130, 139, 141

Kossamak, Queen, 183

Kossotin (Koh Sautin), 162

Kouy Lim, 107

Kraang Laev, 125, 145, 148

kram code, 35–6, 58–61, 66, 89–90, 171–2, 174, 176, 185, 188–9, 190–1, 217

Kratie, 66, 72, 105, 130, 139

kret decrees, 171

Kun, Neang, 85

242 *Index*

Lachevrotière, Henri Chavigny de, 141

Lafarge, Prosecutor General Etienne Camille, 69

land registration, 93–6, 123, 137

land rights, 30–1, 93–6, 104, 110, 123, 128–9

landmarks/guideposts in history, 19

Lange, Matthew, 4, 5–6, 192–3, 199, 201

Lao Issara, 173–4

Laos, xiii, xiv, 8, 9, 13, 14, 37, 39, 52–3, 69, 87–9, 92–3, 131–4, 169–70, 172–4, 180

law, 1–4, 7–18, 19–26, 27–8, 32–6, 39–42, 44, 49, 50–76, 77–100, 101–24, 125–49, 150–65, 185–93, 194–211

  balance-sheet assessment of reforms after 1922, 148–9, 163–5, 191–2

  colonial law approaches, 19–24, 57–76, 194–211

  independence in 1953–54, 168, 185–93, 194, 201–2, 209–11

  monarchy's semi-divine source of law declarations, 7–8, 16–18, 23, 26, 28, 30–1, 74, 165, 167–8, 175–6, 178, 180–2, 193, 203–6

  politics, 2, 4–10, 19, 20–2, 27–8, 35–6, 40–1, 79–80, 122, 125–6, 167–93, 194–9, 205–11

  religion, 3, 7–10, 13–14, 16, 23, 74, 128, 132, 155–6, 162, 165–8, 181–2, 196, 202–10

  see also civil; codes; courts; criminal; justice concepts; legal

Law on Criminals, 58–9

Law on the Reorganisation of Justice 1959, 190–1

lawyers, xxii–xxiii, 4–6, 15–18, 24–6, 39–40, 42–9, 56–61, 88, 92–3, 97–9, 118–22, 130–6, 146–7, 150–65, 186–211

  Cambodian lawyers, 153–60, 193–4, 197

  critique, 18, 24, 48, 134, 136, 146–7, 150–65, 186, 190–3, 194–211

  de-registration criteria, 48

  French lawyers, 47–8, 160, 186–7, 193, 200–1, 203

  "harmful criticisms" (*critique injurieuse*), 155–6, 160, 197

  legal representation reforms, 136, 150–5, 163–4, 189, 197, 198

  metheavy term, 155–6, 160, 163

Leach, 125, 145

League of the Rights of Man and Citizen, 24, 48, 146–7, 150–4, 163, 197–8

Leclère, Adhémard, 33–4, 60, 66, 90

Lee, Jack Gin Gary, 16, 195–6

Le Fol (*Résident Supérieur*), 135–6, 153–4legal aid, 136

legal fictions, 15, 19, 25, 45, 170, 195, 202

legal profession *see* courts; judges; lawyers

legal representation, 136, 150–5, 163–4, 189, 197, 198

legal system overview, France, 39–42

Léger, Judicial Adviser, 95, 129, 130, 133, 136–9, 141–2, 156–9, 161–3, 173, 175

legislative powers, 25–6, 39–40, 42, 136, 158, 167–8, 174–8, 187–8, 190–2, 214–15

Le Myre de Vilers, Governor, 59, 62–3, 67, 197

localisation histories, 20–1

Index   243

Loos, Tamara, 16, 54, 60, 88, 208–10
Lortat-Jacob, Robert, defence
     lawyer, 18, 48, 134, 146–7,
     150–61, 197–8
Lovea Em, 107
loyalty rewards, 30
Luang Prabang, 39, 52–3, 169, 172
Luce, Louis Paul (*Résident
     Supérieur*), 78
Ly Eng, 120

Maghavan, Prince, 97–9
Maine, Henry Sumner, 111, 195
Malaysia, xxi, 7, 12, 14, 16, 31, 37,
     51, 74–5, 172, 196, 198, 205,
     206–8
male suffrage, 176
Malraux, André, 144–5
mandarins (officials), xviii, 27–8,
     32–6, 91–2, 106–8, 124, 142–3,
     146, 197
Manière, Laurent, 143
maps, xiii, xiv, 94–5
marriages, 30, 77, 95–6
Mar Tes, *Oknha*, 156–7, 186
Merry, Sally Engle, 20
Meyer, Charles, 190
Michel, Prosecutor General Gabriel,
     1–2, 21, 47, 98, 116–21
Mikaelian, Grégory, 11, 17, 30, 32,
     35–6, 60, 66–7
Minister of Colonies, 121, 134–5,
     151–3
ministers, xv, 8, 14, 21, 25, 32–6,
     40–6, 50, 70–3, 79–91, 96–114,
     121–7, 132–7, 141–5, 151–62,
     171–82, 185–92, 196, 207
"mixed" French/Cambodian
     citizens' cases, 53–4, 61–4, 67,
     68–71
modernised-laws narrative, 7, 12,
     15–17, 18, 20, 23, 26, 69, 209–10

modernity, 23, 209–10
monarchy, xxiii, 1–11, 16–18, 21–6,
     28–37, 49–76, 88–90, 96–100,
     131, 140–2, 148, 155–9, 165–96,
     202–11, 216–17
     ceremonial-only role, 70–6, 90,
        195, 203–4
     independence of 1953–54, 7–8,
        18, 24, 25–6, 166–93,
        209–10
     pre-colonial court hierarchy,
        32–6
     semi-divine source of law
        declarations, 7–8, 16–18, 23,
        26, 28, 30–1, 74, 165, 167–8,
        175–6, 178, 180–2, 193,
        203–6
monetised market economy issues,
     110–11, 122–3, 136–7, 152–5,
     199
Mongkut, King of Siam (Rama IV),
     29, 54, 60
Monivong, King, 130, 131, 132,
     152, 165, 169, 171–2
Morché, Henri, 92, 96, 145
Morice, J., 186, 189–92
Moroccan protectorate (1912–56),
     11, 13, 39, 75, 143
Mount Bogor colonial retreat, 1
Moura, Jean, 27–8, 32, 36, 57–60,
     75
Muller, Gregor, xxv, 11, 29–34, 43,
     53, 55, 58, 61–4, 84
murders, xvii, 89, 125–6, 145–50,
     156, 162, 197
Murray, colonel Edward Dymoke,
     173

Nagaravatta, 132
Nak, Judge, 162
Napoleon I, Emperor of France, 36,
     89–90

244   *Index*

Napoleon III, Emperor of France, 6, 29, 36, 38, 54
Napoleonic Codes, 12, 15–16, 66–7, 89–90
Narbonne, Louis Charles Motais de, 134
National Archives of Cambodia (NAC), xv, xxv, 213
National Assembly, 18, 42, 48, 152, 166–7, 177–80, 181–2, 185, 187, 190–2
National Geographic, 142–3
nationalism, 8, 15, 22–3, 25, 29, 130–2, 148, 164–5, 168–74, 206
Neak Mian Bon, 132
Netherlands, 14, 16, 38, 54, 172
New Year celebrations, Buddhism, 146
Nginn, Judge, 159
Nguyen dynasty, 51–2, 118, 119, 206
Nhem, *Oknha*, 82–3, 86, 99–100
Nicolas, Raoul, 135, 161–2
non-elites, 21–4, 30–1, 35–6, 57–8, 64–7, 78, 98, 101–7, 110–23, 125–6, 132, 145–6, 153, 159, 164, 166–7, 203
Norodom, King, 3–11, 15, 21–2, 25–6, 29, 31, 38, 49–76, 77–9, 84–5, 98–9, 104, 135, 172, 195–6, 202–4
Norodom Sihanouk, King/Prince, xxiii, 7–8, 17–18, 24, 26, 130, 165, 166–70, 172–4, 175–93, 205–6, 208
    Samdech Upayuvareach post-abdication title, 167, 181–2, 183
Norodom Suramarit, King, 182–3

offence types, 73, 89–91, 109, 112, 114–16, 137–41, 144–5, 152, 155, 160–2, 197
Oknha elitist title, 82–3, 85–6, 156

opium, 47, 51, 103–4
Osborne, Milton, 10, 29, 37, 50–2, 57, 59, 63–6, 70, 74, 87, 103–4, 169–70, 172–4, 183
Ouk, Chou, 84–5
Ouk, Minister of Justice, 50, 98–9
Oung, Governor, 82–4
Outrey, Ernest (*Résident Supérieur*), 78, 98–9

Palais de Justice, 1–2, 12, 15, 25, 125–30, 142–5, 148–9, 150, 155, 163
Pan, Rithy, 42
patronage, 4, 11, 17–18, 28–30, 43–5, 49, 58, 79–87, 100–4, 111, 124, 128, 149, 193–5, 198, 201–3
Peareang, 113–16, 120–1, 123
Penal Code, 59, 71, 73, 89–90, 114, 136, 152, 155–6, 158, 197, 216, 217
Penh Nouth, 150, 156–64, 186, 190, 196, 198–9, 203
Penn, Judge, 2, 15, 88, 126
Perkins, Kenneth, 210
Pétain, Marshal, 169
Philippines, 200
Phnom Penh, case statistics, 138–40, 161
police surveillance, 156
politics, law, 2, 4–10, 19, 20–2, 27–8, 35–6, 40–1, 79–80, 122, 125–6, 147, 167–93, 194–9, 205–11
polity in 1863, 28–32
Pol Pot, 173
Pommier, René, 73
Popular Tribunals, 191–2
post-colonial law, xxii, 3–6, 17–18, 168–93, 194, 199–200, 201–2, 209–11

Index

Pou, Saveros, 35–6

Prajadhipok, King of Siam (Rama VII), 131

Preap Choun, 147

Preas Chey Chestha, King, 59

pre-colonial Cambodia, xviii, 5–7, 14, 18, 20, 22, 27–36, 73

Preschez, Philipe, 172, 176–9, 181–2, 183

Presidential decrees, France, 42, 62, 69–71, 72–3, 217–18

Prey Veng, 106–8, 113–19, 139, 151, 154

private law concepts, 66–7

property rights, 30–1, 93–6, 104, 110, 123, 128–9

protection and civilisation, colonial narratives, 1–29, 35–9, 43, 49–61, 66–7, 74–6, 86–8, 121, 125–6, 130–2, 141–3, 153, 165–8, 185, 194–202, 210

protection-mission colonial narra-tive, 1–7, 9–18, 22–9, 35–9, 50–7, 75–6, 86–8, 130–2, 141–3, 167–8, 185, 194–5, 210

provincial governors
  résidents (colonial administra-tors), 25, 103, 105–9, 112–13, 115, 116–18, 122
  see also governors

public law concepts, 66–7

punishments, 10, 58–9, 72–7, 89–91, 108–9, 112–15, 123, 135–8, 145–6, 152, 155–64, 197

Pursat, 34–5, 118, 139, 162

racial hierarchies imposed by colonial powers, 12–15, 19–20, 25, 28–32, 42–5, 49, 55, 62–3, 69–75, 95–8, 119, 157–8, 164–5, 169, 195–6

railways, 130–1

Rama I, King of Siam, 29

Rama IV, King of Siam, 29, 54, 60

Rama V, King of Siam, 16, 37, 52–3, 88

Rama VII, King of Siam, 131

Rama VIII, King of Siam, 131

rape, 86–7, 142

Réalités Cambodgiennes, 183

reforms, critique, 44–9, 129–30, 142–3, 148–9, 150–65, 170–93, 194–211

Regency Council, 183

registries of births/deaths/marriages, 77, 95–6, 137

religion, 3, 7–19, 23, 26–31, 74, 128, 132, 155–6, 162–8, 173, 175–6, 178, 181–2, 193, 196, 202–10

résidents (colonial administrators), 2, 25, 34–5, 53–7, 62–78, 82–7, 91–126, 127, 135, 142, 145–50, 151–7, 163–4, 174–5, 198–9
  governors, 25, 103, 105–9, 112–13, 115, 116–18, 122
  summary justice powers, 72–6, 107, 118

Résident Supérieur, 1–2, 21, 25, 34–5, 44, 47, 62–3, 68, 70–112, 115–22, 125–6, 131, 134–6, 141–3, 146–7, 151–3, 158, 172–4, 197–204

road improvements, 130–1

Rodier, Governor, 67

Romerio, François, 47, 164

Rous-Serret, *Résident* Charles, 106–7

royal law, 35–6, 88–90, 96–100, 155–6, 165, 167–70, 190–3, 202–3, 205

Royal Ordinances, 56, 59–62, 68–71, 77, 90, 96, 116, 117, 126, 128–9, 155, 172, 189, 192, 204, 216–17

royal prerogative, 90
rubber, 5, 10, 32, 130–1, 138–41, 196
rural jurisdictions, 93–4, 97–8, 100, 103–24, 130–3, 140–1, 170–93, 194–211
Russia, 131

Saigon, xiii, 9, 37, 43–4, 47, 55–6, 62, 67, 98, 118, 146, 158
Sala dambaung (Courts of First Instance), 78, 91, 103, 114–17, 127–8, 132–3, 136–41, 158–64, 175, 203
Sala Domruout (Appeals Court), xviii, 33–4
Sala Lukhun/Chau Krom Sala (Judges Court/Royal Court), xvii, xviii, 32, 82, 85, 91, 127–8, 140
Sala Okret (Criminal Courts), xviii, 103, 112–14, 123–7, 138, 142, 145, 159–64, 186, 190–1
Sala Vinichhay (Court of Annulment (formerly Cassation)), 2, 14, 126–7, 133, 138, 140–1, 175, 203
Salles, André, 34
Sangkum Reastre Niyum (People's Socialist Community), 181–5, 189, 192
Sarraut, Governor General Albert, 47, 116, 121
School of Administration, 116–17, 162
Second World War, 23, 25–6, 47, 116, 128, 132, 163, 164–9, 172–5, 178–9, 193, 205–7
Sedley, Stephen, 178
sentences, 89–92, 108–9, 112–15, 123, 135–8, 145–8, 152, 155–8, 160, 163–4, 172, 197

separation of power, 3, 7, 13, 17–18, 39–40, 57, 68, 73, 78, 91, 98, 103, 117–22, 129, 141–3, 148–51, 159, 163, 189, 197, 203
Siam/Thailand, xiii, xiv, xxi, 7–9, 16, 20, 28–9, 37–9, 52–5, 60, 69, 78–9, 88, 131–2, 196, 200, 206–10
Siem Reap, 37, 105, 138–9, 144
Silvestre, Achille (*Résident Supérieur*), 117, 158
Singapore, 51, 196
Sino–Cambodian Society of Industry and Commerce, 156
Sino-Khmer commercial group, 31–2
Sisavang Vong, King of Luang Prabang, Laos, 169, 172
Sisowath, King/Prince, 1–3, 9, 25, 29, 76–81, 83, 90, 96–102, 112–13, 115, 125–8, 130, 134, 148, 165, 196, 203–4
Sisowath Monireth, Prince, 174, 175–6, 183
Sivotha, Prince, 9, 29
slavery, 20, 30–1, 57–8, 63, 84–5, 119, 195–6, 198
Sok Bith, 146
Son Ngoc Thanh, Prime Minister, 172–4, 179
Sonn Sann, National Assembly President, 179–80
sophea officials, 107–8, 112
Sorn Samnang, xxii, 116, 123
Sot, *Moha Vinichay* (Senior Judge), 82–3, 86
Srey, Judge, 34–5
sruk khmer term, 28–30
Straits Settlements, 16, 51, 196
structural issues, 130–1, 140–1, 199–200, 210
Stuart-Fox, Martin, 52, 131, 169, 172–4, 180

Stung Treng, 105, 119, 139
summary justice powers, 72–6, 107, 118
supervision networks, 132–43, 153–4, 163–4, 175, 203–4
Supreme Council of the Magistracy, 187–8
Suwannathat-Pian, Kobkua, 7, 38, 74, 198, 205, 207–8
Svay Rieng, 72, 105, 118–19, 139, 145, 154

Takeo, 72, 105, 139, 154
taxes, 5, 10, 20–1, 30–1, 44, 50–1, 53, 63–4, 94, 98, 101–7, 111–24, 126, 131–2, 145–8, 203
Thailand/Siam, xiii, xiv, xxi, 7–9, 16, 20, 28–9, 37–9, 52–5, 60, 69, 79, 88, 131–2, 196, 200, 206–10
Theravada Buddhism, 28, 209
Thibaw, King of Burma, 51, 66
Third Republic, 25, 36, 38, 39–42, 44–5, 164–5, 171–2, 205–6
Thomson, Governor General Charles, 63–4, 78
Thongchai Winichakul, 20–1, 28
Thun Theara, 28–9
Tonkin, 10–11, 13, 14, 37, 39, 48, 51–3, 62–3, 64, 87–8, 92–3, 133–4, 173
torture, 57, 58–9, 86–7, 147
Toung, 113–14
Tourane/Danang, 13, 39
traditions, 6–7, 12, 17–18, 23, 29–32, 59–60, 66, 75, 84–8, 98–9, 106–7, 121–7, 142–3, 149, 157, 167–70, 194, 201–11
Treaty of Amity, Commerce and Navigation 1856, Siam/ Thailand, 54
Treaty of Amity, Commerce and Protection (Treaty of Protection)

1863, 6, 9–12, 15, 29, 38, 49–58, 61–6, 69, 75–6, 142, 151, 168, 174, 178, 183, 195, 202, 215
tribunaux résidentiels, 72–3, 97–8, 100, 118
Tu Duc, 37
Tully, John, xxv, 1, 5, 10, 18, 30–1, 37, 57, 63–4, 66, 70, 79, 87, 101–4, 111–12, 116, 130–2, 148, 156, 164, 169–70, 173–4, 179–80
Tunisian protectorate (1881–1956), 11, 13, 39, 210–11
Tunku, Abdul Rahman, 207

Um, Prime Minister, 86–7
Unfederated Malay States (UMS), 74, 206–8
United States (US), 7, 51, 54, 183, 185, 192, 200, 210

Var, Governor, 106–7
Varenne, Governor General Alexandre, 151–3
Vernéville, de (*Résident Supérieur*), 70
Vichy rule, 23, 25, 164–5, 167–70, 172–5, 205–6
Vickery, Michael, 166, 169, 190
Vientiane, 39, 52–3
Viet Minh, 174
Vietnam, xiv, xxi, 7–15, 20, 28–32, 37–9, 51–5, 59, 62–71, 87–8, 92–9, 121–2, 131–4, 157–8, 161–74, 180–5, 192, 203–6
Vietnamese inhabitants, 9, 15, 20, 31–2, 50, 54–5, 62–3, 69–73, 95–8, 107, 119, 122, 131, 139, 157–8, 170–3, 186, 200, 204
village-level tribunals, 33–5

violence perspective, colonisation
viewing "modes", 19–20, 194–6
"volunteers" for military service,
103–4

Whiting, Amanda, 8, 207–8

Yama (god-king), 127
Yem Sambaur, Prime Minister,
178
Yukanthor, Prince, 87
Yuthevong, Prince,
176–7
Yuvan, 169–70

ASIAN STUDIES ASSOCIATION OF AUSTRALIA
Southeast Asia Publications Series

Previously published ASAA titles:

Anti-Chinese Violence in Indonesia, 1996–1999, by Jemma Purdey, 2005

Other Malays: Nationalism and Cosmopolitanism in the Modern Malay World, by Joel S. Kahn, 2006

History in Uniform: Military Ideology and the Construction of Indonesia's Past, by Katharine E. McGregor, 2007

Cham Muslims of the Mekong Delta: Place and Mobility in the Cosmopolitan Periphery, by Philip Taylor, 2007

Javanese Performances on an Indonesian Stage: Contesting Culture, Embracing Change, by Barbara Hatley, 2008

Kuala Lumpur and Putrajaya: Negotiating Urban Space in Malaysia, by Ross King, 2008

Kampung, Islam and State in Urban Java, by Patrick Guinness, 2009

Tai Lands and Thailand: Community and State in Southeast Asia, edited by Andrew Walker, 2009

Workers and Intellectuals: NGOs, Trade Unions and the Indonesian Labour Movement, by Michele Ford, 2009

Madurese Seafarers: Prahus, Timber and Illegality on the Margins of the Indonesian State, by Kurt Stenross, 2011

Development Professionals in Northern Thailand: Hope, Politics and Practice, by Katharine McKinnon, 2011

The Contours of Mass Violence in Indonesia, 1965–68, edited by Douglas Kammen and Katharine McGregor, 2012

Surabaya, 1945–2010: Neighbourhood, State and Economy in Indonesia's City of Struggle, by Robbie Peters, 2013

Squatters into Citizens: The 1961 Bukit Ho Swee Fire and the Making of Modern Singapore, by Loh Kah Seng, 2013

Being Malay in Indonesia: Histories, Hopes and Citizenship in the Riau Archipelago, by Nicholas Long, 2013

Money, Power, and Ideology: Political Parties in Post-Authoritarian Indonesia, by Marcus Mietzner, 2013

The Khmer Lands of Vietnam: Environment, Cosmology and Sovereignty, by Philip Taylor, 2014

Taming the Wild: Aborigines and Racial Knowledge in Colonial Malaya, by Sandra Khor Manickam, 2015

Resilience and the Localisation of Trauma in Aceh, Indonesia, by Catherine Smith, 2018

Soul Catcher: Java's Fiery Prince Mangkunagara I, 1726–95, by M.C. Ricklefs, 2018

Unmarked Graves: Death and Survival in the Anti-Communist Violence in East Java, Indonesia, by Vannessa Hearman, 2018

Haunted Houses and Ghostly Encounters: Ethnography and Animism in East Timor, 1860–1975, by Christopher J. Shepherd, 2019

Workers and Democracy: The Indonesian Labour Movement, 1949–1957, by John Ingleson, 2022

To Remain Myself: The History of Onghokham, by David Reeve, 2022